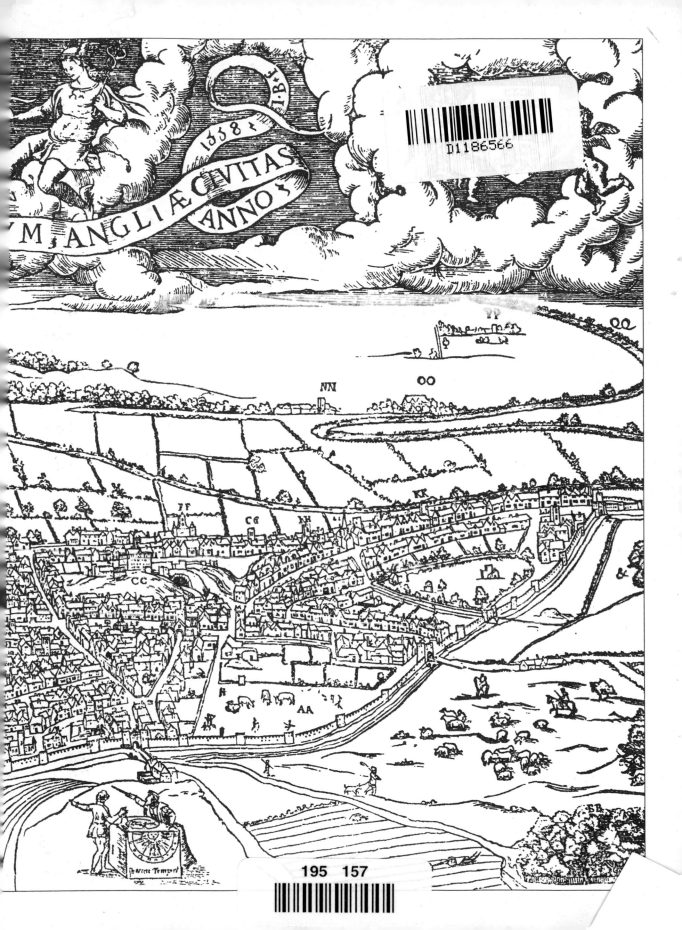

A History of
NORWICH

Norwich Castle

A History of
NORWICH

Frank Meeres

Phillimore

1998

Published by
PHILLIMORE & CO. LTD.
Shopwyke Manor Barn, Chichester, West Sussex

ISBN 1 86077 083 5

Printed and bound in Great Britain by
BOOKCRAFT LTD.
Midsomer Norton

Contents

List of Illustrations

Frontispiece: Norwich Castle

Acknowledgements

This book is dedicated to the late Alan Carter, who was the first person to awaken my interest in the history of Norwich. I have been fortunate enough to listen to many able and enthusiastic speakers since, of whom I would like to mention particularly Brian Ayers, Chris Barringer and John Pound.

The book would never have been written without the help of Clare Brown, Helen Jones and Irene McLaughlin who have typed all the text and helped prepare the indexes and the graphics.

I am extremely grateful to the Norfolk Record Office and the County Archivist Dr. John Alban for permission to reproduce documents and photographs in their care.

This book is a 90,000-word distillation of an original text of almost 150,000 words. A typescript of this longer version is available in the Norfolk Record Office.

1

The Beginnings

The earliest known reference to Norwich is not in a document but on a coin of King Athelstan who reigned from 925 to 939. There are only five known written references to Norwich before the Norman Conquest in 1066 and yet by that time it was already one of the largest cities in the country. What little we know of the beginnings and early history of the city is derived from archaeological evidence and from the study of place-names. Of course it is very difficult to make systematic excavations in a place like Norwich. It is still a flourishing city and the only possible digs are on sites cleared for redevelopment. These often have to be rushed as the developers naturally want to exploit the site when they can. Even so some major archaeological work has been done in the city in the last twenty years, firstly by the Norwich Survey in the period 1971 to 1978 led by Alan Carter and more recently by the Norfolk Archaeological Unit led by Brian Ayers.

The popular opinion of Norfolk is that it is a flat county but in fact parts of it are far from flat: indeed Ayers has called Norwich one of the hilliest cities in England.[1] *The Growth of a City* sums up the geology: East Norfolk is composed of sands, gravels and clays overlaying chalk. Much of it is drained by the rivers Yare and Wensum and their tributaries, and when most of the plateau was heavily forested these rivers would have provided easy routes inland from the coast.[2] The basic reason for Norwich growing up where it did is that given by A.L. Poole: 'The commercial importance of [towns such as Norwich] was largely due to their position on tidal rivers at points where they could be bridged. Goods could thus be carried far into the interior of the country and thence distributed over a wide area'.[3] There is a map in Great Yarmouth Town Hall showing the Yare estuary as it might have been about A.D. 1000. The map was drawn in about 1600 and so has no claim to historical accuracy but the impression it gives is the right one: in Roman and Saxon times Norwich stood at the head of a large shallow estuary, the mouth of which stretched from Caister on Sea to Burgh Castle.

Evidence of man in the greater Norwich area has been found in all periods since the end of the last Ice Age. There are few finds from the Palaeolithic era (roughly 50,000 to 10,000 B.C.), though hand axes have been found at Carrow and one was turned up at Morse's Rose garden in Eaton in 1943.[4] The main evidence for man's activity in the Norwich area in the Mesolithic and Neolithic periods (approximately 10,000-2,000 B.C.) is the finding of flint tools. Flints have been found on Mousehold Heath and hand-axes at Carrow.

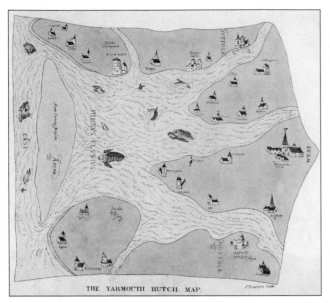

THE YARMOUTH HUTCH MAP.

J. Barire lith

1 *Drawing, based on the Hutch map, of the Yare estuary in about A.D. 1000*

Low-lying sites in the valleys close to the later city include the important religious centre of Arminghall which was discovered from the air by Wing-Commander Insall in 1929. It proved to be a horseshoe of eight holes that once contained huge timber posts each over a metre across and sunk into the ground to a depth of well over two metres. Each one weighed about seven tons. Charcoal from these posts gave a radiocarbon dating of about 3,000 B.C. These may have been tall carved totem poles or they could have had lintels across the tops like the large stones at Stonehenge. Alternatively they could have been connected in some way to form a tower. The entrance to the henge through the surrounding ditches faces south-west and would have been facing mid-winter sunrise. The henge is close to several burial mounds. Its site is on a promontory above the meeting place of the waters of the Tas and the Yare.[5] A barrow in the same area was cut through by the Norwich southern bypass. Although nothing was found, careful analysis of stains in the soil showed there had been an individual in a wooden coffin buried here in the third millennium B.C. This represents one of the earliest known examples of an individual burial.

Mysterious deep shafts with Neolithic material have been found at Eaton: these consist of 21 vertical shafts some eight metres deep as well as the usual pit and post holes. The function of the shafts is completely unknown. They could be wells or ritual features or, as Rodney Castleden suggests, they could even be natural–ancient solution pipes into which Neolithic occupation material has fallen. If so, Eaton Heath is a normal Neolithic settlement site with a radiocarbon date of about 4,000 B.C.[6] However Paul Ashbee thinks the shafts are huge post-sockets and that the site was an artificial grove.[7]

No settlement sites of the Bronze Age (approximately 2,500-800 B.C.) have been found but there is considerable evidence of the presence of these people. In 1979 the Norfolk Archaeological Unit excavated a site within the city boundary at Bowthorpe which air photography had shown as a circular crop mark. It turned out to be the remnant of a Bronze-Age round barrow, dated to about 2,000 B.C. by radiocarbon dating. Here again the archaeologists could detect that there had once been a body in a coffin. Signs of 11 more graves were found around the edge of the barrow. The best preserved of these was found to contain a body resting on a hay-filled pillow in a coffin made of oak planks. A thousand years later the barrow was again used for a burial but practices had changed–the ashes were found of a cremated body covered by a large urn.[8] Two round barrows, of an original group of four, survive on Eaton golf course and bronze tools and weapons have been found all over the area. The finest discovery in Norfolk from the Iron Age (800 B.C. to A.D. 43) is now at Norwich Castle but was actually found in Snettisham. This is a collection of magnificent gold torcs or necklaces that could well have belonged to some member of the ruling family of the tribe of the Iceni who lived in the Norfolk area. Rescue archaeology along the route of the southern bypass revealed a fine Iron-Age longhouse in this area not far from the later Roman town at Caistor St Edmund.

The Romans

Julius Caesar had a preliminary look at Britain in 55 B.C., but the invasion and conquest began in A.D. 43 under the emperor Claudius. The Iceni tribe did not surrender easily. In A.D. 47 the Roman governor attempted to disarm them, which provoked a serious uprising. When their client-king Prasutagus died he left the Roman emperor co-heir to the kingdom along with his own two daughters, but the Romans treated the Iceni as defeated enemies. After the king's daughters were raped and his widow Boudicca beaten, the whole tribe rose up and sacked Colchester, London and St Albans before being finally defeated by the Roman armies. Roman authors disagree about Boudicca's fate. Tacitus says she took poison, but Dio Cassius says she died from disease and tantalisingly adds that the British gave her a rich burial: unfortunately her grave has not yet been found.[9]

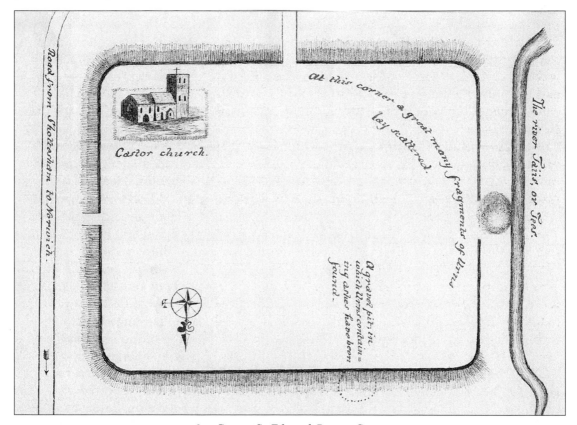

2   *Caistor St Edmund Roman Camp*

It is not known where the centre of Iceni power in the county actually was. Ashbee suggests that their chief camp may have been where Norwich Castle now is.[10] It would have been superseded by the new town at Venta which was probably founded soon after Boudicca's rebellion was defeated. There was never a Roman town at Norwich: indeed much of the Roman material found in Norwich (including Roman bricks built into the fabric of the Cathedral) is probably re-used from Caistor as suggested by the old rhyme, 'Caistor was a town when Norwich was none, Norwich was built with Caistor's stone'.

Venta was the major settlement in the area in the Roman period. The main stone buildings of the town–market, public hall, baths–were put up in the second century and elaborate town walls were erected in the third century. However the story of Venta is not one of peaceful and uninterrupted progress. The forum was at one time destroyed by fire and remained derelict for over 50 years before being rebuilt on a much smaller scale. The third-century walls only enclosed half the area of the original town, another indication of decline. It is possible that the association of wool with the Norwich area goes all the way back to Roman times. There is a fourth-century reference to the Roman army being supplied with cloth from a state weaving mill at Venta. This could be Caistor, but equally it could be one of the two other towns in Britain called Venta (Winchester and Caerwent).[11]

The Roman town of Caistor, the henge at Arminghall and the hill fort at Tasburgh, which is probably Iron Age in date (but could be much later), appear on the map as a straight line. They make one of the most convincing of the many 'lines of power' suggested by ley-line enthusiasts.[12]

Roman roads probably crossed on the site of the later city of Norwich. The archaeologists have found evidence for an east-west road running from Brundall entering the city near Pilling Park, continuing through Mousehold House grounds and down Gas Hill to a river crossing on the site of Bishop Bridge. It is not known if this crossing was by a bridge or a ford. The road continued along Bishopgate: this section would have been on a causeway through marshland. It then continued along the line of St Benedict's Street and Dereham Road.[13] This line is still preserved at Tombland Alley and became part of the much later Saxon grid pattern of streets largely destroyed by the Normans who built their cathedral right on the former Roman road. A road running north from Caistor may have run up along Long John Hill and along the Ber Street ridge, or perhaps along King Street and Magdalen Street.[14]

Pottery of Roman date has been found in the Magdalen Street area, perhaps indicating, as Malcolm Atkin suggests, a farmstead in the St Augustine's area.[15] There have been other finds in the Yare Valley at Eaton and in the Wensum Valley at Lakenham and Earlham, probably also farmsteads. Two rich Roman burials were discovered at Stanley Avenue in Thorpe in 1950: one included three coins of Nero. Two skeletons that were found under Woodlands Park off Dereham Road in 1861 were probably of the third or fourth centuries.[16] Pottery fragments and Roman coins have been found all across the city but these could of course have been dropped years or even centuries later.

Saxons and Danes

As the Roman empire fell apart the Saxons invaded and eventually drove the native British into the fringe regions of Cornwall, Wales and Scotland. However they probably did not slaughter the British but slowly merged with them. Two early Saxon cemeteries very close to Caistor suggest that people continued to live there after the Romans had left.[17]

Alan Carter and others have suggested that Norwich may at this time have been slowly growing out of a number of small settlements. He postulated four of these called Needham, Westwick, Conesford and Coslany. The archaeological evidence for this is small but there is the evidence of the place-names themselves. The name 'Westwic' occurs in 12th-century documents and the form of the name suggests it originated before 850.[18] So did the name 'Coslania' (which according to Alan Carter means 'piggies' long island' and could well have been meant as an insult).[19] A pagan Saxon cemetery has been found on the higher ground north of the river where Eade Road now is: perhaps the people buried here were living down by the river in Coslany.[20]

The place-name 'Conesford' means the 'King's Ford': the name is used now for the area at the southern end of King Street but there is nowhere in that area suitable for a ford. Possibly the name was originally given to the crossing at what is now Bishop Bridge. Until recently it was thought that the largest of the Middle Saxon settlements which eventually became Norwich was that called 'Needham' (meaning 'poor meadow' or 'poor homestead').[21] It was thought this might be centred beneath the later Norman castle. However digging on the Castle Mall site has failed to find any evidence for it. For this and other reasons, Brian Ayers suggests a different origin of Norwich, not as four settlements that have merged but as ribbon development along the banks of the river.[22] If it had a centre it could have been on the north bank by what is now Fyebridge—Malcolm Atkin points out that finds at Fishergate suggest an eighth-century settlement there.[23]

The Danes conquered the east of England after the murder of King Edmund in 869. The only Norfolk town mentioned at this period is Thetford, where the Danes spent the winter in 869 before slaughtering Edmund after a battle.[24] This is generally thought to have been at Hoxne, although a few authorities think Hellesdon a more likely site for this decisive victory. The martyrdom of King Edmund can be seen

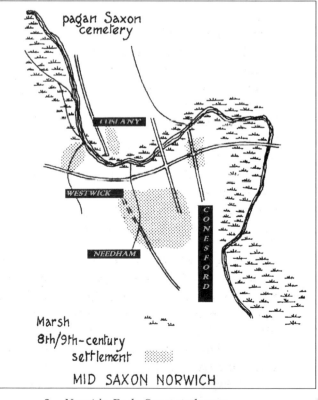

3   *Norwich: Early Saxon settlements*

Lines through Time 1: 870 to 1066

Death of King Edmund, Danes conquer East Anglia	870	
Death of Alfred the Great	899	
Edward the Elder drives Danes from East Anglia	917	
Athelstan becomes King of England	924	Coins are minted in Norwich
Death of Athelstan	937	
	c.980	First written reference to Norwich
	1000	
	1004	King Sweyn burns Norwich
Eastern England surrenders to King Sweyn	1013	
	1016	Death of St Walstan
The Norman Conquest	1066	

carved in stone in the spandrel of the west door of the church of St Lawrence. He is shown being hit by many arrows and the wolf, which according to legend, guarded his body, can be seen peeping out from a cave.

One of the main indications of the Danish occupation of Norwich is the evidence of Danish place names, such as the ending 'gate', referring to a street and not a gate, as in Fishergate, Colegate, Cowgate and Pottergate. Other examples are the name 'Thorpe' which is Danish for a new settlement and the name 'Cowholme' from the old Danish word 'holme' meaning water meadow.[25] One street name in Norwich has two Danish elements–Finkelgate. 'Finkel' may mean 'crooked' or, as Sue Margeson suggests, it could come from the Danish word for 'cuddles' and be the equivalent of 'lovers lane' (a role the street retains even today).[26]

The Danish settlement was north of the river and was defended with a bank and ditch. This has actually been found in St George's Street but the other boundaries are not known.[27] The pattern of the streets suggests it may have been along the curving road now called Cowgate, but the boundary may have been along Peacock Street instead. Where Anglia Square now is there was once a wood called Mereholt, which means 'boundary wood' and which may mark the northern edge of this settlement.[28] There have been a few finds in the city reflecting the period of Danish occupation such as a cross shaft with Scandinavian-style decoration found on the site of St Vedast at Rose Lane and now on display in the Castle Museum.[29]

The Danes were driven out of East Anglia by the English armies of King Edward the Elder in 917. However this did not lead to the restoration of an independent kingdom of East Anglia: it became part of the kingdom of the West Saxons. The name 'Northwic' first appears for certain on coins of King Athelstan, Edward's son, who ruled from 925 to 939. Mints were only set up in 'Burhs', the essential features of which were fortifications and a market. No-one knows if the term means the 'Wic' or trading area to the north of the river rather than the south, or whether the word means it was the north 'Wic' of the kingdom in contrast to the south 'Wic' at Ipswich.[30]

At last we have come to the earliest written reference to Norwich. This is in the *Book of Ely* written in the 980s. When the Abbot of Ely wanted to buy land in Cambridge, he was informed 'that Cambridge and Norwich and Ipswich and Thetford were of such liberty and dignity that if anyone bought land there he did not need witnesses'. This shows that Norwich was already regarded as a 'civilised' town.

Danish raiding started up again in the late tenth century. The second earliest written reference to Norwich is in the *Anglo-Saxon Chronicle*. This tells us that in 1004 the Danish King Sweyn 'came with his fleet to Norwich and completely ravaged and burned the borough'–so Norwich was definitely a borough by this date.[31] Sweyn was avenging Danes who had been massacred in England including his own sister Gunhilda who, Ralph Mottram says, had been murdered in Norwich: however, he does not give any evidence for this.[32] Edith Henderson imagined the scene–

> Norwich suffered terribly from the cruelty of Sweyn and his warriors. They came to the little fishing town here at the foot of the hills of the Yare estuary; and when they sailed away, the red flames were leaping from the homesteads, spreading from hut to hut, filling all the sky with a fierce red glare.[33]

After this raid the Danes came back again and again and in 1013 the whole of Eastern England surrendered to King Sweyn. The English King, Ethelred, fled abroad. Sweyn died in the same year but his son Canute invaded and eventually won the entire kingdom for himself. He was also king of Denmark and (from 1028) of Norway as well: Otto the Black says, 'Canute is the foremost sovereign under Heaven.' The same poet has a mention for Norwich, but the battle he describes is otherwise unrecorded, 'Gracious giver of mighty gifts, you made mailcoats red in Norwich ... still you pressed on, blunting swords upon weapons; they could not defend their strongholds when you attacked'.[34]

A late Saxon skull on display at the Castle Museum could be that of a victim of this battle. It has a large hole made by a battle axe or heavy sword. The label says grimly, 'This one shows no trace of healing and death must have occurred almost at once'. It was found near the site of St Catherine's chapel in Thorpe.

Canute, of course, was much more than a Viking raider. He secured his place in the line of English kings by marrying the widow of his predecessor Ethelred the Unready and devised a code of law based on those of earlier Anglo-Saxon kings. Under Canute, as under Athelstan, money was minted in Norwich. Over 300 coins minted in the city in his reign are known (compared, however, with over 1,500 each from Lincoln and York).[35] In the time of Canute, England was part of an empire centred on the North Sea. Eastern towns like Norwich must have benefited enormously from this, just as towns on the west coast gained from the opening up of trade with America 500 years later.

Ships landed goods at the wharf on the south side of the river near St Martin at Palace Plain. There may have been a market here but the main Saxon market was at Tombland: the name probably means 'open' or 'empty space' and has no connection with tombs. It may not have been the name that the Saxons called it–the earliest written evidence for the name Tombland is in about 1250.[36] This must have been the heart of the late Saxon town with the palace of the Earls of East Anglia along its southern side and in the centre the church of St Michael Tombland, the richest in the city according to Domesday Book. When the underground lavatories were being dug here in the late 19th century a walrus-ivory cross was found which probably came from St Michael's church. Brian Ayers calls it 'the finest piece of art known from pre-conquest Norwich': it is now in the Victoria and Albert Museum in London.[37] Even today the main roads into Norwich, like King Street and Magdalen Street, lead to Tombland rather than to the present-day market place. No doubt goods brought in from Europe by boat would be sold here and also local pottery from the street of potters or 'Pottergate' area of Norwich.

What were the people who lived in Saxon Norwich like? When the site now occupied by Anglia Television was excavated, 130 skeletons were found buried in a churchyard. The state of their bones gives us some clues about how they lived. Half the burials were of children. Of the adults, 40 were male and 20 were female. This may be because it was not possible to dig up the whole graveyard: perhaps some areas were reserved for males and some for females. The age of death could be calculated: 46 per cent of the males and 67 per cent of the females survived to the ages of 35 to 45 years. Very few people lived beyond the age of 45. The lives of these people were hard: their torsos and arms showed signs of heavy labour. Several suffered from rickets and nine had a bone condition which would have meant a continuous pain behind the eyes. These diseases suggest that the diet of these people was not adequate. Surprisingly, one of the skeletons appears to have been of a negress, perhaps a slave or perhaps a descendant of the small black population of Roman Britain.[38]

Clearly a large town like late Saxon Norwich needed relatively sophisticated organisation. Roberta Gilchrist has estimated that a town of 10,000 people in A.D. 1050 would consume in a year 1,000 pigs, 1,250 cattle and 1,750 sheep. It would need almost two million pounds of grain for bread and a further 200,000 pounds for beer. It would create almost a million gallons of human urine and over 700 tonnes of human excrement each year.[39]

The Christian Church

Some of the citizens of the later Roman Empire were certainly Christian and the Saxons would have found it an established religion at least among the elite. During the late fifth and sixth centuries England seems largely to have lapsed into paganism.

Pope Gregory recommended that Christian churches be built at places already used by pagans as places to worship. This is why church sites are one of the features used by ley-hunters to trace ancient 'lines of power'. A possible example in the city is St Michael at Plea–pagan Saxon burials have been found in the churchyard.

Bede in his 'History of the English Church' says that the first seat of the bishopric of East Anglia was set up at 'Dommoc' by Felix in the middle seventh century. This has usually been thought to have meant Dunwich but more recent scholars have suggested Felixstowe as a likelier site. The bishopric was divided in about 673, the northern part being given its centre at Elmham. The identity of this Elmham is not certain: some people think it is Elmham in Suffolk but as this is only seven miles from Hoxne, the southern centre, it seems more likely to be North Elmham in Norfolk. Because of the Danish occupation there are no known bishops of either see in the ninth and early tenth centuries. After the Christian Saxons re-established their authority in East Anglia, the two centres were at Hoxne and at North Elmham.[40]

One Saxon resident of the Norwich area was Walstan, who became a popular saint in East Anglia. According to legend he was born at Blythburgh, the son of a king, and renounced wealth giving his clothes away and working in the Taverham area as a farm labourer, setting an example by his life of simple poverty. Eventually his parents came to Norwich and issued a proclamation asking if anyone knew where he was. His employer heard this and went to Walstan who, however, died very soon after. His dying wish was that his body be put onto his cart and his two bullocks allowed to take it where they chose. They stopped twice to piss (some versions prefer

to say to rest but Eamon Duffy's translation has an authentic ring to it). At each place a healing well sprang up. They arrived at Bawburgh and by a miracle passed through the wall into the church where Walstan was buried by the bishop and monks of Norwich and many miracles of healing occurred at his grave.[41]

Some of this story is clearly untrue— he is supposed to have died in about 1016 and at this date there were no kings in Blythburgh and no bishop or monks in Norwich. What is important is not whether it is true but that it was believed by everybody in Norfolk in the Middle Ages—a local farm labourer became a much-loved saint among the peasantry. Even today two images of him can still be seen in Norwich: on the bowl of the font now in St Julian and on the screen from St James Pockthorpe now in St Mary Magdalen on Silver Road.

By 1066, the city had between 25 and 40 churches for a population of 5,000-10,000. Two pre-Conquest churches are named in the will of Sifflaed, our fourth

4   *Walstan, a Norfolk saint*

5   *St Benedict, the round tower*

document to mention Norwich—St Mary and Christchurch. Unfortunately the precise date of this Saxon will is not known but it must date from some time between 990 and 1066. Six further churches that already existed in 1066 are named in Domesday Book: All Saints, Lawrence, Martin [at Palace], Michael [on Tombland], Simon and Jude, Sepulchre. Late Saxon churches in the Tombland area are commonly on street corners: this, together with the regularity of the street pattern in this area, suggests some form of planning. The fifth, and final, written mention of pre-Conquest Norwich is in another Saxon will which can be dated to 1035-1038: this merely mentions a house plot in Norwich. That is the sum total of archive evidence for Norwich in the period before the Norman Conquest.[42]

The round flint towers for which East Anglia is famous include some which may be pre-Conquest. The most well known is St Mary Coslany where the windows in the tower are of a typically Saxon style. Others in Norwich are at St Benedict (where only the tower survives) and St Etheldreda. The flint for these churches was no doubt dug locally—some of the workings under Norwich that have caused so much trouble for homeowners in the 20th century probably have Saxon origins. Some people argue that the towers are round because it was difficult to build square towers out of flint. However, it is just as difficult to join a round tower to a square nave. It seems more likely that church builders simply liked round towers. They are found in all the countries surrounding the North Sea, so Norfolk is just one part of an international taste for them.

The discovery of the site of a church in the Anglia Television dig is important as it was completely unexpected from written records.[43] It shows just how inadequate our knowledge of early Norwich still is. It is also important because it can be dated fairly exactly: we know that the buildings in this area were cleared to make way for the Norman castle. There appear to have been three stages of development of the church, the final one being of a nave eight by five metres with a chancel of three metres square. There was a font, which replaced an earlier baptistery. The building, like its predecessors on the site, was of course made of wood. It probably gives a good idea of the kind of building in which most of our Saxon ancestors would have worshipped.

Then came the Norman Conquest and the shape of Norwich was forever changed.

2

Norwich in the Middle Ages

The Normans—as everyone knows—invaded England in 1066, beating the English at Hastings and killing Harold their king. William was crowned King at Westminster on Christmas Day 1066. It is debatable how much effect the change of rulers had on ordinary people. Most aspects of daily life probably went on much as before. For example, there is no sudden change in architectural style. Features which are clearly 'Saxon' in style, such as the openings in the round tower of St Mary Coslany church and the round windows in St Julian's church, could have been built before or after the Conquest. However there is no doubt that the Conquest—and especially Earl Ralph's subsequent rebellion—had a drastic effect on the shape of Norwich. This was caused by three major new elements: the castle, the cathedral, and the New or French Borough: these are all described later.

King William gave the earldom, city and castle of Norwich to Ralph Guader in 1071. Ralph was a Norfolk man with a Welsh mother. In 1075 he married Emma the daughter of William Fitz Osbern and sister of Roger, Earl of Hereford. The marriage feast was celebrated in Norwich and many Saxon nobles were present including Roger and Waltheof, Earl of Northumberland. At the feast, Ralph persuaded them to join in a conspiracy against King William who was in Normandy at the time. Next day Earl Waltheof changed his mind and went to Lanfranc, the Archbishop of Canterbury, who was guardian of the kingdom. On Lanfranc's advice, Waltheof sailed over to Normandy and told the king about the planned rebellion. Odo, Bishop of Bayeux, and Jeffrey, Bishop of Coutances, raised an army loyal to the king. They forced Ralph back into his castle at Norwich from where he took ship to obtain help from Denmark leaving his wife Emma to defend the castle.

The Danes sent 200 ships in support but when King William returned from Normandy they fled without fighting. The King's army then besieged the castle and after three months Emma was forced to surrender: she was allowed to follow her husband to Brittany. At Christmas the King himself came to Norwich and punished those who supported Ralph, some being banished and others having their eyes gouged out. The next year (1076), King William pursued Ralph into Brittany and besieged him in his castle at Dol. However Philip, the King of France, came to Ralph's support and William was forced to withdraw leaving Ralph and Emma unpunished. Ralph's estates and titles were of course forfeited and William appointed

6   *St Mary Coslany*

Roger Bigot constable of Norwich Castle and king's bailiff.

At Christmas in 1085 King William decided to make a great survey of England and this was completed by autumn 1086. This is the well-known Domesday Book.[2] The section for Norwich is the first detailed account of the city, showing what it was like just before the Conquest and 20 years after it. It states that before 1066 there were 1,320 burgesses in Norwich. By 1086 some had fled to Beccles and elsewhere—'those fleeing and others remaining have been utterly devastated partly because of Earl R[alph]'s forfeitures, partly because of fires, partly because of the king's tax, partly by Waleran'. There were 190 empty dwellings in 1086. The building of the castle also made a huge hole in the old city—88 buildings had been cleared for it. It seems that it was already proposed to move the cathedral from Thetford into Norwich: the entry mentions 14 buildings given by King William 'for the principal seat of the bishopric'.

It was probably in 1158 that Norwich was granted its first known charter by King Henry II. This confirms to the citizens of Norwich all the customs and liberties they had enjoyed at the time of the king's grandfather (Henry I) without spelling out what these were. Like many early documents the charter has no date and historians have to use detective work to establish when it was written. The clues are the names of the witnesses and the known movements of the king. If the historians are right, Norwich's first charter must have been granted between April and August 1158.[3]

In 1163 King Henry granted Norwich to Hugh Bigot. When Prince Henry, the eldest son of the king, rebelled in France Hugh supported the son against the father. In 1173, Hugh landed in England with an army of Fleming soldiers. He expected the citizens of Norwich to support him but they remained loyal to their king and he was forced to attack the city. Once he had captured it he burnt it in revenge and held the richest citizens to ransom. The king raised an army against Hugh who surrendered without a fight and soon after went to the Holy Land where he died.[4]

King Henry died in 1189 and was succeeded by Richard, known to history as Richard the Lionheart. It was he who in 1194 gave to Norwich the charter from which the foundation of the city is usually dated.[5] This granted that the citizens of Norwich were to choose their own ruler or 'reeve' each year so that the courts and assemblies

Lines through Time 2: 1066 to 1300

The Norman Conquest	1066	
	1072	Earl Ralph's rebellion
Domesday Book	1086	
	1096	Norwich Cathedral founded
	1100	
Loss of the White Ship	1120	
Death of Henry I leads to Civil War	1135	
	1144	Death of 'Saint' William of Norwich
	1158	Henry II's Charter
	1174	Flemings Capture Norwich
Richard the Lionheart is crowned	1189	
	1194	Richard's Charter
Magna Carta signed	1215	
	1216	King Louis of France takes Norwich
	1225	Friars come to Norwich
	1248	Great Hospital founded
	1266	Disinherited barons sack the city
	1272	Riots between priory and town
King Edward expels Jews	1290	End of Norwich Jewish community
	1300	

were headed by men of the citizens' own choosing and not by the king's appointees. The citizens now held the city at a fixed rent or 'farm' of £108 each year which they paid directly to the king's exchequer and not to the sheriff of Norfolk. Edith Henderson knew the importance of this document:

> That charter is perhaps the most precious document that we have in Norwich, for it is the first real grant of our freedom ... It is just a small strip of parchment with some writing in Latin on it. To see it you would scarcely think that it could really have meant so very much to many generations of Norwich people.[6]

The charter was confirmed in almost identical terms by King John when he succeeded to the throne. He, of course, became involved in civil war with his barons.

7   *Charter of Richard I granted in 1194*

Roger Bigot the constable of Norwich took the side of the rebel barons and Norwich Castle was seized by the king. However the Bishop of Norwich was one of those who remained loyal to King John. John sent the bishop to his French domains to raise an army which would have been large enough to destroy the barons. He did this, but most of the soldiers were drowned during a storm while crossing from Calais. King Louis of France landed in support of the barons in 1216 and John slowly retreated before him, losing his treasure in the Wash a few days before he died in Newark on 19 October. The treasure was never recovered and still lies under the peat somewhere near Long Sutton.

John was succeeded by his child son Henry, and King Louis eventually returned to France. Norwich was given to Roger Bigot once more. In 1228 the citizens petitioned Henry for a new charter which he granted them. This was largely identical to those of Richard and John but with an extra paragraph ordering that everyone in the city should pay royal taxes and not just the citizens. He granted two further charters to the city, the last when he visited Norwich in 1256.

In 1266 the city was again plundered by enemies. The so-called 'disinherited barons' were living in hiding in the Isle of Ely after being deprived of their estates for their support of Simon de Montfort against the oppressive rule of Henry III. (Simon and his followers had been defeated by the king's army at the Battle of Evesham in 1265.) Simon was killed in the battle and his supporters had their lands confiscated. These barons raided Norwich and plundered the city, killing many citizens and carrying others away to their base to be ransomed.

In 1272, long-running quarrels between the people of Norwich and the cathedral priory came to a head following disturbances at the fair held at Tombland on Trinity Sunday. The riots are described from the monks' viewpoint in Bartholomew Cotton's *Chronicle* and from that of the citizens in the *Liber de Antiquis Legibus*. According to

Cotton some of the citizens attacked the priory by climbing to the top of the tower of St George Tombland church and firing flaming arrows into the precinct. The great bell tower that stood to the west of the cathedral was burnt down together with St Ethelbert's church which was just inside the gates. Some of the arrows reached the tower of the Cathedral itself–a distance of about 700 feet. (The present tower of St George Tombland is a 15th-century replacement on the same site as the earlier tower.)

However the citizens claimed that the burning of the cathedral was the fault of the monks and their men. They were standing on the cathedral tower with projectiles and with fire, trying to start fires in the city with their burning arrows. They fled when they saw that the bell tower had caught alight. They left their fire on the central tower and this then spread across the cathedral roof. Meanwhile the prior had fled to Yarmouth and he returned with a group of armed men who killed many of the townspeople.

Edward I himself came to Norwich in September 1272 to sort out the crisis. He decided largely in favour of the monks. Many individual citizens were hanged or burnt while the city as a whole had to pay 3,000 marks at 500 marks a year for the next six years to rebuild the cathedral. This was presumably done by 1278 as William Middleton was enthroned Bishop of Norwich in that year in the presence of the king and queen and many nobles.

The effect of the 1272 fire can still be seen in the pinkish colour of the old cornerstones of the Ethelbert Gate now within the 'tunnel' of the later and longer gate. Some of the pink stones inside the cathedral may also have been caused by this fire but as it was just one of several serious fires that the building has suffered it is impossible to be sure. The monks claimed that many of their documents were destroyed in the fire and there are almost no account rolls surviving before 1272.[7] The Romanesque cloisters had been destroyed in the fire (or at least badly damaged) and they were slowly rebuilt over the next 150 years.[8]

In 1285 Edward I granted the city a charter confirming those of his predecessor. Ten years later he issued a second charter giving the citizens the area called Newgate, roughly corresponding to the present Surrey Street. This had previously been claimed by the cathedral priory and an extra £10 was added to the city's fee farm rent for the privilege of undisputed possession. In 1345 Edward III gave to

8   *18th-century drawing of the Ethelbert Gate*

the city the land lying in the outer bailey of the castle. The small increase in the annual rent that this cost the city was probably worthwhile as the bailey had become a haunt of evildoers just out of reach of the jurisdiction of the city.[9]

The leet records of 1288 show the first known sub-divisions of the city. Forty-six parishes were grouped together into 11 sub-leets and these grouped into four leets. Some parts of Norwich were still outside the control of the city and so were not included–the castle, the Close and St Paul's parish (which was part of the priory fee).[10]

In 1381 the peace of the city was once again rudely shattered, this time by the uprising known as the Peasants' Revolt. People in many parts of England rebelled against a poll tax of one shilling on every man and woman over 16 years old (only common beggars were excepted). The revolt in the Norwich area was led by Geoffrey Litester or Lister, a dyer from Felmingham near North Walsham. A large body of peasants gathered on Mousehold Heath just outside the city. It seems they hoped Sir Robert Salle would become their leader. The chronicler Froissart tells the story:

> There was a knight captain of the town called Sir Robert Salle, he was no gentleman born, but he had the grace to be reputed sage and valiant in arms, and for his valiantness King Edward made him knight. He was of his body one of the biggest knights in all England.
> Lyster and his company thought to have this knight with them, and to make him their chief captain, so they sent to him that he should come and speak with them in the field or else they would burn the town.
> The knight considered that it was better for him to go and speak with them rather than that they should do that outrage to the town. Then he mounted on his horse and issued out of the town

Lines through Time 3: 1300 to 1500

	1300	
	1343	City walls completed
The Black Death	1349	Black Death in the city
	1373	Julian of Norwich's 'Shewings'
Peasants Revolt	1381	Lister captures the city
	1400	
	1404	Charter of Henry IV
	1409	Guildhall begun
Battle of Agincourt	1415	St Andrew's friary burnt
	1417	Charter of Henry V
	1443	Gladman's Insurrection
Battle of Bosworth	1485	
Colombus 'discovered' America	1492	

all alone and so came to speak with them, and when they saw him they made him great cheer and honoured him much, desiring him to alight of his horse, and so he did wherein he did great folly. For when he was alighted they came round about him and began to speak fair to him and said 'Sir Robert you are a knight and a man greatly beloved in this country, and renowned a valiant man, and though you are this yet we know you well, you are no gentleman born but son to a villein such as we are, therefore come you with us and be our Master and we shall make you so great a lord that one quarter of England shall be under your obedience'. Salle refused scornfully, saying 'Would you that I should forsake my natural lord for a company of knaves as you are, to my dishonour for ever. I had rather you were all hanged, as you will be, and that shall be your end.

Salle tried to get back on his horse but the mob seized him. Froissart says he died nobly killing 12 of the rebels first but other chronicles say that he did not die fighting but was captured and executed by the rebels.[11]

Norwich's richer citizens then went to Lister and offered him money to keep out of the city, but he came in anyway. According to Blomefield he entered the city 'with a great throng of citizens that had joined him' and they demolished the houses of nobles and lawyers.[12] They beheaded a justice of the peace named Reginald Eccles and raided Salle's house—his chattels were later assessed as worth £200. Lister established himself in Norwich Castle and forced four captured knights to serve him at meals. He sent men to the priory at Carrow to seize their documents which he had brought back to Norwich and publicly burnt.

The 'fighting Bishop' of Norwich, Henry Despencer, was at his manor at Burleigh near Oakham when news of the revolt reached him. He at once marched towards Norwich gathering supporters and scattering rebels on the way. The rebels retreated to North Walsham where they made themselves a makeshift fort out of carts and furniture. Not surprisingly they were soon defeated by the bishop: Lister was found hiding in a cornfield. He was immediately sentenced to be hung, drawn and quartered. The bishop heard his confession and walked with him to the gallows.[13] Lister's quarters were put on display in different parts of Norfolk and his goods forfeited to the king: his stock-in-trade at Felmingham was valued at 33 shillings.

In 1404 King Henry IV gave a new charter to the city. This took Norwich out of the control of county officials by making Norwich a county in its own right—this privilege had already been granted to Bristol, York and Newcastle. The bailiff was replaced by two sheriffs and a mayor was appointed who, along with four 'Probi Homines' (honest men), exercised the office of justice of the peace. Under the charter Norwich had a mayor for the first time. William Appleyard was mayor for the first three years and he was to hold the office a further three times. Unfortunately the 1404 charter did not define the city's boundaries and so did not resolve the many disputes between the city and various religious bodies about rights in the city and surrounding hamlets. The charter created an advisory body of 24 men but did not say if city officials were to be chosen by the 24 or by all the freemen. The differences were submitted to the arbitration of Sir Thomas Erpingham and he arranged a 'Composition' in 1415. This recommended a Common Council of 60 members elected annually by the citizens and a Mayor's Council of 24 who could do nothing without the consent of the 60. The great wards and little wards which were established in 1404 were to be the basic units of city government for over 400 years.

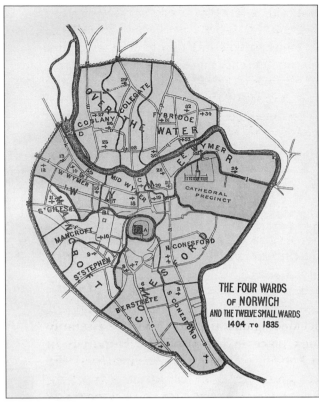

9   *The Great and Little Wards*

In 1417 King Henry V—who two years earlier had fought at Agincourt with Sir Thomas Erpingham as the leader of his archers—gave the city a new charter. This confirmed the charters of his father Henry IV and the 'new composition' made between the citizens in 1415 after Erpingham's arbitration. The 1417 charter set up the way the city was to be governed and its provisions endured largely unaltered for over 400 years. The mayor and one of the sheriffs were elected by the entire freeman citizenry. The council consisted of 60 people—all male, of course—a different number for each ward, presumably roughly equivalent to their population and importance in the early 15th century. The 60 councilmen were elected ward by ward in Passion week each year. Councilmen had to live within the ward for which they were chosen. Although in theory an entire new body of men could be elected every year, in practice there was a fair degree of continuity. The mayor was required to call the councilmen together with the aldermen at least four times a year: usually they met together far more frequently. The council ratified decisions and elected officials such as coroners and clavors (literally 'key-holders', they looked after the city's cash).[14]

The aldermen, sheriffs and mayor formed a body of 26 men with the real power in the city. The 24 aldermen were to be elected by the freemen, six from each ward. If the mayor thought they were not of the 'worthiest and most sufficient' men he could challenge their election but this almost never occurred. What gave city government its continuity was the fact that, once elected, an alderman remained in office for life. In some other boroughs the aldermen acquired the right to choose who was to fill a vacancy and so became a 'self-perpetuating oligarchy'. This never happened in Norwich: its aldermen were always chosen by the freemen.

The sheriffs were elected each year and could not stand again. One was elected by the freemen and councilmen, the other by the mayor, existing sheriffs and aldermen. No citizen who had not first served as sheriff could become mayor.

The mayor was elected on 1 May and took up office in June. Both occasions were marked by ceremony and feasting. The councilmen and aldermen met to choose two aldermen who had previously been sheriff. The aldermen and sheriffs then voted by secret ballot which of the two was to be mayor-elect.

These arrangements continued until 1834 with a few minor changes noted later. They meant that it was essential to be a freeman of the city to participate in local elections–and it was also necessary to be a freeman to vote in Parliamentary elections.

In spite of the apparent clarity of these arrangements there was trouble to come.

Problems began in 1433 with an election dispute. A group of citizens accused the out-going mayor, Thomas Wetherby, and his friends of trying to choose their own man to succeed him in office. Wetherby walked out and the assembly chose its own candidate but they were not sure if the election was valid in the absence of Wetherby who was still the mayor. The assembly then banned Wetherby and his friends from holding offices. In 1436, Wetherby and his friends were restored to the freedom of the city. This led to more trouble at the mayoral election of 1437 when a group of citizens prevented Wetherby and his friends from taking part. The dispute reached the Privy Council and the city's liberties were taken into the king's hands for two years.

Meanwhile disputes continued between the city and religious bodies. In 1429 the mayor, Robert Baxter, secured a written agreement with the cathedral priory, one clause of which was that the city should pay the priory 4s. a year in return for the lease of tithes in Carrow. Like so many of these agreements this was to lead to as many problems as it solved. In 1442 a dispute between the city and the abbot of St Benet's, another of the city's clerical enemies, was decided against the city. The city assembly would not accept this and a further riot took place in January 1443. Hundreds of citizens took to the streets on the occasion known as 'Gladman's Insurrection', the details of which are obscure. John Gladman rode through the city dressed as a king as he regularly did on Shrove Tuesday. This time however something was wrong: this procession was not on Shrove Tuesday but in January. Some of the crowd laid siege to the priory and demanded that they be given the 1429 agreement. They started to pile wood against the gates of the Close and two of the monks, apparently terrified, found the document and gave it to them. As in the Peasants' Revolt, the document was identified with the information it recorded. One wonders whether the priory had made copies as it certainly did of its title deeds. The rioters held the city for a week and would not admit the king's commissioners. However, unlike in 1272, no one was killed in the riot and no one was hanged in punishment.

The city's liberties were withdrawn and remained in the king's hands until 1447. When the corporation and St George's gild were joined in 1452 this was intended to prevent factional rivalry between the city's rulers: any official who stepped out of line risked expulsion from the fraternity.

The Cathedral

Norwich Cathedral is perhaps the finest Romanesque building in England, if only because later bishops did not have the money drastically to alter the work of its founder. This founder was Herbert Losinga. He had been brought up a monk at Fécamp monastery in Normandy and had become prior there. He created a scandal when he paid King William II a large sum of money to be made Bishop of Thetford and to have his father made abbot at Winchester. This is the sin called simony and William of Malmesbury put his disapproval into verse:

In the Church there arises a scandal;
Losinga is first the cause;
A sect is named from Simon,
And they scorn the Church's laws ...

O shame! that the church should be bartered
For money—for sordid pelf!
Son and Father, Bishop and Abbot—
Each a very Simon himself.[15]

Herbert is supposed to have built the cathedral as a penance and probably he did feel guilt since he went to Rome to obtain absolution from the Pope. He moved the centre of the see from Thetford to Norwich in accordance with the papal regulation that cathedrals should be in large towns. The *Chronicles of Stephen* record:

> [Losinga] bought for a great sum a large part of the town of Norwich and, having torn down houses and levelled the ground for a great space, built in an excellent position on the river Yare a most beautiful church in honour of the Holy Trinity.

There was probably already a church named Holy Trinity on the site and part of the Saxon grid plan of the town may have been destroyed to make way for the new building, including the line of the old Roman road along the line of which the nave was placed. Work began in 1096 at the east end: this is the most important part of any church as this is where the high altar is placed. Stone was used from Barnack in Northants and from Caen in Normandy. Rubble core for the walls was collected

10   *The Cathedral Guest House*

locally and includes Roman bricks from
Caistor. The church was built rapidly for
such a huge enterprise with Herbert constantly urging on the monks in his letters
with cries such as

> the work drags on and in providing material
> you show no enthusiasm. Behold the servants
> of the king and mine are really earnest in the
> works allotted to them. They gather stones,
> carry them to the spot ... You meanwhile
> are asleep with folded hands ... failing in
> your duty through a paltry love of ease.[16]

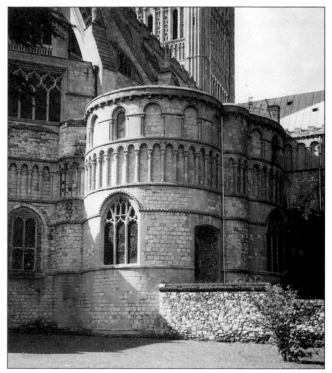

11   *The Cathedral Chapels*

Three small round paintings on an
arch within the cathedral survive to tell
Herbert's story. The first shows Herbert
handing over money, the second his absolution, the third the new cathedral he is
building. Thought to date from about 1190,
this is the first known representation of
the building.

When Herbert died in 1116 the eastern part of the church had been completed
and work had begun on the east bays of
the nave. The work was completed by his
successor Bishop Everard in almost exactly the same style although there are just a few
subtle alterations that mark the new work.

Later building programmes in the cathedral tended to happen only when something
needed to be replaced. The Ethelbert gate was rebuilt at the citizens' expense to replace
the church of St Ethelbert which stood just inside the precinct and which was destroyed
in the 1272 riots. The passage is a very early example of a lierne vault—that is, with
additional rib-vaults springing neither from the main springers nor the central boss. The
outside of the gate is decorated in a pattern made up of stone and squared flints that was
to become a characteristic of East Anglia. The cathedral communar rolls still survive and
record the cost of building work on the cloisters including importing the stone.

The great glory of the cathedral is its collection of carved roof bosses, many of
which have survived undamaged because they were out of reach of later vandals.[17]
Those in the cloister are the earliest—a total of 394 bosses on religious and secular
themes. The largest sequence on one subject is the 102 bosses telling of the Book of
Revelation in the south and west walks. The communar rolls record that a copy of this
work was purchased, presumably an illuminated manuscript whose illustrations were
used as a pattern book. Secular themes include several 'green men' with foliage emerging from their mouths and Eric Fernie has described one curiously contorted figure
among the bosses as that of a defecating man. He is immediately over the entrance to
the slype or passage down which the monks went towards the toilet, so this is perhaps
an example of crude medieval humour.[18]

The nave of the cathedral has over 250 roof bosses telling the Bible story from the Creation to the Last Judgement. These are lively designs and reflect contemporary life. In the Red Sea scene Pharaoh is dressed as a medieval king and has been thrown from a Norfolk cart. The house Rebecca and Joseph stand in front of could be the house of a 15th-century Norwich merchant. In the Last Supper scene there is a plate on the table with two large fish on it, perhaps herrings.[19]

The present spire is the fourth one the cathedral has had. The first was destroyed in the riots of 1272. The second blew down in a storm in 1361 or 1362, damaging the presbytery. The third fell after it was struck by lightning in 1463. The present spire was then built by Bishop Goldwell–it is of brick with a very thin cladding of stone and at 96 metres is the second highest in England.

The damage to the presbytery meant that the upper part of the east end of the church had to be rebuilt. This was done largely at the cost of Bishop Henry Despencer and the work was carried out in the fashion of the day with large windows and with flying buttresses outside. It harmonises wonderfully with Losinga's work of 250 years before on which it stands. There were statues on the heads of the flying buttresses but the present ones are 19th-century replacements.

The Erpingham Gate was built by (or as a memorial to) Sir Thomas Erpingham, a leader of the English archers at the Battle of Agincourt in 1415–he died 'very ancient' in 1428.[20] It has two rows of statues, the outer all female, the inner probably the 12 apostles. The kneeling figure of Sir Thomas was not originally intended for the

12 *Pull's Ferry, medieval watergate of Cathedral Close*

13 *Sketch of the Erpingham Gate*

14 *Dr. Bensly's photograph of the statue of Thomas Erpingham*

niche where it is now: its legs have been chopped to fit it in. Perhaps it came from a chantry chapel over his tomb in the cathedral.

The chapel in front of the west end of the cathedral, now used by Norwich School, was built by Bishop John Salmon in about 1316. The undercroft was used as a charnel house for storing bones both from the priory and from the parish churches in the city—their tiny graveyards were already becoming overcrowded by the 14th-century.

Bishop William Alnwick rebuilt the west entrance to the cathedral—his arms are above the doorway. He left money to build the great window above (the glass itself is 19th-century). Alnwick also built the gate to the Bishop's Palace in St Martin at Palace Plain. The repeated letter 'M' with a crown over it is a sign of the Virgin Mary to whom Alnwick was especially devoted. The carving of a bishop in the vault of the gate may be a portrait of Alnwick himself.[21]

The main medieval buildings that have since gone are the bell tower, the Lady Chapel, the Chapter House and the monastic quarters. The bell tower, destroyed in the 1272 riots, was replaced by a massive new one over 36 feet square, built between 1299 and 1307. After the Reformation it was no longer used and no doubt provided a useful source of stone for later buildings: not a trace of it now remains above ground. The east end of the cathedral had a chapel built by Losinga. This was replaced by a Gothic chapel built by Walter Suffield, the founder of the Great Hospital. This too fell into disuse after the Reformation: only the entrance to it survives inside the cathedral although its outline can be seen outside. The Chapter House was reached from the cloisters and the three bays marking its entrance can still be seen. It too was a victim of the Reformation. Some of the medieval monastic buildings survive within the fabric of the houses of the Close and the Infirmary lasted until the 19th-century. There is a painting by Crome of its demolition and its piers can still be seen in the Close car park.

The cathedral priory was built for a community of about sixty Benedictine monks following a rule based on that of Fécamp where Herbert had been prior. The monks rose at 2a.m. in winter (earlier in summer!) for services and reading until the service of prime was said at daylight. Much of the morning was spent in prayer or reading with an interlude for washing–evidence of these activities can be seen in the cloisters where there are book cupboards in the north-east corner and washing facilities in the south-west corner. The monks then met in the Chapter House for discussion: this was the first time they were allowed to talk. They had their only meal of the day at about 2p.m., eating in silence while scripture passages were read. The afternoon was taken up with work, followed by prayers and a service at about 7p.m. followed by bed. In the 14th century the regime was relaxed and supper was allowed.

Although there were only 60 monks there were many more mouths to feed. The records show up to 250 people eating there each day. These were servants, workmen and guests of the community who combined to make the cathedral priory the largest consumer of goods and also the largest employer of labour in the medieval city. The yearly revenue of the priory was about £2,200 in the early 14th century–this contrasts sharply with the civic community whose yearly revenue never exceeded £270 even at the height of prosperity in the 15th century.

There were also the poor: one of the functions of a monastery was its charity, although they were often criticised for their lack of generosity. Norwich Cathedral Priory gave 10,000 loaves a year to the poor, as well as giving money to the poor at its gate and to prisoners, lepers and others. About 10 per cent of the cathedral income went in charity. It also had responsibility for educating boys and administered St Paul's Hospital: these duties are described later in this chapter.

The cathedral had a fine library although the books given by its founder were largely destroyed in 1272. The replacement was augmented by the bequest of Adam Easton. He had been a monk here and was one of those sent to Oxford University at the priory's expense. He rose to become a cardinal and died in Rome in 1397. His bequest of books, packed in six barrels, arrived at the priory ten years after his death. The most well known of the other monks is Bartholomew Cotton who wrote a *Chronicle* which has already been quoted.[22]

The Castle and the New Borough

Before the Conquest the Earl of the East Angles had a palace on Tombland. The Norman castle made it possible for the new rulers to dominate the native inhabitants who were forced to work on the building, which was originally of earth and wood.

According to Domesday Book nearly 100 houses were destroyed to make space for the castle and its earthworks, and so was at least one church, described in the Introduction. The wooden tower was probably replaced with the stone one we see today in the late 11th or early 12th century. The mound had to be extended but was not given enough time to settle before building was started. This weakness explains the cracks in the east face of the building. The keep, like the cathedral, was built of stone brought over from Caen in France. It is 93ft. by 108ft. and 70ft. high, making it one of the largest Norman keeps in England. Some of the masons worked on both the castle and the cathedral as is shown by masons' marks that can still be

15 *Bigod's tower, Norwich Castle*

seen: for example, some in the east end of the cathedral match those in the basement of the castle keep. Accommodation on the main floor included a great hall, two private chambers, lavatories, a great chamber, a chapel and a store room, with a well 115ft. deep. The building must have been complete by 1122 when Henry I spent Christmas here.[23]

The whole building was in fact refaced in Bath stone by the architect Anthony Salvin between 1834 and 1839. Fortunately there are detailed drawings of all four faces of the castle made by Francis Stone about 15 years before Salvin's work. From these it can be seen that the arcading on the walls (which is very unusual for a military building) is the same now as it was before the refacing. However Salvin did introduce a major change to the look of the castle: he made the stone cladding cover the lower storey which previously had been of exposed flint.[24]

The boundary of the castle fee was marked by a bank and people who lived within the fee came under the direct jurisdiction of the king. As the castle area became less of a fortress, this freedom from the city's control created problems: evildoers of all kinds lived within the castle fee or retreated there to avoid arrest. The area leading up to the castle (roughly where St Andrew's Hill and Opie Street are now) was known as the '*Turpis Vicus*' or 'evil neighbourhood'. It was not until 1345 that King Edward III

16   *Norwich Castle, before the refacing done in the 19th century*

granted the city control of the greater part of the castle fee, reserving to himself only the keep and shire house on the mound.

Earl Ralph used the lands he held west of the new castle to form a new borough. At its formation it had 36 French and six English burgesses. The older parts of the town suffered as a result of Ralph's revolt but his new borough flourished. By 1086 it had 41 French burgesses and 83 others some of whom were also burgesses. The market-place was moved from Tombland to the site in the New Borough that it still occupies.

The market area established after the Norman Conquest extended from St Stephen's church to the present site of the Guildhall. There is no evidence that there was ever a market charter. Presumably all property in the New or French borough which was in the demesne of the Earl of East Anglia and the king at the time of the Domesday survey passed to the commonalty when the city was granted to the citizens by Richard's charter of 1194. A writ of Edward III issued in 1330 upheld the rights of the citizens to profit from vacant places in the city and houses they had built on them by virtue of the fact that the citizens 'by charters of our ancestors former kings of England, which the lord Edward late king of England, our father, confirmed by his charter, hold the said city with the appurtenances hereditarily at fee farm'.

Visitors to Norwich often ask who was the person 'Saint Peter Mancroft' to whom Norwich's market church is dedicated. Mancroft is of course not the name of a person but a place-name. The area of the new borough was known as the 'Magna Crofta' (great field). This name and the siting of the main city market beneath the castle are the legacies of the New Borough of Earl Ralph that have survived in spite of his ill-fated rebellion.

The French borough and the English inhabitants of Norwich appear to have merged very quickly into one unit. Richard of Devizes wrote in about 1190, 'In

17   *St Peter Mancroft*

Durham, Norwich and Lincoln you will hear scarcely any speaking Romance' (i.e. French).[25] Paradoxically, by the later Middle Ages the French language was not spoken only by Frenchmen—it had become the language of the gentry. Sir Thomas Erpingham is one of England's heroes, fighting against the French at Agincourt and yet his wife's will is written in French, as are those of several of her upper class contemporaries.[26]

The Jewish Community

The chronicler William of Malmesbury says that Jews first came to England with William the Conqueror and there is no evidence of an earlier Jewish community in Norwich. The name of Isaac first occurs in the Domesday list of Frenchmen living in the New Borough. The Jewish community in Norwich probably numbered about 200 people at its height, declining to 50 or 60 at the time of the final expulsion from England in 1290. There was an area of Norwich known as the Jewry where the majority of the community lived: this was in the area around Haymarket, White Lion Street and the present Orford Place. This area was close to the market and also to the castle where the Jews were sometimes forced to seek royal protection when there was ill-feeling against them. They had a synagogue here, just off White Lion Street, and some glazed roof tiles and other artefacts from it have been found. However this was not a ghetto and it was never compulsory for Jews to live there. The richest Jews in

18   *The Music House, King Street*

Norwich were the Jurnet family who lived in King Street where the Music House now is: the undercroft of their house still survives.[27]

We do not know to what extent their loans paid for the cathedral in Norwich but they were certainly involved: in the first cathedral register there is a copy of an acquittance by William de Walsham, Prior of Norwich, of all debts due to Isaac son of Jurnet. The date of the document is given as 4978 which is equivalent to the Christian year 1218.[28] A connection between Isaac and the cathedral has often been guessed at, partly because a surviving mason's mark on his King Street house is identical to some on the Cathedral, showing that the same man worked on both buildings. There is some evidence of Jewish physicians in Norwich: there is a record of the house of Isaac the physician on Saddlegate and also of the herb garden of Solomon which Lipman says is the earliest known reference to a private herb garden in England.[29] We also know of Jews in Norwich described as cheesemongers, wine merchants and a fishmonger, but it is not known if they traded solely with fellow-Jews or with the citizens as a whole.

On 24 March 1144 the mutilated body of a 12-year-old boy was discovered on Mousehold Heath. The body was identified as William, who was apprenticed to a skinner in Norwich. It came to be believed that he had been tortured and murdered by the Jews in a form of mock Crucifixion; apparent miracles at his tomb led to the translation of the body to the monks' cemetery, then the cathedral chapter house and then into the cathedral itself. It seems clear that Elias, the prior of the cathedral, had doubts about the story and it was only after his death in 1150 and the election of William Turbe as bishop that the cult was given official sanction.

The cult was never strong outside East Anglia but is significant as being the first known example of the accusation of ritual murder against Jewish communities in Europe; there were to be many later examples in England and Europe in the centuries to come. However, it does not seem that the Norwich Jews suffered immediate persecution. There was an outbreak of violence against the Jews in Norwich in February 1190, probably as a consequence of Crusading fervour stirred up by King Richard: the constable of the Tower of London rendered accounts of £28 7s. 2d. on the chattels of Norwich Jews who were killed at this time. There were further attacks in the 1230s after a Christian boy was claimed to have been forcibly circumcised by the Jews.

In answer to Pope Gregory's renewed condemnation of usury, Edward I in 1275 forbade Jews to lend money at interest. In July 1290 writs were sent to all sheriffs ordering that all Jews must leave England by November on pain of death. They were allowed to take their money and personal property and were to be provided with safe passage across the Channel. They could stay if they converted to Christianity and three women from Norwich are known to have lived in the House of Converts in London after doing so. The synagogue itself, and parts of the Jewry too, appear to have been destroyed by fire. In the late 19th-century, when the basement of the Curat House in White Lion Street was being rebuilt, fragments were found of stone columns, glass and pottery, as well as a layer of burnt material. Some bones were also disturbed during this work and there have been rumours since of the house being haunted by the ghost of a rabbi.[30]

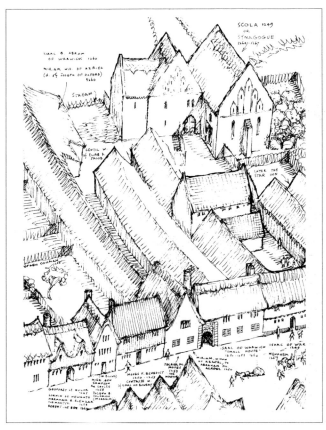

19 *Drawing by A. Chaplin of the area around the synagogue*

Religious Life

Norwich cathedral priory was a Benedictine house, that is the monks followed the rules laid down by St Benedict in the sixth century. As the centuries passed and people made many gifts to the monasteries, much of the ideal of poverty and simplicity was lost.

Groups of friars were established in the late 12th century as a reaction to the wealth and power of the older religious orders. Six orders of friars came to Norwich in the following century: two were fairly short-lived but the other four lasted until the Reformation. The first two orders to arrive were the Franciscans or Grey Friars and the Dominican or Black Friars, both of whom came to the city in 1226. The Franciscans' house was at the top of what is now Prince of Wales Road and the Dominicans' first house was off Colegate. The other two successful friaries were the Augustinian Friars at King Street, and the Carmelite or White Friars north of what is now Whitefriars Bridge.

The Friars Penitential established themselves by Elm Hill but the order was a failure and was suppressed by the Pope in 1307. The Black Friars, finding their Colegate site inconvenient as it had no river frontage, asked the king if they could take over the

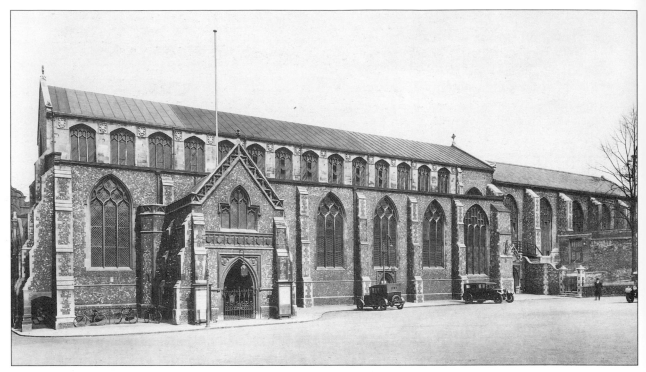

20   *St Andrew's Hall*

house of the Friars Penitential. They were allowed to do so on condition that they permitted the last prior now 'broken with age and nearly blind' to stay there for the rest of his life.[31] They made the site much bigger by taking over surrounding plots of land: this process can be traced through the Norwich City court rolls and has been described by Margot Tillyard. They rebuilt the friary church on a much larger scale but two parts of the previous building survive: the brick undercroft and the building known as Becket's Chapel.[32]

As the site grew bigger the line of Elm Hill was diverted around it which explains the sharp bend at the upper end of Elm Hill today. The church was destroyed by fire in 1413 although the fine east window survived and can still be seen. The friars still had their other site in Colegate and they moved back across the river while a new church was built. This is the building that survives today as St Andrew's and Blackfriars' Halls. A relative of Sir Thomas Erpingham, probably his nephew, was a friar there at the time and Erpingham paid for the rebuilding of the clerestory of the nave in stone: the family arms can be seen between the windows on the outside of the building.

The friars were a preaching order using their church and the yard outside, and also travelling throughout the county. Unlike the cathedral, they did not have large estates to supply them with food and with revenues. Instead they were *mendicants*–that is, they were dependent on charity. The friars were generally popular and almost half the Norwich people making wills gave money to all the four friaries and many asked to be buried in them.

21   *The Arminghall Arch: now in the Magistrates' Courts building*

The other three friaries must also have been impressive buildings. The Carmelite friary in Whitefriars was perhaps the most popular of them all as a burial place. The Augustine friary in King Street had a huge east window which was also paid for by Sir Thomas Erpingham and which contained the coats of arms of all the 107 lords, barons, and knights who had died without issue since the coronation of King Edward III.[33] In 1458 Margaret Wetherby, widow of the contentious alderman, gave 100 marks to build a new library in the friary on condition that her name and that of her husband be inscribed on every bookcase and every window.[34]

Unlike Blackfriars the other three friaries passed into private hands after they were dissolved at the Reformation and the churches and conventual buildings have all been destroyed. All that now remains of them is an arch from an anchorite's cell and an undercroft in Whitefriars; and also the so-called 'Arminghall Arch' now inside the new courts building on Bishopgate, which is also thought to have originally come from Whitefriars.

Of course not all friars lived up to their vows. Walter of Croxton, one of the short-lived community of 'pied' friars, stole charters from the Norwich church along with chalices and money in May 1287. In September 1288 a pied friar called Walter of Norwich stole books from the Westminster house of the order. This was probably the same man.[35] Although 'of Norwich' would be enough to distinguish him in the London house, in Norwich itself there would be many Walters and he would be distinguished by the name of the village he or his family came from. In the same way a man might be identified by his place of origin in one document and by his trade in another–this illustrates how hard it can be to sort out individuals occurring in records before the development of surnames in the early 14th century. Cardinal Adam Easton is simply called 'Adam Anglo' on his tomb in Rome–as the only Cardinal from England, this was enough of a description to distinguish him.

The only female religious house in Norwich was Carrow Priory, a Benedictine house given estates by both King Stephen and King John. It was never a large house: there was a prioress with 12 nuns here at the time of King Stephen and the same number of sisters at the time of the Dissolution in 1538. The last prioress, Isabel Wygun, built the prioress's lodge which still exists as part of the Carrow Abbey complex. The church at Carrow was the largest in the city apart from the Cathedral.[36]

There were many disagreements between the city and its religious neighbours, some of which have already been mentioned. There were also disputes between the city and Carrow Priory, mainly because the city boundaries had never been properly defined: the citizens claimed that the priory was within the city but the priory said that it was not. This led to a bizarre dispute in 1415 after a man called William Koc of Trowse was murdered in Lakenham by a gang of men armed with spades and sticks. His widow Margery raised the hue and cry in the neighbouring townships, but Editha the prioress of Carrow harboured the murderers, presumably claiming that the affair fell within her jurisdiction. As a result she and another nun were actually accused of the murder and spent some time in prison as a consequence. Various courts pondered the rights and wrongs of the case and in 1418 it was decided that the prioress was not guilty of the charge but also that Carrow was in the city of Norwich.[37]

Julian of Norwich

The work of Julian of Norwich is a very well known and important book of mystic devotion, but almost nothing is known of her life apart from the information it contains about her. In it she says she was 'thirty and a half' years old in May 1373 when she received her revelation, so she was probably born late in 1342.[38] It was when she fell ill and was preparing herself for death that she experienced the first of a series of 16 revelations or 'shewings' of God's love and these became the substance of her book. The only known references to her are in three wills–dated 1394, 1404 and 1415–to which money was left to her as anchoress at St Julian's church off King Street. (It should be noted that this church is not named after her but after a much earlier saint–either Julian the Hospitator or Julian, Bishop of Le Mans. Julian took her name from the church not the other way around.) The church of St Julian had been given to Carrow Priory by King Stephen so it is possible that Julian was educated at the priory and brought up to be a nun but there is no archive evidence for this: it is equally possible that she was a widow and a mother. She lived in walled seclusion in the anchorage by the south wall of St Julian's church. The date of her death is not known. Although she is a highly original writer–the *Cambridge Medieval History* calls her the first English woman of letters–she was part of a flourishing school of mysticism in Norwich diocese and her contemporaries included Margery Kemp of Lynn and Richard of Caister, vicar of St Stephen's in Norwich. We know from Margery's own book that she came to Norwich to visit Julian.

Julian describes herself as unlearned and some of her attitudes are probably typical of medieval piety. To her the saints were real people and friends–she writes of St John of Beverley, 'our lord showed him … and brought to my mind how he is a kind neighbour'. She stressed the physical nature of Christ's suffering, dwelling on the drying out of Christ's body as he was dying on the cross. Some of her thinking, however, is surprisingly modern (or timeless): she was able to write of God, 'As truly as God is our father, so just as truly he is our mother'. Her optimism is reflected in her most famous words–'all shall be well and all manner of things shall be well'.[39]

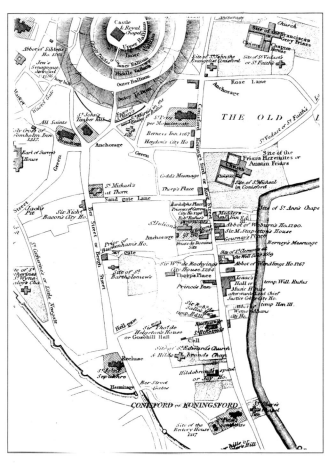

22   *From R. Taylor's plan, showing St Julian's church and anchorage*

She was not by any means the only anchorite or anchoress in the city–references are known to at least 50 between the mid-13th century and the Reformation (only 13 anchorites are known to have lived in London during this period).[40] Some were attached to churches, others lived on or by bridges and gates where they no doubt had functions of cleaning and maintenance and of raising money for minor repairs. Although leading religious lives they had no fixed common rule and, as Blomefield says, some had servants.[41] The names of two of Julian's servants are known and one of them later became an anchoress herself. John Bond in his will of about 1348 leaves bequests to anchorites at the churches of St Peter Hungate, St Christopher and two other churches, and to one at Fyebridge.[42] The cells of anchorites were often built so that the hermit could see the high altar of the church: the 'squint' through which this was done can still be seen on the north wall of what is now Blackfriars Hall.

Another mystic in late medieval Norwich was Richard of Caister, known as 'the good vicar', who was vicar of St Stephen between 1402 and 1409. He had such a reputation for holiness that miracles of healing were reputed to happen at his tomb. He was the writer of the prayer:

Jesus, my Lord, that madest me,
And with Thy blessed blood me bought,
Forgive that I have grieved Thee
With word, with work, with will and thought.

Jesus, in whom is all my trust,
That died upon the cruel tree
Withdraw my heart from fleshly lust,
And from all worldly vanity.

The Parish Churches and Popular Religion

Norwich is fortunate in having a large collection of medieval wills: between 1370 and 1532 the wills of over 1,500 lay people and 300 clerics survive. From these we know that people felt a strong bond to their local parish church. 95 per cent of the testators left something to one or more parish churches and most people named the one in which they chose to be buried. Some left bequests for specific building work and these can help in dating the fabric of a church. For example, three people left money for building the new church of St Andrew between 1499 and 1508. In 1479 William Blackdam left 10 marks towards painting the rood screen in St James Pockthorpe. This is the screen that includes the painting of St Walstan referred to earlier and which is now in the church of St Mary Magdalen.[43]

By the later Middle Ages many Norwich people probably thought the monks at the cathedral were wealthy enough. About one third of the wills mention bequests to it, compared to one half leaving money to all four friaries. Bequests to the cathedral tended to be from the wealthy and also from the county gentry–only six Norwich people asked in their wills to be buried in the cathedral whereas about 150 asked to be buried in one of the friaries. In April 1998 part of the graveyard of Greyfriars was uncovered and analysis of the bones found here will hopefully add to our knowledge of medieval Norwich. Prominent county people buried in the cathedral included John Heydon of Baconsthorpe in 1480 and members of the Boleyn family. There is an indent in the south ambulatory where a long lost brass may (as Arthur Whittingham suggested) have been of Dame Anne Boleyn, who was the great-grandmother of Henry VIII's queen and who died in 1484.[44]

The wills people made reflect their religious beliefs. In the 1490s Roger Aylmer left money for John Fysher of the Norwich Greyfriars to go to Rome and sing for his soul while Katherine Kerre left money for the Jesus mass in Norwich Cathedral, for Thomas Pekke to sing in St Julian and St Peter Southgate, to three named nuns at Carrow Priory, to the anchorite at Blackfriars 'and her maid' and to other named anchorites.[45] Three hundred years earlier Oliver Wyth of Yarmouth made many religious bequests in Yarmouth, Norwich and elsewhere. His Norwich benefactions included Carrow (where two of his daughters were nuns), gifts to anchorites including Lady Margery of St George Colegate and bequests to hospitals.[46]

Religious and charitable bequests are neatly combined in the will of John Cambridge, twice mayor of the city, who died in 1442. He left £10 to be kept in a chest in St Andrew's church which was to be lent out to the poor of the parish for a maximum term of three months. Each time anyone borrowed or gave back the money he was to kneel before the rood and say prayers for the souls of John Cambridge and his family. John Gilbert made many religious bequests including 4d. to each of the sisters of St Lawrence–these were presumably an informal religious group but nothing is known about them. Gilbert left 12d. to each anchorite or anchoress in the city and also money to provide for poor prisoners in the prisons at the Guildhall and the castle and to 'iche blynde and beddered man or woman'. A purely secular charity occurs in the gifts of Walter and John Daniel, the second and third mayors of the city. They built almshouses for the poor in their parish of St Stephen in Great Newgate, later Surrey Street.[47]

Popular religion in these churches was a much more sensuous experience than it is today. All wall spaces would have been painted, all windows filled with coloured glass, all now empty niches replete with painted figures of saints. Each church had a screen across the chancel in front of the altar, with a loft above to which the priest would process at certain times, and above this a huge representation of the crucifixion, with Mary and John standing beside the cross. St Peter Mancroft had an Easter sepulchre where the Host was formally buried each year in a silver image of Christ with his bleeding wounds and a pyx upon his chest. A window in St Andrew still shows a bishop and a muffled female figure with a ghastly grin engaged in a dance of death. Several Norwich churches have passages under their chancels, as at St Gregory and at St Peter Mancroft, or beneath the tower, as at St John Maddermarket. These may reflect the need to preserve rights of way in a crowded city centre but they were also used for ceremonial processions–there is still a niche above that at St Gregory where a holy statue would have stood.

Norfolk was exceptionally rich in shrines. The most famous of all was that at Walsingham which was the most popular in England. Pilgrims to the shrine included most of the kings of England–even King Henry VIII was a visitor there although he was later to have it destroyed. Many of the pilgrims must have visited Norwich where there was the shrine of St William in the Cathedral and St Leonard's Priory had a bejewelled statue of St Leonard, which is mentioned in the surviving account rolls. In 1443 Margaret Paston wrote to her husband who was ill in London: 'My mother promised another image of

23 *The east window of St Stephen's church*

wax of the weight of yourself to Our Lady of Walsingham ... I have promised pilgrimages to be made for you to Walsingham and St Leonard's.'[48] St Leonard's Priory also had an image of King Henry VI which was supposed to have healing powers. The tomb of Richard of Caister in St Stephen's also attracted pilgrims: badges bought at his shrine have turned up in London and Salisbury. People from Norwich travelled to other shrines—pilgrims' badges from the shrine of the Virgin's robe at Aachen have been found in the city.

We have a detailed record of the miracles at St William's tomb as they were all eagerly written down by William of Monmouth, one of the cathedral monks, who was keen to prove William's saintliness. He lists 115 miracles mostly involving Norwich people—57 per cent of those cured came from within 10 miles of the city and very few came from more than 50 miles away. The cases reveal some acts of personal charity—a Norwich tanner allowed a blind man and other poor pilgrims to stay with him without charge. On the other hand a mad woman, taken to the shrine in the hope of a miracle cure, was dragged out of the cathedral so that 'the people who had assembled at the tomb with their offerings might not be hindered by her presence'.[49]

Bible stories re-enacted as drama were organised by the gilds. In 1527 the gild of St Luke complained to the city authorities that it could no longer afford to provide pageants and processions on Whit Monday and Tuesday as it had been doing. The city replied by identifying 12 pageants which it divided out among the various gilds. For example, the grocers and rafemen (chandlers) performed 'Adam and Eve', and the butchers, fishmongers and watermen performed the 'Holy Ghost'.[50]

Some of these religious dramas are reflected in the ways in which scenes are portrayed on the cathedral bosses. The subject is discussed in Rose and Hedgecoe with photographs of some of the bosses concerned.[51] M. Anderson thinks that the design of the 'Red Sea' boss imitates the painted cloths that were used for the sea in such dramas. She also saw scenes from religious plays in the glass in St Peter Mancroft—'St John is led to prison by a gaoler who wears what is obviously a mask in the shape of a pig's snout'. In the portrayal of the Massacre of the Innocents in the same church, 'Herod sits on something more than just a throne, but not quite a building, and a red fabric thrown over the front of it might have been the curtain used to shut him off from later scenes in which he did not figure'.[52] A play performed on Corpus Christi Day that featured Herod is mentioned in a Paston letter of 1478.[53]

Signs and portents were taken very seriously. In 1274, according to notes made by the antiquary John Kirkpatrick, 'on St Nicholas' Eve were great earthquakes, lightning and thunder, with a huge dragon and a blazing star'.[54] Another chronicler describes an event in 1394:

> This year an exhalation of fire (two words lost, probably 'appeared in') many places of England, which, when a man went alone went as he went, and stayed as he staid, but if many went together, it appeared afar off, sometimes it was like a wheel, sometimes like a barrel and sometimes like a log.

The same writer tells us that in 1401 'was seen a blazing star first betwixt the east and north sending forth his fiery beams towards the North'.[55] Today we might class these appearances as Unidentified Flying Objects, but of course that terminology was not in use then.

Trade and Industry

Norwich attracted traders and adventurers from the earliest times. An early medieval poem says:

> For metals is Exeter famous,
> And York for her broad wooded plains.
> While Chester is proud of her Frenchmen,
> Norwich boasts of her Irish and Danes.

Specific information on how livings were made in the city is very sparse. A French chronicler says that the reason the Flemings took Norwich in 1174 was because Norwich men 'for the most part were weavers, they knew not how to bear arms in knightly wise'. Central taxation records (the Pipe Rolls) refer to Norwich citizens trading in dyed cloth in 1202 and that of 1204 includes Norwich in a list of seaports. The city had an obligation to provide 24 herring-pies to the king every year. It is not known when this obligation began but it continued until 1806 and reflects the sea-going nature of Norwich trade. A copy of an agreement of 1286 between woad merchants of Amiens and Corbeil in France is recorded in the *Book of Customs*: woad is a blue dye which is also used as a fixative for other dyes.[56]

Some old street names come from the trades that once congregated along them—this concentration of trades comes from a time before the survival of written evidence. The name Pottergate is of course the street of the potters; another street named after a trade is Parmentergate (now called Mountergate) named after the leather dressers who presumably congregated in this area of the city. These trades have been confirmed by archaeologists who have found knives and specialised tools of leather workers and iron combs and spindles of textile workers.

City court rolls record transfers of ownership of property and survive from 1285. Serena Kelly has used these to obtain information about working patterns. Between 1285 and 1311 some 966 people appear in these rolls with their trade given. They include 247 ecclesiastics of various kinds, 173 leather workers, 144 textile workers, 97 merchants, 60 metal workers and 43 bakers, suggesting that there was still a very wide mix of occupations and Norwich had not yet developed its specialisation in the textile trade.[57]

Before 1300 the leather industry was as important as the textile industry—three branches of it were banned from forming gilds between 1288 and 1293 (tanners; fullers and saddlers; cobblers). The story of St William tells us that he was apprenticed to a skinner in 1132—he is England's first known apprentice. He was only eight when he became an apprentice—his biographer implies this was a normal age to do so.[58]

There was a large sheep population in Norfolk from at least the time of Domesday Book and by the late 13th century Norfolk weavers had developed a light-weight cloth called worsted which was in demand throughout England and also for export. Worsted weavers are found in Norwich and elsewhere by 1329. Worsted is not the name of a cloth but of a type of yarn spun 'in his oile' from the tops of pasture wool.

It was used for various purposes but above all for textiles. The first known document mentioning worsted is in 1295 when it was already known in Dublin. Blomefield dates the great growth in worsted to a slightly later year:

> This year, 1336, is memorable for the great increase of the Flemish stuffs, or worsted manufacture, which proved the most advantageous trade to the nation in general, and this city and county in particular, that ever was introduced among any people ... that it was first of all introduced at Worsted [sic], I make no doubt, from its name, which occurs in the most ancient things I meet with, in relation to it, it being as plain that it had that name on that account, as the name of Norwich-stuffs at this day, for the same reason.

Blomefield is probably thinking of the Act of 1337 by which King Edward III encouraged foreign weavers to come to England, promising privileges to 'all the cloth-workers of strange lands of whatsoever country they be' who came to Norwich and other large towns.[59]

In later centuries dornyx weaving flourished too, the earliest known reference in Norwich being 1493. This originated in Doornijk, now called Tournai, and produced a fabric suitable for beds and hangings generally woven in colours on the loom.

Of about 1,850 names enrolled in the Free Book before 1400 only 20 have place-names from outside Norfolk and Suffolk and seven of these were from the Continent: this underlines the isolation of Norwich from the rest of England in the Middle Ages. Trade with Europe was booming. In 1295 three Flemings—Bernard Pylat, Nicholas de Lo and John Waterbal—are known from Flemish archives to have been engaged in trade with Norwich drapers. English cloth was shipped to Holland and Zeeland by merchants from those countries and by Norwich merchants.[60]

The kind of imports coming into the city can be illustrated from the records of a 14th-century tragedy. On 19 October 1343 a boat loaded with men and goods coming from Yarmouth to Norwich sank near Cantley and 40 people were drowned. The river was part of the city of Norwich all the way down to Hardley Cross, so the case came before a Norwich inquest. The sinking was blamed on the rain, the strong wind and the overloading of the boat. The boat was loaded with sea coal, salt, barrels of iron from Sweden, wood from Riga, onions and herrings.[61] It is thought that the bricks used to make the Bridewell undercroft were imported from Zeeland.

The strong trading links with Europe are illustrated by John Asger who was mayor of Norwich in 1426. His brass in St Lawrence's church describes him as 'once a merchant of Bruges'. It seems that he was there when he was elected mayor: an Assembly Book minute of 27 May 1426 records that the expenses in riding to Bruges for him were to be paid by the community.[62] By the 15th century English merchants in Low Countries towns were organised under English governors—William Hemstede, John Austin, Thomas Ritser and John Reinier were among the merchants who refused to pay towards the salary of governor John Wareyn in Middleburgh in 1421. All four came from Norwich and they disliked the growing power of London merchants like Wareyn. The merchants employed factors to look after their interests when they were back in England—Richard Hart of Norwich lost £20 in 1467 because his factor in Middleburgh was slow in reclaiming the debt from a merchant there who had since died.[63]

There was a circuit of large fairs in East Anglia that traders would go to. A merchant from Bordeaux sold some wine to men from Norwich at Boston fair in 1273.

He failed to get his money and searched in vain for them in Boston and Norwich throughout 1274. In May 1275 he finally caught up with them at the fair at St Ives and they were brought to justice there–the case is recorded in the court rolls at the Public Record Office in Kew.[64]

The occupation of many Norwich citizens must have been farming. The walls built in the 14th-century included a good deal of farm land and the citizens also had grazing rights beyond the walls in Eaton and Lakenham. The cathedral records include an agreement of 1205 between the prior and the citizens of Norwich about land described as pasture in the suburb of Norwich, extending towards Lakenham, Harford Bridge and Eaton. The prior acknowledges that the citizens have the right to pasture their animals: they are to pay him one penny a year for each cow or ox feeding in the pasture of Lakenham or Eaton (two pennies a year if they feed in both pastures), with the same charges for every five sheep. In return the citizens grant to the prior two areas of 40 acres and 33 acres in the same common from which he may take heath, broom, furze and fodder and may dig turves.[65]

On the east side of the city Mousehold Heath covered 6,000 acres extending from Norwich into eight country parishes. By 1086 it was wooded only at the Norwich end where Thorpe Wood is assessed in Domesday Book as having 'wood for 1,200 swine'. This is one of the largest assessments in Norfolk. King Henry I gave the wood to the Bishop of Norwich in 1101 and Bishop Herbert was keen to preserve it–he wrote to his servant: 'As to making a present of Thorpe Wood to the sick or everyone else I gave you no orders … for I appointed you the custodian of the wood not the rooter up of it'.[66]

In 1156 Pope Adrian referred to 'the Heath and all the wood' and by the 16th century the heathland extended over the whole plateau, only the steep slopes being still wooded. The Heath was grazed and bits dug up for chalk and flints. The Assize Roll of 1268-1269 records that Walter Pye and his wife Margery were crossing 'the heath of Muscholt' on the way from Norwich to Thorpe when they had an argument: 'Walter struck the aforesaid Margery with a certain stick on the head so that she immediately died.'[67] This is the first known reference to the heath's name. Its meaning is not certain. 'Holt' means 'wood' and 'muse' could be derived from 'mossy' or 'mousey'. Another school of thought is that it is derived from 'monks' as the cathedral Priory owned part of the heath.

An Assembly order of 1354 shows how the country could invade the city, perhaps helped by the ravages of the Black Death:

> Whereas great injuries and dangers so often have happened before this time in the city of Norwich and still happen from day to day in as much as boars, sows and pigs before this time have gone and still go vagrant by day and night without a keeper in the said city, whereby divers persons and children have thus been hurt by boars, children killed and eaten, and others buried exhumed, and others maimed, and many persons of the said city have received great injuries as breaking of houses, destruction of gardens … [68]

The market was regulated by the leet courts and later by the city authorities through the mayor's court. Dealers were grouped according to their wares–the drapers in one spot, the fishmongers in another. Some markets were held elsewhere–cattle, sheep, poultry and cheese on the south side of St Peter Mancroft now called Haymarket; horses

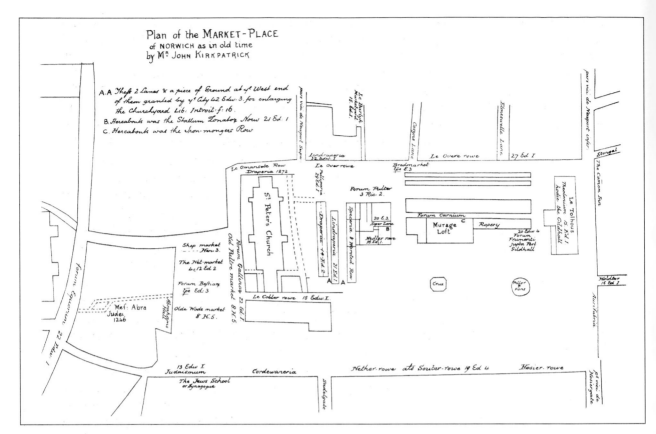

24 *John Kirkpatrick's plan of the medieval Market Place*

at Rampant Horse Street from at least the 13th century, according to title deeds–*Rampant Horse* is the name of an inn. Pigs were sold at All Saints' Green until the time of Edward I when this market was moved to Hog Hill (now Orford Hill) and All Saints' Green was used for the timber market. The word 'maddermarket'–where the dye of that name was sold for colouring cloth–occurs in documents from the mid-13th century.

Market stalls were known as solds or selds and the size of the stalls is occasionally given in title deeds. In 1385 the cathedral prior leased to Bartholomew de Appleyard and other citizens of Norwich two market stalls: their measurements are given in the lease. One in the meat market was 17ft. 3in. by 9ft. 4in., the other in the fish market was 10ft. 3in. by 4ft. 6in. They paid a combined rent of 13s. 4d. a year for the stalls.[69] As the city began to acquire property in the late 14th century it became the owner of the market and of other key sites. In 1392 Henry Lominour and two others gave to the bailiffs and the commonalty three messuages, 42 market stalls and 4s. of rents in the city 'for doing and supporting certain charges and works of piety in the city aforesaid, every year for ever'.[70] In 1398 the abbot of Wendling leased to the city for 600 years his messuage with its quay in Conesford, for a rent of 13s. 4d. a year.[71]

Once the markets and staithes were established the city could issue orders insisting they were used and they also insisted that traders had to be freemen of the city.

The charter of 1194 is the first to refer to the citizens of Norwich rather than the burgesses but they are not defined. In the charter of 1285 'citizen' is synonymous with 'freeman'.

From the city's point of view, the important thing was for all its inhabitants to be freemen. Only freemen could trade in the city, train up apprentices or take part in city government. They were exempt from paying tolls at the great fairs and markets. Their freedom was of course recorded by the city authorities and these records survive from 1317. People who did business in the city without becoming freemen were fined. At the leet court in 1289 Hugh de London was fined 12d. 'because he buys and sells in the city and is not of the freedom'.[72] There were four ways to become a freeman. The most common were to be the legitimate son of a freeman or to work for seven years as an apprentice to a freeman. The other two ways were by purchase or by free grant of the corporation. In 1462 the right to vote was extended to freemen living in the hamlets.

If a craft was oversubscribed the entry fee was raised to deter applicants and in times of depression the fee might be reduced. Trade matters were regulated at the leet courts and after 1404 at the mayor's court.

Hudson and Tingey have compiled a list of trades and occupations mentioned in city records in the last half of the 13th century.[73] There are about 150 of these including some highly specialised skills such as bell-founder, goldsmith, parchment dealer as well as surgeons and apothecaries: all these people would no doubt be serving the needs of people in the surrounding villages as well as those in the city. In the 15th century Norwich included specialised trades such as bell-founding and glass-making. The most famous bell makers were the Brassyer family, whose monuments can be seen in the church of St Stephen. One of their bells, thought to date from about 1490, was in the tower of the church of St Julian when it was bombed in the Second World War. The bell survived and can be seen in the reconstructed tower.

Women could not sit on the council but they could have trades: Helen Moundeforde describes herself as a glazier in her will made in 1458. Very occasionally women are found in the registers of 'freemen'. They include Petronilla de Bokenham in 1366 and Isabella de Weston the following year—unfortunately the person's status and trade is not recorded in these early freemen's records. In 1445-6 Elizabeth Baret, single woman, was enrolled as a worsted weaver. However, the role of women as part of the workforce was not always appreciated—in 1511 the worsted weavers in the city rioted against women who were thought to be taking their work.[74]

Norwich was an administrative centre as well as the centre of the Archdeaconry Court of Norwich (which covered about half the parishes in the county) and also of the Consistory Court of the bishop (which covered all of Norfolk and Suffolk). The latter sat in the Ethelbert Gate leading to the Close. These courts brought business into the city and help to explain the large number of inns in the Tombland area.

Noisy and smelly trades tended to be located on the edge of settlement. Even so there is an anti-pollution verse of about 1350 in a Norwich Cathedral manuscript now in the British Library:

Swart Smoky Smiths Smirched with Smoke
Drive me to death with the din of their dints
Such noise at nights heard no man never
such crooked codgers cry after 'coal! coal!'
and blow their bellows till their brains are all bursting.

Serena Kelly found that in about 1300 the smiths were concentrated on the edge of the built-up area north of the river, no doubt both because of the noise and the risk of fire.[75] In the 12th and early 13th centuries iron was being smelted from nodules dug from the gravel, while by about 1300 the emphasis had shifted to the working of imported material. The leather industry and the fulling and dyeing of cloth needed a lot of water and these trades were concentrated on both sides of the river in the west (upstream!) part of the city–there was a fulling mill next to the Duke of Norfolk's palace in the 17th century. Most other trades were not zoned by this time: there was no longer a concentration of potters along Pottergate, nor of cutlers along the street called Cutlers' Row. However even in 1300 there was a concentration of butchers and leather-workers in the Ber Street area–this street was associated with butchers right down to the 20th century.

Brewing was of course an important activity from the earliest times. Pottery cisterns holding between one and two gallons of beer or ale were found in almost all the Pottergate houses. On the Alms Lane site described in more detail later, a large hearth associated with finds of germinated barley suggests there may have been a brew-house here. Ale was the staple drink but the making of beer with hops imported from the Low Countries is known from the late 14th century. In 1390/1 Floritus Taylor was fined two shillings in the leet court for brewing beer. In 1459 Norwich Assembly granted a monopoly of beer brewing to one man–'it is granted that no foreigner or anyone else shall brew beer for sale in the city except him. Except that every citizen shall brew beer for his own and domestic use.' The distinction between brewing for home use and brewing for sale must always have been blurred and the Assembly made various edicts about brewing which were no doubt largely ignored. In 1471 they ordered that brewers should brew neither with hops nor gawle 'nor none other thing that may be found unwholesome for man's body'. In 1498 they issued an order regulating prices of beer: 7d. for a firkin of best beer and 5d. for a firkin of small beer.[76]

Fishing in the river was a source of food, though far more fish sales seem to have been of salt fish brought up from Yarmouth. Margaret Paston wrote to her husband, 'As for herring, I have bought a horse-load for 4s. 6d. I can get no eels yet'. One house in the city is recorded as owing a render of at least two thousand herring.[77] As has been said, the city paid an annual tribute to the king of 24 herring pies. The person carrying them to the king was given 4d. and one pie by the city and six loaves, six dishes from the kitchen, one gallon of wine, one gallon of beer, oats and hay for his horse, some wax and six tallow candles at the king's court. An order of Henry III told prior Simon of the cathedral priory that he must permit the citizens of Norwich 'to have a common of fishing in the river of Norwich which they ought and were accustomed to have it, as they say', so obviously there had been a dispute about fishing rights between the city and the priory.[78] Over 3,000 fish remains were recovered at the Alms Lane site, mainly herring. The only important freshwater fish eaten was the eel. Many oyster shells were found. The importance of fish is perhaps shown by the fact that in Gladman's procession a man dressed as Lent wore white and red herring skins and his horse bore oyster shells. This reminds us that no one would have eaten meat during the 40 days of Lent.

The charter of 1256 included a clause 'that no gild shall be held in the city to the detriment of the said city'. The enforcement of this explains why the corporation was able to keep the crafts firmly under its own control: no strong craft or merchant gild system sprang up in Norwich as it did in many other towns. The most important gild in Norwich was a religious gild rather than a trade one. The gild of St George, founded in the closing years of the 14th century, rose to political prominence by the 1420s and was joined to the city government in 1452. Gild members gathered in the Cathedral on St George's day each year. The gild offered a stipend of 8d. a day to any brother or sister who fell into want. In 1417 the gild received a charter from Henry V which changed it into a corporate body and allowed it to obtain lands and rents. It then issued a set of ordinances that include the first mention of its famous procession: the dragon is first mentioned in the accounts of 1420. The gild included clergy, noblemen and high-status tradesmen and also people of lower status such as blacksmiths and reeders.

Civic Buildings

The city was enclosed with a bank and ditch in 1253. The city walls and gates were completed in 1343 but according to the *Norwich Walls Report* Conesford or King Street gate is mentioned in a deed of 1175 so there may have been much earlier defences. The walls were completed mainly through the generosity of a citizen named Richard Spynk. They form two arcs, the one on the south extending from the river at Carrow to the river at New Mills (in all 1.5 miles), the other from the river near St Martin at Oak to the river at Barrack Street (in all 0.75 miles). The walls were about 20 feet high with battlements. Towers and walls are made of flint bedded in lime mortar with brick arches. It has been suggested the brick might be a later addition to strengthen the walls against artillery about 40 years later. However Alan Carter was sure it was part of the original fabric.[79]

The city agreed to release Spynk from all tolls and dues because of his generosity in repairing the walls and furnishing them with espringolds and other weapons of war. The two boom towers at Carrow were built at the same time as an integral part of the city's defences. Spynk's charter of 1343 mentions 'two great chains of good Spanish iron across the river ... so that no barge or boat might come in or depart without leave nor against the will of those who have to govern the city'.[80] As this suggests, the function of the walls was not just military defence–controlling the number of ways in and out of the city made it easier to regulate traffic and make sure the appropriate tolls were paid.

The walls were not always properly maintained: the Assembly Book for 1420 refers to trees growing on the land of John Swanton near Conesford gate 'to the injury of the walls and towers there'.[81]

In the early 14th century the city owned only the Tolhouse in the market and a common building on Tombland, about which almost nothing is known. Towards the

25 *The city walls: Barrack Street Tower*   **26** *The city walls: The Boom Towers*

end of the century the city began buying property. It then ordered that all flesh and food should be sold at the common stalls. All ships and boats were to be loaded and unloaded at the common staithes–and, of course, had to pay tolls. The city had always had a quay at Fyebridge, used mainly for boats bringing shellfish. The common staithe was purchased in 1379, followed by the new common staithe bought in 1397: both had a crane. These staithes were both along King Street, downstream of the one at Fyebridge, access to which must have been severely restricted when Bishop Bridge was built.

The city also bought a block of buildings between the Market, Pottergate, Dove Street and Lower Goat Lane. Part of the property was formerly an inn and seems to have continued as such–from 1409 it is called the '*Common Inn*'. By an Act of 1404 all merchants had to house with hosts assigned to them by town authorities and traders visiting Norwich no doubt stayed at this inn. The northern part of the property became the Worsted Seld, the only place in the city where country weavers could sell their produce. City revenue was also spent on other projects–Cow Tower was rebuilt in 1399, the Market Cross built in 1409, the murage loft in 1411, and the Guildhall at the same time.

27   *Bishop Bridge*

The Guildhall was built on the site of the old Tolhouse, the brick undercroft of which can still be seen beneath it. It was begun in 1407 and is by far the largest building of its kind in England outside London. One account roll survives describing the expense of building–that for 1411-1413.[82] The building must have been almost complete as, of a total expenditure of just over £100, half was spent on lead for the roof. Additions to the building were made throughout the century and major repairs were needed when the roof of the Mayor's courtroom collapsed in 1511. Some 15th-century glass still survives, now gathered together in the windows at the east end of the Council Chamber.

Cow Tower–formerly known as the Dungeon Tower–is made entirely of brick on a stone plinth and was originally about 50 feet high. It was used as a tollhouse by the priory, then as a prison by them, and later sold to the Great Hospital. The Master of the Hospital granted it to the city in 1378 and it was then repaired–accounts for the purchase of new bricks still survive among the city records.[83]

Bishop Bridge is the only surviving medieval bridge in the city. It is mentioned in an Agreement of 1331 between the citizens and the priory: the prior was to be allowed to build houses on the bridge itself and along both sides of the river but must allow the citizens access to the river for their horses beside the arches of the bridge. It was maintained by the priory until 1393 when it was handed over to the city. The two angle turrets of the gate on the bridge are still marked by the semi-circular projections of the parapet wall. When work was being done on the bridge

28   *Cow Tower*

in 1998 a portion of the wall over six feet high was uncovered on the south side of the bridge.

The earliest city seal 'dating from the time of the bailiffs' has a castle on the front and a lion on the back. The seal made in 1404 has the present design on the front, the castle above the lion. The arms of the city can be seen in the frieze of stone carvings on the outside west wall of St Andrew's church, the stones of which are much older than the wall in which they are now embedded. The castle bears no resemblance to Norwich Castle but the elongated lion is like those put outside City Hall almost 600 years later.

An increasing pride in the city is reflected in an increase in record-keeping. In 1398 the city paid 3s. 6d. for 'a book made for the Community, for parchment and binding the said book'. The *Liber Albus* was begun in 1426 and 'all

29   *The city arms on the east wall of St Andrew's church*

the material evidences and memorable occurrences were entered there by the command of Thomas Ingham the mayor and ever since other things have been added as they happened'.[84]

Housing and Diet

Very few houses from the Middle Ages survive in Norwich and these are of course the houses of the gentry. There are no documentary descriptions of houses so our knowledge is a mixture of archaeological evidence and hints from documentary sources.

Few houses were of stone. Between the Norman Conquest and 1330 there are about twenty known written references to stone houses.[85] One is recorded in 1254 as being between Tombland and the cemetery of St Cuthbert's church. The family who lived there were even called 'de Stonhous' after it, a sign of its rarity. The present Black Horse bookshop marks the site of a stone house called 'le Heybothe' which must have been large—in 1283 it included three shops. In 1285 Nicholas de Ingham and Gundreda his wife gave their son Walter their stone house in Fyebriggate. Most of these medieval stone houses have disappeared but parts of two do survive—the Music House or House of Isaac the Jew in Norwich and the stone house discovered by excavation in 1981 and now preserved under the new Court Buildings. There is no documentary reference for this one so there may have been other ones for which we do not have any records. Leet court records give a few details about houses. In 1288 Robert Scot is reported as being wont to climb over outer walls by night and break through house walls and do other felonies, suggesting that the walls were not very solid—they were probably of wattle and daub.[86] According to the Chronicle of the Norwich monk Bartholomew Cotton, a flood in 1290 'overturned some houses and bore them along' and a flood in Norwich in 1273 is said by a Bury chronicle to have done more harm to Norwich than either the raid of the disinherited barons or the depredations of royal officials after the 1272 riots.

The leet roll of 1263 has a description of what must have been a relatively up-market house. Katerine, the widow of Stephen Justice, accused eight people of breaking into her house on 22 November 1263 and doing damage and robbery and burning the body of her husband which lay on a bier.[87] The house was on Fyebridge Street in St Clement parish—it stood around a yard. The principal room was the hall where meals were taken and the men of the household slept. The private chamber was reached through the hall: this is where the more valuable possessions were kept and where the women probably slept. The constant danger of fire in a city where housing was of flimsy material and roofs of thatch is shown by a legal case in 1264 when William de Eblaster and others burnt down the house of John de Ballaya by setting fire to its gate. To make sure they were successful they stole the clappers and cut the ropes of the bells in the nearby churches of St Peter Parmountergate, St Vedast and St Cuthbert. This was to stop any passer-by seeing the house on fire from raising the alarm by ringing the church bells.[88]

Although the area inside the walls of the city was so big and large parts of it were not built upon, suburbs beyond the walls were developing as early as the mid-13th century around the city gates. There are references to 'suburbs of Norwich' in cathedral deeds of 1250 and 1261. A deed of 1295 mentions a lime kiln in the suburb of Norwich outside Conesford gate and a deed of 1297 refers to a suburb outside Westwick gate.[89]

The court rolls already referred to as registering changes of ownership of property describe the location of houses by naming owners of adjoining properties. By putting this information together it is possible to map who owned what property in Norwich from 1285 onwards. This has been done by the Norwich Survey for the period between 1285 and 1310 and these maps are now in the Norfolk Record Office. The property sizes are given only occasionally: a typical property in the built-up parts of the city might be 10 feet by 30 feet, with the short side fronting the street.

There is nothing to suggest that only citizens could buy and sell property and there was no restriction of gender–single women and widows frequently did so. There was an age restriction–in 1310 the age of majority in Norwich is given as 16 years. Each transaction involved a small cost–a penny to the bailiffs from buyer and seller (the 'outpenny' and 'inpenny'), 2d. for an endorsement on the title deed that it had been enrolled, and 4d. for the actual enrolment. Wills bequeathing property were also enrolled and as Norwich Consistory Court wills do not survive before 1370 this is the earliest series of surviving wills for the city–however, usually the only part of the will to be enrolled was that relating to the bequest of property in the city.

A total of 1,900 enrolled deeds survive for the period 1285 to 1311.[90] One of the main functions of enrolment was to make sure that a wife explicitly gave her consent to the sale–in this way she gave away her right of dower in the property which might otherwise lead to complications later. Both husband and wife would normally come to the court: in one entry in 1289 when Nicholas de Tolye sold a piece of land it is explicitly said that his wife Alice did not give her consent and did not come to the court.

The enrolled deeds suggest that there was an active market in small pieces of undeveloped land at the end of the 13th century. These were probably used for quarrying sand and flint or chalk and gravel, and for the extraction of iron ore. Recent excavations in Norwich have given us a good picture of daily life in the houses of a class of people not much recorded in surviving documents. These finds are described in more detail by Malcolm Atkin.[91]

In Pottergate the archaeologists have found a 57-metre frontage destroyed by fire. These houses were probably burnt down in the fires of 1507 described in the next chapter and the site then undisturbed for the following 150 years. The artefacts found are mainly from the kitchens and they suggest the increasing material wealth of the early 16th century. They include metal cooking vessels, pottery storage vessels and jugs, some made locally, others of a style imported in massive quantities from the end of the 15th century.

At Alms Lane, it appears that the area was used until the 13th century for quarrying and rubbish dumping and was then occupied by iron-workers and brewers. By about 1300 the site was built-up, the houses progressing from single-storeyed to two-storeyed clay wall houses. After about 1500 the houses were rebuilt in flint and brick with timber-framed first floors. Very delicate analysis of tiny bones found on this site helps us piece together the daily life of our ancestors. Some 22,686 fragments of animal bones were recovered, mainly cattle with a much smaller number of pig bones. One rabbit bone from the 12th or 13th century was found: rabbits were only introduced to England in Norman times. They obviously caught on—rabbit bones were common from the late 13th century to early 16th century. Many bird bones were analysed, mostly fowl and geese probably raised on the site.

In the early Middle Ages houses would be using peat for fuel and massive amounts were needed, brought into the city by water. The cathedral account rolls show that the priory was using up to 400,000 peat turves every year and this use of peat, together with rising sea levels, led to the formation of the Norfolk Broads. In 1272 William de Dunwich left 10s. for buying turves for the poor.[92] In the house of Katherine of Norwich in 1336-7, faggots were used for brewing, turf for cooking and logs for heating the hall and chamber.[93] By the end of the

30 *The flint wall of the Bridewell*

Middle Ages the peat was no longer so easily accessible and people turned to wood or coal brought from a distance. Eventually the artificial nature of the Broads was forgotten—Sir Thomas Browne in the 17th century did not know that they were man-made.

Some larger houses of the gentry do survive. The house now called the Bridewell was built in about 1370 by the Appleyard family who supplied Norwich's first mayor in 1404. The long wall of knapped flint running parallel to St Andrew's church is still impressive as are the vaults of the cellars. Strangers' Hall is a house of many different periods which contains a mid-15th-century hall built by a merchant named William Barley. It was not uncommon for the rich to have poor people living in their households. The will of Sir Thomas Erpingham's servant John Middleton who died in 1417 shows, apart from the servants, five poor people dwelling in Erpingham's house. There were 13 poor people in Katherine of Norwich's house, living on a diet of maslin bread and herrings.[94]

Norwich is famous for its brick-built undercrofts: more than eighty are known, probably built in the 15th century to provide level fire-proof platforms for timber-framed houses. As much of the city was later destroyed by fire, many are much older than the houses that now stand on them.[95]

31 *Dragon Hall: the doorway*

Non-domestic survivals include Dragon Hall in King Street, a merchant's hall probably owned by Robert Toppes who was four times mayor of Norwich and who died in 1467. A list of his debtors drawn up at his death survives and shows he had interests throughout the county.[96] The house has a 14th-century doorway with a 15th-century surround. Inside, the hall is on the upper floor. It has a tie-beam roof with crown posts and spandrels in one of which is carved a dragon still with its original paint. The timbers of this roof were dated by dendrochronology in 1987: they are all of the 1420s. Digging in the same year showed the site to have been occupied since at least the 11th century. The Britons' Arms in Elm Hill has a medieval doorway facing the churchyard. The house is timber-framed with fireplaces in the individual rooms like a series of 'bed-sits'. It may well have been a *beguinage* or group of religious-minded women dwelling together. These groups are common in Europe but not otherwise known here. Blomefield says there was such a group living on the north side of the church-yard of St Peter Hungate, as this house is, but it is not known from what source he took this information.[97]

Problems of maintaining cleanliness and water supply occasionally show up in the records or in the archaeology. The toilet arrangements of the Norman stone house found under the present Court building consisted of a garderobe or shaft, the bottom of which was open to the river which washed it clean.[98]

Drinking water came from the river, the cockeys or from wells. There was a common well in the centre of the city, a little to the north of White Lion Street. It was uncovered in 1888 and was reported to be 50ft. deep and 'lined at the bottom with great stones like a Church'. There were various pits and ponds within the city, the names of some of which survive, as in Muspole Street named after the Muspool situated where the street joins Colegate. In 1289 William le Skinner was fined in the leet court for throwing the bodies of cats into the pit called Lothmere: this was in the street now called Bethel Street.[99]

The City Assembly issued regulations about keeping the city and the river clean. On 21 March 1380 they declared–'It is ordained that no one, of whatsoever condition he be, shall carry any muck by ships or boats, by day or night by the King's river and if he does he shall be heavily amerced.' The fine was 20 shillings for the first offence, 40 shillings for the second, and for the third 60 shillings and loss of citizenship.

> Also that if anyone has cast or collected together any muck and refuse in the market place or in any places and localities of the city he shall remove it or cause it to be removed before the feast of the Nativity of St John the Baptist [24 June] under the penalty of 40d. and for every day afterwards 40d.[100]

There were some attempts to light the streets at night from as early as the 14th century. The City Assembly of 14 December 1453 ordered:

> that all the inhabitants of the city shall keep and find lights before their doors and gates from the feast of the nativity of the Lord until the feast of the Epiphany [that is, from Christmas to 6 January]. And the said lights shall be lighted at the 5th hour after noon and their lights shall last until the 9th hour.[101]

We know what one person in the medieval city was wearing. A carved wooden figure of a young man of about 1400 is in the Castle Museum. It was a supporting bracket in the White Swan in St Peter's Street until that was pulled down. The label tells us:

> The figure is wearing a short closely fitting garment probably a 'cote hardie' buttoned down the front from neck to hem. It has a decorated or dagged edge. The belt is a knightly girdle, worn by noblemen between about 1350 and 1410. He also wears a simple hat with rolled brim. The raised bands below his knees show his hose rolled down. This is often illustrated in illuminated manuscripts.

Examples of rings, fasteners, belt buckles and the metal parts of shoes have been found in excavations, as have items of personal hygiene such as combs (of bone, antler and ivory), tweezers and nail cleaners or toothpicks, sometimes with ear-scoops at the other end.[102]

Health

The first hospital in Norwich was probably at the cathedral as Benedictine monasteries were required to look after the poor and sick. The monks themselves were looked after by their infirmarer but other people would be dependent on the charity of the almoner.[103]

The Hospital of St Paul—often called Norman's after its first master—was established in the early 12th century by a grant from Prior Ingulph and the monks of Norwich Cathedral. It was endowed with land in St Paul's parish, together with property in Sprowston, between what is now Mousehold Heath and the river Wensum. Richard de Beaufo, Archdeacon of Norwich, gave the hospital all his estates, tithes and advowsons from four parish churches in Ormesby. This was augmented by a personal gift from Henry I of the tithes and lands belonging to the royal hall at Ormesby. Theobald, the Archbishop of Canterbury, gave his support too, promising an indulgence of eight days, remission of penance to visitors making gifts during the festival of the patron saint.

The hospital aimed to support up to 20 poor and frail people until they were well enough to make way for others. It was also intended to house poor travellers overnight

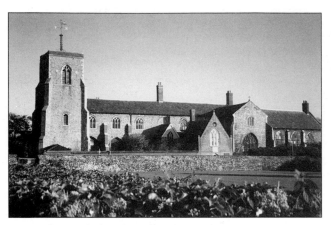

32 *The Great Hospital: a 'church' with chimneys.*

and provide them with an evening meal and bread in the morning for their journey. It may also have admitted sick and pregnant women in addition to the 20 sick. Indeed St Paul's was the only hospital in the city that specifically catered for pregnant women and nursing mothers. The hospital was run by 'sisters' who were themselves poor women in need of alms. About a third of the people of Norwich who left wills between 1370 and 1532 left something to St Paul's, often a few pence, sometimes with household items like bedding or furniture.

The Norwich city archives contain the earliest known reference in England to a barber and the second earliest to a surgeon. The barber was John Belton, mentioned in a document of 1163. The surgeon was Ralph de Morley: he is mentioned in a deed relating to his house in King Street in 1288 and also in the cathedral infirmarer's roll for 1313-4, when he was paid for attending sick monks.[104]

The Great Hospital, which still functions at its original site in Bishopgate, was founded in 1249 by Bishop Walter Suffield. He dedicated it to the Holy Trinity, the Virgin Mary, her mother St Anne and all the saints, but first and foremost to St Giles. The hospital was to make at least 30 beds available to the sick poor, to distribute food to 13 paupers (outside in summer but in winter they might eat inside by the fire), and three or four sisters were appointed to look after the sick. The hospital had only a small chapel at first but in 1270 they were given the parochial rights of the church of St Helen. They demolished this church, greatly enlarging their own chapel to serve both their sick poor and the parishioners of St Helen's.

Towards the end of the 14th century the present chancel and tower were built. The panels of the ceiling are painted with eagles which are often said to commemorate the visit to Norwich of King Richard II and his wife Anne of Bohemia. However, Anne's arms bore double-headed eagles: those on the ceiling of the Great Hospital have single heads. The hospital became more and more a centre for celebration of divine services rather than a place to care for the poor and sick.

Hildebrand's Hospital, also known as Ivy Hall, was one of the few hospitals in Norwich founded by a layman, Hildebrand le Mercer, a wealthy Norwich merchant, at the beginning of the 13th century. It was intended as a hostel for 'poor people wanting lodging.' The hospital was in King Street and was well supported at first but declined and the receipts at the Reformation were only 14s. a year.

Shortly before 1348 a priest named John de Brun endowed a hospital and chapel in St Stephen's parish, on the site now occupied by the Assembly House. However, it very soon gave up any charitable activities and became a college for secular clergy.

Leprosy was a common and much-feared disease in the Middle Ages. Although it could be confused with other skin diseases, medieval diagnosis seems generally accurate: work on burials both at Castle Acre and at St Mary Fyebridge in Norwich show cases of definite leprosy. There were six leper hospitals in Norwich, all on the outskirts of the city. The best known is that of St Mary Magdalen on the Sprowston Road, north of Norwich. This was founded by Bishop Herbert and part of the building still survives, currently in use as a library. The hospital had its own cemetery, part of which was excavated when Gilman Road was built. The hospital derived its income from land and from an annual fair known as the Rush Fair.

Another leper hospital was just outside St Stephen's. This hospital was owned by the priory at Horsham St Faith which appointed its master. There was a third at St Giles' Gate, which in 1308 consisted of 'seven cottages where leprous people dwell' and which was described as a 'sykehouse' 250 years later. The three other houses were outside the gates of St Benedict's, St Augustine's and Magdalen Street. In 1448, Henry Wells left money for a new chapel at the last of these: Henry describes himself as a leper and his executors as 'leprosos'. Eight years later, provision was made for Richard de Walsham, a monk at the cathedral priory, to lead a solitary life in a specially built house in the grounds of St Leonard's. He had contracted leprosy and doctors and physicians were unable to cure him.[105]

The most dramatic health disaster—and one that must have had almost the impact of a nuclear war—is the plague known as the Black Death which spread through Europe from the Middle East, reaching England in 1348. It was resident in this country for just over 300 years, disappearing after the epidemics of 1665: it is not known why it arrived when it did or why it disappeared. The bacillus responsible for the disease is primarily an internal parasite of rodents, carried to human beings by fleas from rats. Contamination can occur from bites by the flea or through its excrement being deposited on scratches on the skin. A blister forms at the site of the infection, developing into a blackish carbuncle. Lymph glands in the armpits, neck or groin swell and suppurate forming the buboes that give bubonic plague its name. Usually 60 per cent to 80 per cent of those infected died, half within eight days of infection.

The Black Death had a devastating effect throughout Europe: it is estimated that between a third and a half of the population died in a year. Unfortunately it is very difficult to get at exact figures because no records were kept of deaths or burials. Blomefield quotes the chronicler Weaver, saying that the Black Death came to Norwich on 1 January 1348 (1349 new style) and in that year some 57,304 people died there 'excluding religious and beggars'.[106] This precise sounding figure is clearly ridiculous—the population of the city at this time cannot have been more than 25,000—but the plague's effect is dramatically captured in the *Norwich Book of Pleas*:

> In the year of our Lord 1349, God almighty visited mankind with a deadly plague, which began in the south parts of the world and went through the north part thereof, attacking all nations of the world; this plague equally destroyed Christians, Jews and Saracens, killed the confessor and the confessed; in many places this plague did not leave the fifth part of the people alive, it struck the world with great fear, so great was the pestilence, that the like was never seen, heard, nor read of before, for it was believed that there was not a greater number of souls destroyed by flood in the days of Noah, than died by this plague.'[107]

Once established the plague did not go away: there were further outbreaks in 1361-2 and in 1369. In Norwich the population could have fallen from as many as

25,000 in the 1330s to as low as 6,000 in the 1370s. The suggested figure of about 25,000 is taken from work by Elizabeth Rutledge on the tithing rolls and related documents. This is considerably higher than earlier estimates and suggests that death rates in the plagues could have been even higher than previously thought.[108]

Some after-effects of the disaster can be found from the archives. Communar rolls for the cathedral show that work on the cloisters came to a sudden stop on 25 June 1349: it did not start again for six years. In the episcopal visitation of 1368 it is specifically said that the church of St Matthew on Bishopgate is now ruined and that the parishioners had used the church of St Martin at Palace from the time of the great pestilence. Due to the plague and the fall in population one church sufficed and the parish of St Matthew was formally united with that of St Martin in 1377.[109]

A city court roll for 1357 records that many shops and market stalls had been untenanted for so long that they had fallen into ruin. After 1369 the churchyard of St Peter Mancroft was extended, taking in part of the old cloth market. In the heart of Norwich, the dead had more need of space than the living. However life, of course, went on and the short-term results of the plague could even have benefited the survivors. There would have been less pressure on food and accommodation and labour would have been in short supply, leading to an increase in wage rates.

There were many other waves of infectious disease—Margaret Paston mentions epidemics of pestilence in Norwich in 1465, 1471 and 1479 in letters to her husband in London. In her 1471 letter she wrote—'I fear there is great death in Norwich, and in other borough towns in Norfolk, for I assure you that it is the most universal death that I ever knew in England.'[110]

Crime and Punishment

The control of law and order was attempted by a whole series of local and national courts depending on the location and nature of the crime and status of the criminal. In the period after the Conquest there were probably separate courts for the English and French communities, but the earliest courts for which records survive are the city leet courts.

The leet court dealt with minor offences against the law of the land and with all breaches of the customs or bylaws of the City. Judgement and punishment in more serious cases was reserved for the county court or the next visit of the king's judges. The whole adult male population was bound to organise itself into small bodies of men: a person became an adult at the age of 12. The members of each tithing were mutually responsible for their good conduct and were collectively held responsible for all offences committed in their immediate neighbourhood. This system was called Frankpledge and twice a year the sheriff of the county took a View of Frankpledge to make sure that every adult male had enrolled in a tithing.[111]

From the later 12th century, the View of Frankpledge was accompanied by a report or presentment of any offences which had been committed since the last View. One man from each tithing (called the Chief or Capital Pledge) made presentments on behalf of his group and offences were punished by fines. In theory this jurisdiction belonged to the king but it was granted to boroughs at an early date. In Norwich the

View of Frankpledge probably passed to the citizens under King Richard's charter of 1194. In 1223 the four original leets of the city (Wymer, Westwick, Mancroft and Coslany) were divided into sub-leets for the purpose of exercising the jurisdiction of presentment of minor offences.

Records for the Norwich leet court survive from 1288. They include a tithing roll for the leet of Mancroft of about 1311, giving the names of the members of each tithing. This shows that the number of tithings remained the same but as people came and went the number of men in each tithing changed. Leet roll entries give insights into the daily life in Norwich in the late 13th century:

> Ralph Perconal found and keeps a plank cast up by the river and has not delivered it to the Bailiffs … The anchorite of All Saints has stopped up the Cockey so that no one can pass by there … All the men of Sprowston sell sausages and puddings and knowingly buy measly pigs and they sell in Norwich market the aforesaid sausages and pigs, unfit for human bodies.[112]

The leet court lost its importance after the charter of 1404 when the new sheriffs began holding Tourns at which presentments were made from the four leets, by now called wards. During the 15th century the magisterial power of the alderman evolved into the Mayor's Court which took over responsibility for punishment of minor crimes.

From the late 12th century the king's justices travelled the country hearing serious criminal and civil cases. The surviving assize rolls in the Public Record Office illustrate the kinds of cases that appear and show that often they developed into power struggles between crown and city.

The assize roll of 1286 records a complex and gruesome case. The jurors presented that Walter Eghe was indicted at the city leet for possessing cloth stolen from the house of Richard de la Hoe and for other larcenies. Two days later he was led before the king's bailiffs and the commonalty of the city in the Tollbooth. He was questioned about the theft and the bailiffs and the commonalty found him guilty: they took him outside and hanged him. However, when he was cut down and taken to the church of St George Tombland to be buried, he revived. He could hardly be dragged out of the holy building so he remained inside, guarded by men from the parishes of George Tombland, Peter Hungate, Mary the Less, and Simon and Jude. He stayed inside for 15 days and then managed to escape across Tombland into the cathedral priory where he stayed until the king pardoned him.

The king clearly thought the city authorities were in the wrong. They were asked by what right they had hanged Walter when he had not been caught in the act and they had heard no man's suit against him: it appears that the king did not dispute their right to hang people but that he did not like the way they handled this particular case. He took the matter seriously and seized the liberties of the city into his own hands, where they remained until the next Parliament when the City's liberties were restored to it.[113]

There was no imprisonment as a punishment—the only sentence was death—but people would be held in Norwich Castle while waiting for the next visit of the king's judges. The case of Richard Sapling indicates the poor conditions there. He came before the judges in August 1308 and produced a parchment which had the king's seal attached but which was completely unreadable. He claimed it was a charter of pardon which he had been given by King Edward at Carlisle in January 1307. Unfortunately he had been kept in the north tower of the castle over the winter exposed to the elements and 'during that time his charter was in water except for the case of the seal.' The court had faith in central government's record keeping as it ordered the chancery rolls to be searched and a transcript to be made by Michaelmas, but they were too optimistic. The transcript still had not turned up when Sapling appeared in court again in May 1309 and this time the transcript was ordered to be produced by October and Sapling was returned to the castle.[114] Another sad case is recorded by a graffito scratched on a stone in the castle. It is from the 12th century and written in French. It translates as:

> Bartholomew
> Truly wrongfully
> and without reason
> I am shut in this
> prison

Jurors were capable of being merciful to the obviously insane. In 1307 Peter Monk bought a horse from Andrew Friday for eight shillings in Norwich market. As the horse was worth 20 shillings, Peter was suspicious and it turned out that Friday had stolen it from a Raveningham neighbour of his three days earlier. However, evidence was produced that Friday was mad:

> they [the jurors] say that he is a lunatic and in the waning of the moon he becomes insane ... They say that 15 days before the theft Andrew cut down all the trees at his home in Raveningham and replanted them in the ground.

Because of his madness, Friday was taken back to the castle to await the king's pardon.[115]

Courts of Quarter Session began in 1361 when justices of the peace were enabled to try felonies and trespasses without a separate commission of gaol delivery. In 1363 the justices were ordered to hold these courts four times a year. Norwich courts were held at the Guildhall and the court for Norfolk was held at the Shire House on the castle mound, before adjourning to other towns in the county.

Two hundred years after the Eghe case criminals could still try to use churches as sanctuary. In January 1492 the City Assembly ordered their members of Parliament to speed up an Act to take a man named Eastgate out of the church of St Simon and St Jude where he had taken sanctuary and could not be dislodged.[116] Sanctuary for criminals was not finally abolished until 1623.

Education and Culture

The image of a schoolmaster severely caning a boy is a common one in carvings of the Middle Ages and there is one on a misericord in the cathedral. This is appropriate as all the three medieval schools in the city were connected with the cathedral.[117] During the 12th century it was common for parents to present their young sons as 'oblates' to live in a convent and it was usual for a Benedictine monastery to provide teaching for these boys to make them ready to become monks. This school was known as the Cloister School. Bishop Herbert himself had been brought up at the monastery of Fécamp in Normandy. His surviving letters reveal his concern for the education of the boys at Norwich Cathedral.[118] The second school was the Almonry School, intended for the education of poor boys. In 1408, when John Hancock was master, there were about two dozen boys, who were taught grammar and song.

The third school was the Episcopal School. The Lateran Council of 1179 ordered all cathedrals to provide a master to teach their clerks and poor scholars, and later it was ordered that the masters be given a benefice so that they could afford to teach without charging. This school was situated in Holme Street, very close to where the *Adam and Eve* inn now stands. John Hancock was appointed here in 1403 and he seems to have taken the profits of the estate and hired people to teach at the school, while he continued to act as master of the Almonry School. Hancock was rector of St Mary in the Marsh in the Close as well. He was a wealthy man and gave money for the building of the cathedral cloisters. When he committed suicide in the 1430s he had the enormous sum of £100 in his possession which was taken by the priory and became yet another cause of argument between it and the city.[119]

There may have been some teaching of girls at Carrow Priory but no record of this survives. No doubt educated clergymen in the city taught those children whose parents wished it. One Norfolk man whom we know about is St Godric: he was born at Walpole in about 1065 and his life was set down in writing very soon after his death. He was a successful merchant and great traveller, visiting Santiago, Rome and Jerusalem. He may well have been unable to read or write but he learned Latin prayers from his parents and memorised large chunks of Latin texts. However, when he wound up in the monastery of Durham the educated monks there laughed at his pronunciation of the Latin words—or perhaps at his Norfolk accent![120]

Literacy became more common in later centuries—bone pens have been found on sites in the city from the 14th century. The gild of St Katherine in the parish of St Simon and St Jude included both literate and illiterate (with women included in both categories). Its regulations required that 'every brother and sister that is lettered' say the placebo and dirige for a dead member of the gild while 'every brother and sister that be nought lettered' should say the paternoster and Ave Maria—these were so well-known that they could be said without recourse to a written text.[121] Thomas Salter, who died in London in 1558, said in his will that he was making a bequest to the sisters of the Hospital of St Paul in Norwich because 'a verie good devoute sister of the said house … was the first creature that taught me to know the letters in my book'. Her name was Katherine Peckham and she had taught him 72 years previously, that is in about 1486.[122]

By the 15th century, writing was a commonplace activity amongst some sections of society. One of the most important collections of household letters is that of the Paston family of Norfolk. The *Paston Letters* were first published in 1787, edited by their owner John Fenn.[123] He dedicated the book to King George III. The king asked to see the letters and Fenn took them to him in three bound volumes: in return he received a knighthood. Fenn's original collection was of 155 letters but many other letters from the family for the second half of the 15th century have turned up since and over a thousand are now known. The letters give a great deal of incidental information on life among the gentry and merchants of their time and have already been quoted several times in this book. 'They are important not only for our understanding of the events of that turbulent period in our history, but also of such matters as our understanding of social conditions and conventions of the time, the history of education, the development of constitutional law and even of the development of the English language.'[124] The letters have been published in many different editions and are essential reading for those interested in this period of history.

A more consciously cultured resident of Norfolk a generation later was the poet John Skelton, rector of Diss in the early 16th century. One of his most famous poems the *Boke of Phylyp Sparowe*, was written at Carrow Priory in 1505 and is about a pet sparrow that was eaten by a cat:

> I wept and I wayled
> The tears down hailed
> But nothing it availed
> To call Philip agayne
> Whom Gib our cat hath slayne
> Gib I say our cat.

Not quite Shakespeare perhaps, but a very popular piece of light verse. The pet sparrow belonged to Jane Scrope who had taken refuge in Carrow Priory after the execution of her stepfather John Wyndham for treason in 1502.[125]

Archaeologists have found signs of other leisure activities. A flute from Bishopgate was probably home-made from a swan's wing bone: it had four finger-holes and had been well used. The flute is in the Castle Museum. Counters and gaming pieces have been found made of bone, pottery and chalk. Dice have been found on several sites, some of proper cube shape, others asymmetric with the numbers five and six on the sides likely to turn up most often.[126]

The 14th century was perhaps the greatest period for East Anglian art. Illuminated manuscripts probably from Norwich include the Gorleston Psalter and Stowe Breviary in the British Library, the Ormesby Psalter in the Bodleian Library in Oxford and the Book of Hours in the Norwich Castle Museum. These books, with their gilded decorative borders and marginal grotesques, are the kind of thing that the cathedral monks would have produced but there is nothing to link them definitely to Norwich.[127]

One beautiful illuminated book that can certainly be linked to Norwich is the Helmingham Breviary, also in the Castle Museum. It is a service book of about 1422 and features the dedication of the cathedral as one of its days of special importance. On one page of the book there is an illuminated initial in which a monk holds a scroll on which are some words in Latin. They translate as 'Holy Mother be a remedy to Robert.' There is documentary evidence that a Brother Robert gave a 'new and great breviary' to the monks' cell at St Leonard's in 1422–this must surely be that very book.[128]

Then, in 1507, fires devastated Norwich.

3

Tudor and Stuart Norwich

The Tudor period begins strictly in 1485 when Richard III was killed at the Battle of Bosworth and was succeeded to the throne by his conqueror Henry VII. The new king visited the city at Christmas 1485 and the city made him a handsome present of £140. Gifts also had to be provided for the many nobles who came with him—entertaining royalty was a very expensive business. The king then went on to Walsingham on pilgrimage.[1]

In the early 16th century the city was devastated by fire. Blomefield says there was one in 1505 and two more in 1507.[2] According to the cathedral almoner's account for 1505, only 33s. were received in rent from houses normally bringing in £5 because 'many tenements are burnt': after the 1507 fires the rents obtained shrunk to 19s. 4d. a year from the same properties.[3] The first of the 1507 fires began on 25 April and lasted for four days. Blomefield tells us that it began near the *Popinjay* on Tombland and spread from there towards St Andrew's and into 15 parishes south of the river. It also spread across the river to St George Colegate. The second fire, according to Holinshed, started on 4 June in the house of a French surgeon named Peter Johnson in the parish of St George Colegate. In all, 718 houses were destroyed in the fires. A poem by John Skelton conveys the extent of the disaster:

> England's chief ornament in ashes lies;
> O city, what of thee can now be said?
> A few fair things survive that thou hast bred;
> A life is brief, and frail all man's estate.
> City farewell: I mourn thy cruel fate.[4]

Disputes between the city and the cathedral priory that had lasted for hundreds of years were finally resolved in 1524 after arbitration by Cardinal Wolsey. The priory's Pentecost fair was surrendered to the king and granted to the city. The tenants of the prior, or his successors, within or upon the outer walls of the priory were to be free to buy and sell in their houses and shops all manner of merchandise without impediment by the mayor in the same manner as any other citizen of Norwich during the term of the fair which ran from sunrise on the vigil of Pentecost to sunset on the Monday next after the feast of Holy Trinity. (An attempt by the City Council to put up stalls on Tombland in the 1950s led to High Court actions which established that Tombland was a permanent open space.)

33   *Elm Hill: only the Britons' Arms (on the right) predates the 1507 fires.*

It was under the 1524 settlement that the estate later known as the Town Close passed to the city. The king licensed the priory to convey to the commonalty 80 acres of land, with an extra six-feet-wide strip around it for a ditch and hedge, and also the right to lead beasts along the highway to Harford Bridge and as far as the water near the bridge.[5]

The Tudor period was a time of great changes in the religious landscape of the city and of the whole country. Monasteries, friaries and other institutions were abolished and their estates taken by the Crown. The monasteries dissolved included Norwich Cathedral Priory. The last prior and 21 monks (with one monk from Thetford) formed a dean, six prebendaries and 16 canons: only three of the former monks were not included in the new foundation. Norwich was the first monastic cathedral to be refounded and the Crown later decided it had been too generous. In 1547 the chapter was forced to surrender to the Crown again on the grounds that the Bishop of Norwich—as successor to the founder Herbert Losinga—had not given his consent. A new foundation charter was issued. This time the Crown kept back some of the estates of the former priory, which it later sold for profit.[6]

Carrow Priory was dissolved at the same time: there were only 13 nuns there at the time of the dissolution. The friaries soon followed and the land was taken into the hands of the king who sold it off to private individuals, apart from the Black Friars' building which was bought by the city.[7]

There was a crisis in Norfolk in the summer of 1549: Kett's rebellion. The revolt grew out of minor rioting in Wymondham to develop into a national crisis for the hard-pressed government of Edward VI. On 6 and 7 July there was unrest in Wymondham following festivities and there on the next day a small band of peasants began pulling down fences of recently enclosed fields. A local lawyer called John Flowerdew bribed them to attack the fences of an enemy of his, a tanner and small landowner called Robert Kett. Somehow Kett made himself the leader of the band and, after he had destroyed some of his own fences himself, they destroyed Flowerdew's fences. They then marched towards Norwich, attracting more discontented country-men to their side. The city refused them permission to enter and they skirted the walls and camped on Mousehold Heath.[8]

Lines through Time 4: 1500 to 1600

	1500	
	1501	Market Cross built
	1507	Fire destroys much of Norwich
Henry VIII is crowned king	1509	
Battle of Flodden	1513	
	1524	Agreement between City and Priory
Dissolution of Monasteries	1538	Cathedral priory becomes Dean and Chapter
Henry VIII dies	1547	Hospital granted to the city
	1549	Kett's Rebellion
Mary becomes Queen and restores Catholicism	1553	
Elizabeth is crowned Queen	1559	
	1565	'Strangers' invited to the city
	1570	First book printed in Norwich
	1578	Queen Elizabeth visits Norwich; plague
	1582	Water pumped from New Mills to the Market
Mary Queen of Scots executed	1587	
Spanish Armada	1588	
	1600	

At first the camp was peaceful: there were about 10,000 men camped on the Heath for a total period of seven weeks. The camp was centred on a large oak tree called the Oak of Reformation, roughly where the Water Tower off Quebec Road now stands. From here the rebels held services, administered justice and even appointed governors for 25 hundreds in Norfolk and Suffolk. Some of the men were supported and actually paid by their village communities: for example, North Elmham church-wardens' accounts record that men from this parish were being paid 3d. a day and also paid for food and beer to go to the camp.

Kett's rebellion occurred at the same time as a rebellion in south-west England (which is one reason why the central government was slow to put it down) but was

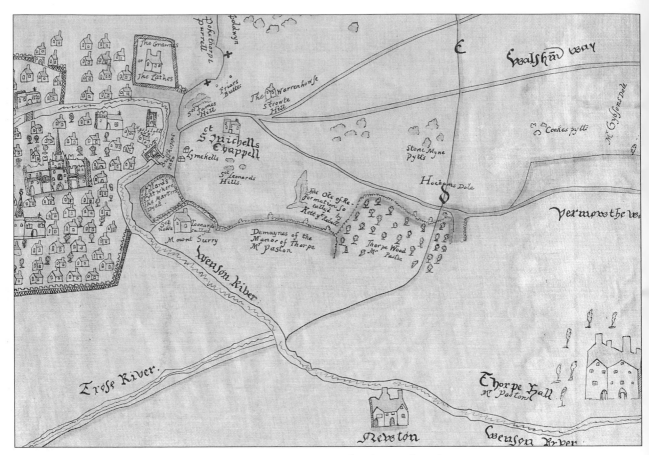

34 *Kett's Norwich: drawing based on a plan of 1589.*

very different in character. The western rebellion was concerned about religious changes such as the abolition of the monasteries and the destruction of images, wood screens and paintings in parish churches. However, the Norfolk rebels were not interested in religion. The 29 articles of complaint they drew up were entirely concerned with economic matters, mainly complaints against overbearing lords of the manor and including the famous statement 'we pray that all bond men may be made free'.

The rebels attracted the support of the poorer people of Norwich too: Blomefield says, 'the scum of the city … were on the rebel's side.'[9] On 21 July the rebels were offered a pardon if they dispersed peacefully but they rejected the offer, saying they had done nothing wrong and therefore had no need of the pardon. They then proceeded to raid the city over the next two days, capturing the mayor and leading citizens and imprisoning them in Surrey House (at the top of what is now Gas Hill). The government was now, of course, committed to battle. An army of about 1,400 men under the Marquis of Northampton reached the city and fought with the rebels in a battle centred on the Bishopgate area on 1 August 1549.

Although the rebels lost about 140 men to the Marquis's 50 they forced the Marquis and his army to withdraw from the city. Among those killed on Bishopgate

Street was Edward, Lord Sheffield: he was buried at the nearby St Martin at Palace church and a plaque on the outside wall of the cathedral close records the spot where he died. The burial register for St Martin at Palace records the burial of Lord Sheffield and 35 other unnamed casualties of the battle.[10]

Many of the leading citizens of Norwich fled to London with the Marquis's army, leaving the city in the hands of the rebels. They rifled the richer houses and set fire to parts of the city. Blomefield says: 'all the houses in Holmstrete were consumed with fire on both sides thereof, with St Giles' hospital … and divers other buildings in many places were burnt; and had not the clouds by God's special providence commiserated the city's calamity, and melting into tears, quenched the flames, the whole city had been laid in ashes.'[11]

Clearly the government could not allow the situation to continue. A much larger army of 12,000 Englishmen and 1,200 Swiss mercenaries was already in the field commanded by the Earl of Warwick, having been raised to fight the Scots.

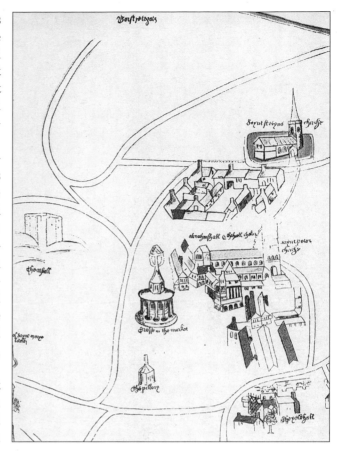

35 *Detail of the Sanctuary Map of 1541, showing the Market Cross*

This army was diverted to Norwich. The rebels and soldiers clashed in the streets and 320 people were killed.

On 24 August the rebels were forced back up onto Mousehold Heath. For the next two days they attacked the city with guns from Warwick's army that had lost their way and wound up in rebel territory. They mounted them on the Hill above Bishop Bridge from where they battered down a great part of Cow Tower. Six people killed in these skirmishes were buried in the garden of a Mr. Spence off Holme Street: this is recorded in the St Martin at Palace burial register but their names are not given.[12] The high ground of Mousehold Heath gave the rebels a natural defensive site but of their own accord they retreated to an area called Dussindale (now an industrial park off the Yarmouth Road near St Andrew's Hospital). They appear to have done this because of a traditional prophetic rhyme:

> The Country gnoffes Hob, Dick and Hick,
> with clubs and clowted shoon
> shall fill the vale
> of Dussin's Dale
> with slaughtered bodies soon

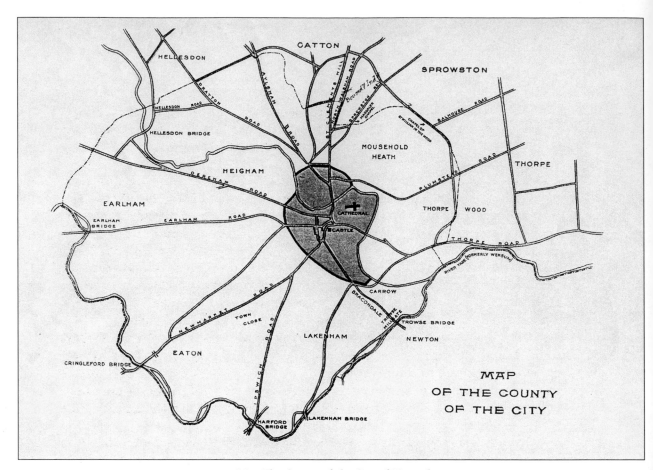

36   *The County of the City of Norwich*

As with so many prophetic utterances, this was tragically ambiguous and when the trained army of Warwick caught up with them it was the rebel peasants whose bodies filled the vale.

The rebels were severely punished–about 300 were executed, some on the Oak of Reformation, others on the Market Cross in Norwich. Robert Kett himself was captured not at the scene of the battle but in a barn at Swannington. He and his brother William were taken to London for trial. They were kept in the Tower of London, where the former protector Somerset was also in prison awaiting his trial and execution. Ironically, he had initially been in sympathy with the rebels' demands. The fate of the Kett brothers was a foregone conclusion. Robert was hanged from the top of Norwich Castle and William from the steeple of Wymondham church: their chained bodies remained hanging for many months as a grim warning.

In 1556 a charter was granted to the city by Philip and Mary and this defined the boundary of the city for the first time and this boundary remained almost unchanged for 450 years.[13] This was the first formal authentication of a boundary that the city had long claimed. The base of an earlier–15th-century–cross can still be seen outside the

Boundary public house and there is another, much restored, near the Sweetbriar, Drayton and Boundary Road junctions.[14]

The 'Strangers' in Norwich

There has always been movement of people between Norwich and Europe. Nicholas le Mouner of Amiens appears in the Norwich City court roll of 1287 when he bought a house in Fyebridge from which he no doubt ran the woad trade already mentioned. He appears to have lived in Norwich with his wife and family until his death in about 1330.[15]

In the 1560s the Netherlands was a colony of Catholic Spain and the governor, the Duke of Alba, was persecuting Protestants in the colony. In 1565 the city authorities arranged for 30 households of religious refugees from the Netherlands to settle in the city. Six of the households were French-speaking Walloons and the other 24 spoke Dutch or Flemish. More refugees followed: a return of aliens made in 1568 and preserved in the Norwich city archives lists 1,132 Flemings and 339 Walloons in the city. By 1579 there were 6,000 'strangers' in a population of about 16,000–so that they made up over a third of the population, the largest percentage in any town in England, although the actual number of immigrants settling in London was greater.[16]

In 1570 John Throgmorton and other Norfolk gentry tried to raise a rebellion against the incomers but there was little response from the people of the city: the strangers were in Norwich to stay. However, many limitations were placed on the life of the new immigrants. Under the Orders issued by the city in 1571 they were not to walk in the streets after the curfew had rung. They could not become freemen of the city on the same terms as the 'natives' until 1598.

Most but not all of the immigrants were weavers. They were organised by a committee known as the Governors of the Drapery and by their church leaders. They appointed 'politic men' (eight Dutchmen and four Walloons) to be their representatives in dealings with the English. Some followed other trades or professions: Leonard Forster mentions four silver beakers made as communion cups for the Dutch church in about 1580 by a Dutch goldsmith in Norwich called Peter Peterson.[17] One of these cups is in the Castle Museum in Norwich, another in the Rijksmuseum in Amsterdam. Peterson's will was proved in Norwich in 1603. He asks to be buried 'in the chapel where I do usually sit in the Parish of St Andrew where I was born in the city of Norwich' so he was a second generation immigrant.[18]

The first printer in Norwich was Anthony de Solempne who came over from Brabant with his wife and two sons in 1567. He is known to have published eight works between 1568 and 1570: all except one are in Dutch. The only work he published in English was a broadsheet of poetry by Thomas Brooke in prison on the night before his execution in 1570. Ironically, Brooke was awaiting execution for his part in Throgmorton's rebellion against the immigrants. Solempne became a freeman of Norwich in 1570 and in the same year became entitled to sell Rhenish wine. He seems to have given up printing. Two further Dutch books printed in Norwich may have been by another printer named in the list of aliens of 1568, Albert Christian from Holland.[19]

37 *St Stephen's Gates, drawing by John Kirkpatrick*

Bishop Parkhurst allowed the French speakers to hold their services in the chapel of the Bishop's Palace, but later bishops were not all so tolerant to them. Bishop Wren wanted to close the foreign churches and make the immigrants worship in their local parish churches. Indeed, by the 1630s it appeared to be England that was intolerant of puritan leanings. The Netherlands were now independent and offered religious freedom not only to those Dutch and Walloons who decided to go back, but also to Englishmen who found the High Church Anglicanism of King Charles I unacceptable. Some of them later returned to found the first Congregationalist churches in Yarmouth and Norwich when the political climate became more favourable in the 1640s.

The Dutch community worshipped in the Blackfriars church in St Andrew's Hall, the French in the Bishop's Palace until 1637, then in the unused church of St Mary the Less in Queen Street until 1820.

Some pottery has been found in Norwich excavations that is of a distinctly Dutch style. This includes some early 17th-century 'slip' ware that experts are sure was made in Holland and must have come over with the strangers. Slip is a thin clay that can be painted on to an unfired pot to decorate it. The pot is then glazed and fired in a kiln.

The Dutch brought several other benefits to Norwich. They are famous as gardeners: as early as 1575 a Dutch gardener, Joos Brake, settled in Norwich and was employed by local gentry to lay out their gardens. In the 17th century, according to Thomas Fuller, an especially famous rose was grown in Norwich having been brought here by the Dutch. Florists' feasts took place every year in the city in the 1630s and are said to have been introduced by these flower-loving immigrants.[20] The 16th-century Dutch are said to have brought canaries with them. By the early 18th century canary breeding was a Norwich hobby and the Norwich 'plain-head' canary had become a recognised breed. Even today Norwich City football team take their colours and their nickname from these imports of 400 years ago.

Queen Elizabeth I visited Norwich in August 1578. The procession entered by St Stephen's Gate. The queen was in the city for almost a week. She knighted the mayor, Robert Wood, and said, 'I have laid up in my breast such good will, as I shall never forget Norwich'.[21] The city has three traditions about the visit, all probably false. She did not stay at the *Maid's Head*, as is often claimed, but at the Bishop's Palace in the Close. The tradition that she dined in the cathedral cloisters with local nobility (whose family arms are now painted on the wall there) is based on a misreading of Blomefield.[22] The final tradition is that she brought the plague with her entourage from London.

There *was* a major outbreak of plague in the city in 1579, but, as Hudson and Tingey point out, this was several months after Queen Elizabeth's visit.[23]

In 1611 the city was the scene of a major tragedy. Blomefield says:

On the 18th of June (it being the gild-day) a sumptious pageant was prepared at the new mayor's gate on Tombland, and certain fireworks, as had been usual, were fired off in the evening, some of which breaking, frighted the people (who were very numerous) to such a degree, that hurrying away in crowds for fear of hurt, there were no less than 33 persons trodden down and pressed to death, as the register of the parish of St Simon and Jude declares.

The burial register names six people buried on 19 June 1611 and adds: 'Thes 6, and 27 more, weare all slayne at the fyer works in Tumbland, Mr. Tho Angwishe then entering his mayoralty.' As a result of the tragedy fireworks were banned from future celebrations.[24]

The Crown enforced a change in the way the city was run in the early 17th century. The freemen had selected junior aldermen as one or both of their nominees in seven of the ten mayoral elections prior to 1618. The magistrates invariably

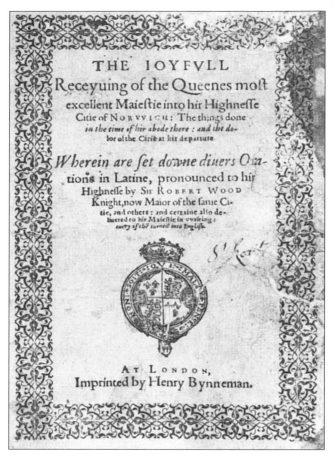

38   *Queen Elizabeth I visits Norwich*

elected the most senior of the two. In 1618 the freemen chose Richard Rosse who ranked tenth in seniority and Henry Fawcett who ranked seventh. Indeed Rosse had only been an alderman for one year though both men had been on the common council for at least fifteen years. Rosse was chosen and this led to an Order from the king that in future the most senior alderman who had not been mayor before must be chosen. This, of course, meant the end of free elections, but no effort was made to make Norwich a closed corporation in which the magistrates chose their own successors, as happened in some other towns.[25]

The magistrates and councilmen had control over two lectureships at St Andrew's and they always sponsored Puritans. The space in front of St Andrew's Hall once used for preaching by the friars was used as a preaching yard by the city. It was called the 'green yard'–an obvious challenge to the open preaching space of the cathedral, also called the 'green yard'. In 1622 Bishop Harsnett forbade Sunday morning sermons and lectures in the city. He ordered parishioners to attend sermons at the cathedral. In 1623 more than 300 citizens presented a petition lamenting the loss of sermons–unfortunately the names of those signing the petition have not survived. Monday and

Lines through Time 5: 1600 to 1714

	1600	
Queen Elizabeth dies	1601	
Gunpowder Plot	1605	
	1608	Norwich Public Library opened
	1615	Thomas Tunstall executed
	1618	Children's Hospital founded
Pilgrim Fathers sail to America	1620	
Charles I is crowned king	1625	Plague in Norwich
Civil war breaks out	1642	
	1644	Cathedral desecrated
	1648	'The Great Blowe'
Execution of Charles I	1649	Girls' Hospital founded
Restoration of the Monarchy	1660	
Plague in London	1665	Plague in Norwich
Great Fire of London	1666	
	1671	Charles II visits Norwich
	1682	Death of Sir Thomas Browne
	1687	Doughty's Hospital founded
William and Mary succeed James II	1688	
	1693	Old Meeting House built
	1706	*Norwich Post* started
	1708	Duke of Norfolk leaves the city
	1711	Norwich Workhouse Act
	1714	Bethel Hospital built

Friday lectures continued at St Andrew's. A group of 12 influential Norfolk men established a corporation to buy advowsons of churches to put in Puritan ministers. They bought the advowson of St Peter Hungate and put in a leading Puritan William Bridge as rector. Puritan preaching flourished in the city in the 1630s.

Matthew Wren became bishop in 1635 and cracked down on Puritans. He compelled all the magistrates to attend the cathedral service and sermon every Sunday morning. Wren suspended eight Norwich ministers including Bridge and carried out a visitation designed to enforce uniformity of worship in parish churches. A correspondent wrote to Wren, 'for our Norwich Puritans, though they be more civil, yet they are as malicious, and more crafty, than those of Ipswich'. There were successes on both sides—Bridge went to Holland but the corporation managed to restore the Puritan sympathiser John Carter to St Peter Mancroft. When Laud reported to the king that Bridge had fled to Holland, the king scribbled in the margin, 'Let him go: We are well rid of him'. He returned in 1641 to become preacher at Yarmouth.[26]

Wren's policies are thought to have driven about 500 people out of the city, some to Europe and others on to America. Registers of travellers embarking from Yarmouth in the years 1637 to 1639 survive and have been published. They include three master weavers who went to America. One was Francis Lawes, who took with him an 18-year-old apprentice called Samuel Lincoln: President Abraham Lincoln was descended from him. Another important Norwich Puritan was Thomas Allen of Norwich St Edmund who emigrated to New England in 1638, where he married the widow of the founder of Harvard College. He returned to take charge of St George Tombland in 1651.[27]

Although the majority on Norwich corporation was disposed towards Puritanism, Wren did have a body of support. When in autumn 1636 the mayor and a majority of the corporation petitioned the king in favour of non-conforming ministers, no fewer than 12 addressed a letter to Wren recording their dissent. Several of these were among the Royalist minority expelled from the corporation a few years later.

On 28 July 1642 Captain Moses Treswell appeared in the city with a Commission for levying 100 volunteers for the royal forces.[28] The mayor's court ordered him not to beat his drum and when he refused to obey he was arrested and sent to London as a prisoner. The magistrates ordered that in future the city gates were to be locked and a double watch set up. They then took steps to defend the city. The walls were repaired, several gates blocked up and the rest were to be locked at 9 o'clock each night. Some royalist supporters left Norwich to be with the king, including Augustine Briggs who survived the war to become a Norwich MP in the reign of Charles II.

On the council there was then a purge of Royalists—Rosse and three others were removed in March 1643, William Gostlin was in prison in Cambridge and John Anguish's health was failing. In May 1643 John Freeman was impeached by his ward but he managed to hang on to his rank of alderman. In April 1644 Alexander Anguish was ejected on a trumped-up charge of fraud and corruption.

In September 1641 the House of Commons had passed an order forbidding people to bow at the name of Jesus, allowing the removal of communion rails and calling for the removal of images. The cathedral officials took away the communion rails themselves to prevent riots, but in November 1643 a mob led by two aldermen and one of the sheriffs forced their way into the cathedral, smashed stained glass windows and burnt relics, surplices and hymn books. Bishop Hall wrote:

it is tragical to see the furious sacriledge committed under the authority of Linsey, Tofts the
sheriff and Greenwood: what tearing down of monuments: what pulling down of windows and
greavs: what defacing of arms: what demolishing of curious stonework that had not any
representation in the world but the cost of the founder and skill of the mason ... the ordnance
being discharged on the guild day the cathedral was filled with musketeers drinking and
tobacconing as freely as if it had been turned into an alehouse.[29]

Joseph Hall had become bishop of Norwich in 1642. His son Edward died in the
same year and is buried in the cathedral. The revenues of the see, and the bishop's
small private income, were seized. Hall was evicted from the palace, but lived in a
house in the Close and preached when he could throughout the summer of 1644. He
then retreated to a house in Heigham owned by a family named Browne, which later
became known as Bishop Hall's. He lived here for about 10 years preaching sometimes in Heigham parish church, where he was buried after his death in 1656. The
church, with his monument, and much of the house, by then the *Dolphin Inn*, were
destroyed by German bombs almost 300 years later. The inn, unlike the church, has
since been rebuilt.

The churchwardens' accounts for Norwich St Lawrence include the following
entry for 1643–'Laid out to Goodman Perfitt for putting out the superstitious inscrip-
tions on the church windows and the pulling down of crucifixes 1s. 8d.' In March 1644
the Mayor's Court ordered religious paintings from the churches of St Swithin and St
Peter Mancroft to be publicly burnt in the Market Place.[30]

The revenues of the cathedral were also seized and the chapter ceased to function
in May 1649. The cathedral is supposed to have been used for billeting troops and a
musket ball may still be seen embedded in Bishop Goldwell's monument in the nave.
In 1650 the Yarmouth corporation petitioned Parliament that 'you will be pleased to
grant us such a part of the lead and other useful materials of that vast and altogether
useless Cathedral in Norwich, towards the building of a work house to employ our
almost starved poor, and repairing our piers'.[31]

Some records do survive to show which side people were supporting in the
struggle between King and Parliament. Donors to the Newcastle Collection of 1644
and signatories to the Solemn League and Covenant of the same year show that
support for Parliament was strongest in Wymer and Over the Water wards and weak-
est in Conesford and Mancroft wards.

In 1648 occurred the most violent event in the city during the Civil War period,
known to history as 'The Great Blowe'. The events can be pieced together from a
collection of 278 depositions of witnesses and participants in the events leading up to
it.[32]

The mayor in 1647-8 was John Utting who had Royalist sympathies. In December local apprentices petitioned him that Christmas Day be celebrated. In April 1648
a petition of Puritans complained that their ministers were being slighted and demanded that the remaining pictures and images in Norwich churches be removed.
Three of their leaders including Thomas Ashwell went to London and succeeded in
getting an order from Parliament that Utting should be dismissed from his office and
taken to London. In Norwich a petition in favour of Utting was raised and throughout
Sunday 23 April rumours spread that he was about to be taken. A crowd estimated

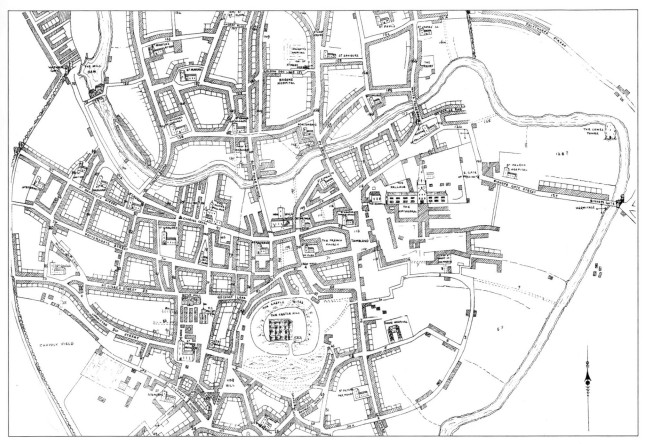

39 *Market Place and Committee Street, from John Kirkpatrick's version of Cleer's map of 1696*

at about 2,000 gathered and broke into Ashwell's house, opposite the churchyard of St Michael at Plea. They stole arms that they found there and moved onto the houses of other 'enemies', Thomas Browne (not the doctor of that name) and Adrian Parmenter who lived on the Market Place. From there they moved to the Committee House which stood where the Bethel Hospital was later erected.

This was where the county arms and armour were stored: it was under the charge of Samuel Cawston or Cawthorne. He locked the gates and doors but in the tumult a shot from inside the building killed a boy in the crowd outside. The enraged mob broke in and began pillaging the contents. There was a large store of gunpowder, some of which was seen spilled on the stairs, while a man was seen to rush out carrying a hat full of powder. Not surprisingly, a huge explosion took place. A report in the *Commons Journal* says that 40 people were killed. The burial register for St Peter Mancroft records the burial of three people 'slain by gunpowder' on 24 April. Seven other victims were buried at St Stephen including a youth called Henry Wilson who may have been the boy shot outside the Committee House. Churchwardens' accounts for both St Peter Mancroft and St Stephen record the expense of repairing windows blown out by the blast.[33]

Troopers of Colonel Fleetwood's command had arrived in the city at about the time of the explosion. It appears that the rioters hoped to trap them and kill them—the Brazen gates and Ber Street gates were shut with the soldiers inside the city. However the troopers were too strong and rounded up and captured the rebels. The next day John Utting rode to Parliament of his own accord, presumably to avoid further trouble.

The sessions records of December 1648 name 66 people charged with involvement in the riot. Eight were sentenced to be hanged: William True, Charles Emerson, Anthony Wilson, Edward Graye, Henry Coward, Christopher Hill and two brothers Thomas and John Bidewell. The rest were fined, imprisoned or both. The eight were executed on the Castle Ditches on 2 January 1649 along with Anne Dant and Margaret Turrell, two old women who at the same sessions court had been sentenced to death for witchcraft. The register of St Lawrence records the burial of one of the eight men hanged at the Castle Ditches on 2 January 1649: 'Buried Charles Emerson, executed in the Castle Ditches as one of the pretended mutineers when the then Committee House was blown up with 80 barrels of powder'.[34]

Utting was sentenced by Parliament to six months in the Fleet prison in London and the Norwich town clerk John Tooley to three months. They were also fined £1,500 between them, the money 'to be given to the City of Norwich to be disposed of by the Mayor, Aldermen and Common Council for the public use of the town'.

After the Great Blow there was another purge—anyone who helped spread the petition defending Utting or who took part in the riot was forbidden to vote and could not be elected to office: those already in office were to be displaced.

The Assembly welcomed the execution of Charles I in 1649, sending a letter of congratulation to Cromwell. However, there was still a Royalist presence—Mackerell says that 24 people were tried at St Andrew's Hall in the same year for planning an insurrection in favour of Charles II; some were hanged in Norwich, others in towns throughout the county. One, Major Roberts, was hanged outside the door of his own house in the Market Place. In March 1655 there was an unsuccessful Royalist uprising in the county: Norwich magistrates put the city on alert and set up night watches.[35]

In 1658 the Assembly sent a letter to Cromwell praising his rule and after his death they sent a letter of support to his son and successor Richard Cromwell. They wrote of Oliver, 'his piety, his wisdome and valor soe eminently appeared in him whilest he lived as the memory thereof will remayne to future ages, the loss of wch head will make the whole body to tremble'.[36] However in January 1660 when General Monck and his army approached London from Scotland, the City of Norwich sent him an Address in effect supporting the Royalists although the return of the king is not actually mentioned. The Address has 794 signatures including 14 aldermen and 25 councilmen. The Assembly celebrated the return of the Stuarts with the ringing of bells. By the Corporation Act of 1661 those improperly ejected from office over the last 20 years were to be restored. This had already happened in Norwich in most cases and only four aldermen, including Adrian Parmenter, were dismissed from office.

Charles II visited Norwich in September 1671 amid scenes of great popular enthusiasm. This was the first royal visit for almost one hundred years: the mayor gave his king a present of 200 guineas.[37] Six months later Charles passed the Declaration of Indulgence which suspended the penal laws against catholics and dissenters: however dissenters could only worship in places approved by the government and catholics only in their own homes.

By the late 1670s the city was drifting into opposition to the crown and to the established church. Conventicles were well attended and non-conformists had made significant inroads into the magistracy. Politically the dominant theme of the period was the triumph of the local Tory party and the extension of Lord Yarmouth's influence in the town. His nominees won each of the five Parliamentary elections held: however the Whigs won three of the four elections for mayor in the same period, so there were inevitable disputes.

Whitehall drew up a new charter for the city which was issued in April 1683. This gave the king the right to dismiss any official he chose. As a result, 10 aldermen were removed from office, including every one elected for the wards of Conesford and Over the Water since 1677.

Arguments between Whigs and Tories were at their height in the early 18th century.[38] On the death of an alderman in August 1704 the freemen twice elected the Whig Thomas Dunch. However the Tory mayor William Blyth and his party in the court of aldermen disallowed the voters' choice and swore in a Tory instead. In May 1705 Parliamentary elections were held and two Whigs, Waller Bacon and John Chambers, were elected, perhaps as a protest against the mayor's high handedness. However Blyth was not finished: he persuaded the sheriff to make a double return as Chambers and Bacon were not freemen of the city and so could not be elected as its members of Parliament. The whole dispute came before the Commons who decided in favour of the Whigs both for Parliament and for the aldermanic vacancy. Blyth was made to kneel in the House and ask for pardon. However the Tories won back both Norwich seats at the 1700 election and held them in 1705. The way elections could be manipulated was illustrated ten years later. Tories were elected to both seats in 1713 and the Whigs responded by making great efforts to increase the number of freemen (who were of course the only people who could vote). The number of freemen was 25 per cent greater at the election in 1715 than it had been in 1710: Whigs were elected to both seats.

Trade and Industry

Visitors to Norwich were impressed by its activity. Baskerville wrote in 1681, 'as to Norwich, it is a great city and full of people' and Celia Fiennes wrote in 1698 'the whole City lookes like what it is, a rich thriveing industrous place'.[39]

In the 1590s one in seven new freemen was connected with the textile trade. This rose to one in three in the 1620s and to about half in the 1670s. Norwich was still an agricultural centre and all textile and similar work stopped during harvest—a Norwich bylaw ordered all worsted weavers to leave off work for about a month. Fishing remained important to the city as a source of cheap protein. When a special harvest of herrings was brought up river to Norwich in 1666 the town clerk wrote that 'twelve herrings a penny here fills many an empty belly'.[41]

40 *Probate inventory of Robert Wales, a Norwich grocer*

We have seen how weaving was boosted in the city by bringing in the 'Strangers' and this applied to other trades as well. Eighteen citizens of Norwich of a wide range of trades started the craft of making felt hats in 1543. They brought over six or seven Frenchmen who were skilled in the work. Later some of these same citizens were among the group who floated the making of russells; this time people with the appropriate skills were brought over from Flanders. (Russell is a woollen fabric whose name is probably derived from Rysell, now called Lille.)

Ten dornix weavers appear in the Norwich freemen's records in the 17th century and some of them left probate inventories. John Hayward who died in 1626 had three looms, a draft loom and a warping stage; he left dornix yarn, 11 yards of dornix and over 100 yards of woolsey cloth. Thomas Barker, whose house was in St Michael Coslany, was a much richer man: there were at least eight rooms in his house, five of which were heated as well as attics and out-houses. He seems to have bought and sold cloth as well as making it.[42] In the 1620s Norwich and Yarmouth houses were exporting 70,000 pairs of stockings a year, mainly to Rotterdam.

The inventor of the spinning jenny was Nicholas Doughty of Norwich who in 1644 claimed to have 'contrived an ingen for the more speedy spininge of yarn'. By the early 18th century it was in common use in Norwich.[43]

Norwich gets a mention in Pepys' *Diary*. On 16 June 1664 he wrote: 'Home after I had spoken with my cozen Richard Pepys upon the Change about supplying us with beupers from Norwich, which I should be glad of, if cheap. So home to supper and bed.' 'Beupers' is an old word for bunting out of which flags were made. Pepys (who, it will be recalled, worked for the Admiralty) was continually complaining about a shortage.

Baskerville wrote about the market in 1681:

they not as in London allowing markets in several places, make it vastly full of provisions, especially on Saturdays, where I saw the greatest shambles for butchers' meat I had ever yet seen … They setting their goods in ranges as near as may be one above another, only allowing room for single persons to pass between.

However, he thought the prices were excessive: 'They asked me for one pike under 2 foot 2s. 6d. and for a pot of pickled oysters they would have a shilling'.[44]

Towards the end of the period the number and range of shops in the city became much greater. William Browne who died in 1700 had a coffee-room in his house and in the same year the Corporation let out part of St Andrew's Hall to be used as a coffee-house. From the early 18th century coffee-pots and tea-kettles turn up in Norwich probate inventories. Booksellers tended to be near the Guildhall just as Jarrold's is now. William Oliver traded there and a sale catalogue printed after his death in 1689 survives. His books included religious works, poetry, handbooks on gardening, romances and a selection of joke books. The importance of Norwich as a shopping centre is reflected in a very rare survival at 15 Bedford Street. There is a Tudor shopfront here, still clearly recognisable, although it has been much restored.[45]

The corporation regulated trade by limiting it to freemen and reserving to itself the right both to give and to take away the freedom. In the *Assembly Book* of 1602 it is noted that Thomas Norford, beer brewer, was disenfranchised for unseemly words and bad behaviour: the next year he submitted and was made a freeman again. In 1609 it is recorded 'that John Cockshead being known to be a notorious drunkard and of late charged with blasphemy, shall be utterly discommuned and disenfranchised for ever'. Changes of trade are also recorded in the Assembly Books. For example, in 1554 Robert Collard and Thomas Swanton who had been enrolled as cordwainers asked to be enrolled as a fishmonger and as a haberdasher instead: the Assembly agreed. The *Assembly Book* for 1708 records that on 21 June five people were summoned for keeping shops in the city although they were not freemen.[46]

In 1603 alderman Robert Gibson was both removed from his place as alderman and disenfranchised. His offence came about when the mayor rode through the city asking people to remove hangings because of the plague (they were thought to harbour infection). Gibson refused to do so. He taunted the mayor, 'I would see who dare pull them down' but the mayor was a match for him, replying 'that dare I'; he proceeded to pull the hangings down himself. Gibson was himself a benefactor to the city, building the conduit from St Lawrence's well for public use—and all at his own expense as the surviving inscription is careful to inform us.

The city authorities had to deal with the increasing number of people living in the suburbs. They were thought to be taking advantage of the city but not contributing their fair share towards it; some city people still think this about those who live beyond the city boundaries. The Assembly Book of 1553 says that 'many evil disposed persons' have lived in the city until they have been made freemen and have then moved out into the country, coming back in to buy or sell goods. It was ordered that people living outside the city could only trade within it as 'foreigners' and not on the same terms as the freemen who actually live there.[47]

In 1622 new *Ordinances for Crafts* were issued by the city. They grouped all the different trades practised in Norwich into 12 'Grand Companies'. Each Grand Company was assigned to a particular Small Ward, the two aldermen of that ward acting as gild masters. The division of trades reflects the social structure of the city. The greater merchants were assigned to Conesford, the richest ward, lesser merchants and goldsmiths to Mancroft, the cloth-makers and related trades to the manufacturing ward of Wymer, and the lowest trades to Over the Water, the poorest of the wards.[48]

The Town Close estate which, as has been said, was given to the city in 1524, was also regulated by the city authorities. In the *Mayor's Court Book* for 1637 it is recorded that John Witherland and William Garrard are appointed to ditch and hedge the Town Close. In 1641 four aldermen were appointed to see how many cows and horses were kept in the Town Close and make a list of their owners. Any cattle that should not be there were to be put in the pound. As early as 1536 the Assembly had decreed that only citizens could keep any 'great beast in the common close of the city'. Any animal belonging to a non-citizen was to be forfeit and the owner fined 40d. Half the fine was to go to the person finding the animal, which must have been a great encouragement to 'sneak' on wrong-doers.[49]

The roads were not made up and could be terrible in winter: however, there was regular communication between Norwich and London. On 20 July 1665 an advertisement proclaimed that all passenger coaches between London and Norwich were to stop: this was because of the Plague. In 1681 a coach was running from the Saracen's Head in Aldgate to Norwich. Walter Rye quotes a case heard before the Mayor in 1566 which tells how a man in London intending to travel to Norwich, hired four Hackney horses from the *Windmill* in London. From the details given 'it would seem that the price was a shilling a day per horse, with a minimum of 9 shillings, which would imply the average journey to and from London took nine days or more'.[50]

Some people were prepared to travel further in search of work. The London *Lord Mayor's Waiting Books* include the names of people going to serve as apprentices in America between 1682 and 1692. Six are from Norwich—three male and three female—and they are bound to people in Maryland or Virginia for terms of four or five years. There is at least one case of poor children being sent to America at public expense. The accounts of the overseers of the poor in St John Maddermarket for 1658/9 include this entry: 'pd to send away 2 of goody Blunt's Sons to new Ingland £1. 10s.'.[51]

The Poor and the Sick

The Tudor authorities were very aware of the problems of dealing with the poor, which had suddenly become much greater with the dissolution of the monasteries and hospitals run by monks and nuns. They were keen to distinguish between the 'impotent' poor who could not work because of sickness and the 'idle' poor who chose not to work and should be punished. In 1547 an Act was passed saying that the impotent poor were to be relieved in the places where they were born by the charity of the parishioners. This was the start of the poor law system that prevailed for the next 200 years. The poor were examined to see where they came from and then removed to that parish. An extreme case is that of a blind cripple called Mary Ambree. Upon examination it was decided that her true place of settlement was Newcastle and, after several weeks in Magdalen Gates lazar house, she was duly sent all the way back there.[52]

The 1547 Act said the sick poor should be provided with suitable 'houses' which in Norwich meant continuing with the Great Hospital and the Lazar houses. Henry VIII had intended to dissolve the Great Hospital and give it to the city. He died before this could be done but his successor Edward VI granted the site of the Great Hospital to the city by Letters Patent of 7 May 1547 so that:

> the aforesaid late hospital of St Giles shall henceforth be a place and house for the poor there to be maintained, and it shall be called God's House or the Poor's house in Holmestrete in the City of Norwich, of the foundation of ourself and King Henry the Eighth our father for ever.

The 1547 Act also said what should be done with the idle poor. They were to be punished and might be forced to wear iron collars round their necks or legs. There are a few references to this punishment being ordered by the mayor's court but for an actual crime rather than merely being 'idle'. In 1559 a servant called Thomas Huson was ordered to wear a 'clogg' on his leg after he had eaten someone else's chicken. When another servant, William Bannocke, confessed that he had run away three times from his master, the court ordered 'that he shall have a ryng aboute his necke according to the statute'.[53]

The Tudor poet Thomas Tusser seems to have thought the city was especially harsh in the way it treated its poor. He wrote in 1557:

> At Norwich fine, for me and mine, a citie trim
> There strangers wel may seem to dwel,
> That pitch and pay, or keepe their day,
> But who that want shall find it scant so good for him.

Norwich had experimented with a poor rate in the 1540s but its real attempt to deal with the problem of poverty came in 1570. First the problem was analysed by making a Census of the Poor. Then came the radical solution, the 1571 Orders for Control and Relief of the Poor (note the order of the two priorities). These said that the ratepayers of the city felt aggrieved that:

> the city was so replenished with great numbers, poor people both men, women and children to the number of 2,300 persons who for the most part went daily abroad from door to door counterfeiting a kind of work but indeed did very little or none at all.

These 'sturdy beggars … being overgorged they cast forth the rest into the straight so that they might be followed by the sight thereof in pottage, bread, meat and drink which they spoiled very voluptuously'.[54]

Begging was forbidden and a Bridewell was set up, at first in the St Paul's Hospital building, for which the Corporation took over responsibility in 1565. It became the city Bridewell in 1571. The Orders for the Poor say that men could be set to work grinding malt and women to 'spinne and carde'. In 1583 the Corporation bought the house now called the Bridewell from the Sotherton family. This was the house formerly of the Appleyard family in St Andrew's and a Gothic decoration made of wood can still be seen over the original Bridewell entrance. The mayor's court book says:

> Whereas the inhabitants of this city of long time have been at great and excessive charges in maintaining the poor people within the same city which increase more and more by reason that so many young idle persons and bastards do daily increase, and no convenient house hath been provided for a Bridewell to keep and stay the said idle persons to some honest work and labour: the magistrates therefore of the same city have provided and bought the great house of Mr. Baron Sotherton situate in St Andrew's nigh the churchyard there, in a place most fit for such a purpose.

In 1573 all the unemployed had to go to the Market Cross with their tools to be available for work. The mixing of firmness with kindness is shown by the appointment in the same year of a bone-setter to treat free those who could not afford to pay for treatment.[55]

The measures seem to have worked, at least in the short term. Sir John Harrington called Norwich 'another Utopia' in which 'the people live so orderly, the streets kept so cleanly, the tradesmen, young and old, so industrious; the better part so provident ... that it is rare to meet a beggar there, as it is common to met them in Westminster'.[56]

The Census of the Poor is a fascinating document for its insight into how the urban poor were living. The census names a total of 2,359 paupers, perhaps 14 per cent of the population, 'a uniquely comprehensive listing'. However, it does not include the 'strangers'. City authorities expected everyone to work in some form until death. Pelling estimates that people in Norwich over 60 years old stood a two-in-five chance of poverty. There were no pensions, of course, so anyone who was not earning had to depend on their family or on their fellow-workers. Places of birth are recorded for less than a third of the poor—of these more than half were not born in the city. Some of the poor were in their own homes but most were tenants of prominent citizens.

The Census shows that very young Norwich children knitted or spun or were learning these skills. The Census describes children as young as six as 'idle', implying that they could have been working. Some of the families in the Census are explicitly said to be dependent on the income of a child. The mayor's court exercised powers now associated with social workers. In 1622 a Norwich mother who was beating her child had it taken away and had to pay for its maintenance by someone else. Eleven years later the same court ordered John Roote, who had hurt a child's eye, to have 1s. 8d. a week taken out of his wages and paid to the child's mother.[57]

Two major charities were founded in the 17th century—the Children's Hospital and Doughty's Hospital. The Children's Hospital was founded under the will of Thomas Anguish who died in 1618 leaving a house and estate in St Edmund's for the purpose. Other citizens gave or bequeathed money and the house was opened on Fishergate in 1621 when 14 boys were admitted. The number increased to 21 in the 18th century and to 30 in 1798. The hospital benefited again under the will of Thomas Tesmond. He died in 1626 leaving 69 acres in Bixley to the Corporation to fund sermons. The residue of the income was to go to the Children's Hospital.[58]

Anguish seems to have intended his hospital to be for both boys and girls but there is no evidence that girls were ever admitted. In 1649 mayor Robert Baron left £250 for the training up of 'women children' and in 1656 Henry Whitingham of London left £200 for the same purpose. The girls seem to have been lodged in St Andrew's Hall until 1664 when they moved into the house on what is now Golden Dog Lane. Accounts survive from 1653 when there were only two girls there: by Blomefield's time there were 21 girls in the hospital. The Mayor's Court Book for

1675-6 records that the girls in the Girls' Hospital were set to work spinning wool on great wheels under the tuition of a 'knowing person'.[59]

William Doughty wrote to the Mayor's Court from Dereham in 1677 saying that he intended to live in Norwich and would like to be free from rates and charges. The court agreed: presumably he had already promised to endow a hospital in the city. Doughty died in 1688 leaving £6,000 to trustees to buy a piece of land and build a hospital for poor old men and women. He made some specific orders—it was to have a court in the middle with a gate so narrow that a cart could not come into the court; the hospital was to be run by a bachelor as master (this clause of his will was very soon forgotten) and was to accommodate 24 men and eight women. It should not cost more than £600 to buy the site and put up the building. The rest of the money was to be used to buy land in Norfolk 'not subject to be overflowne with the sea'; did he forecast the problems of global warming and rising sea levels? He calculated that the land would provide an income of £250 a year to keep up the buildings and give the old people 2s. a week each and a gown when they first came to the hospital.[60]

Each parish in the city was responsible for its own poor. A fairly typical case is that of Jane Lusher and her children in St John Maddermarket. She was paid three shillings in 1636/7 'in her sickness' but she died soon afterwards, leaving three or-phaned children. The parish then paid 'the widow Cooper' 10 pence a week to look after the children. Probably two of them died soon after; in the following year Mrs. Cooper was receiving money for just one Lusher child and the end of the story comes in the same year when she was given a further two shillings 'for the burial of it'. The overseers were always keen to shift responsibility for a poor person elsewhere if they could. An entry in the St Andrew's overseers accounts in 1673/4 says bluntly: 'Paid Mary Hastings at several times and to goodie downes to get her oute of the parish 00. 13. 6.'.[61]

Treatment of the poor in Norwich was revolutionised by an Act of 1711. Under the Act the whole of Norwich was made into one parish for the poor, apart from the Close and the strangers' congregations which were excluded. Guardians of the Poor were set up, comprising the mayor and aldermen and 32 people chosen by the free-men, eight being chosen from each ward. The poor were to be maintained in work-houses in St Andrew's Hall, a wing of the former Duke's Palace and outside St Augustine's Gates.

Records relating to medical practice in Norwich have been analysed in several articles by Margaret Pelling. In the Middle Ages the sick had been given licences allowing them to beg. Norwich introduced a compulsory poor rate in 1549 to replace this system and seems to have been the first provincial town to do so. The scheme was not effective and licences continued to be issued. However the Corporation accepted responsibility for the sick poor. They were not usually institutionalised, but people—often poor women—were paid to 'keep' the patients until they were cured. Some of the women were employed in an ancillary role, others had sole responsibility for the patient.

Professional help was also provided. In 1573 the Corporation paid Richard Durrant to live in the city and attend to 'the relief of such as shall fortune by misfortune to have their legs, arms, or the bones of other parts of their limbs to be broken [and] of such as be poor and not able to pay for their healing'.[62] The Norwich Book of the Poor shows that about 11 per cent of the adults named in the book are sick or disabled. From these figures Pelling estimates that people in Norwich over 60 had a one-in-four chance of being severely disabled. She comments that 'a minimum of 7 per cent of the urban population at any time might be grossly infectious, repulsive, confined within doors, bedridden, or unable to see'.[63] However, the city already had a reputation as a centre of healing. Simon Bushe, aged 12, was brought to Norwich from Scottow on a cart by someone who told him he would have 'meat enough in Norwich and a surgeon to heal him'. He may well have been right—in 1580 the mayor's court ordered that a lame boy be given a joint of veal or mutton twice a week while he was recovering. The surgeon given responsibility for the boy had the appropriate name of William Fever.[64]

Only nine medical doctors are known to have practised in Norwich between 1501 and 1600 but the city is known to have 17 qualified doctors between 1603 and 1643. This may just be because of better record-keeping; Bishop Redman's visitation of 1597 was one of the first serious attempts to ensure that all practitioners were licensed. The first evidence for the systematic licensing of midwives comes from as late as the 1630s. Some of the doctors became nationally known. Henry VIII's personal physician was William Butts who was born in Shouldham Thorpe in about 1483 and brought up in Norwich. He was the first medical man to be knighted.[65]

Another famous Norwich-born doctor was John Caius. His career is summarised in the *Pocket County Companion*:

> Dr. John Caius, born at Norwich 6th November 1510, was the founder of Caius College, Cambridge. His name was Kaye or Key, which he Latinised to Caius. In 1547 he became a Fellow of the College of Physicians, of which he was afterwards President; and was likewise physician to Edward VI, Queen Mary and Queen Elizabeth. He died 29th July 1573 and was buried in the chapel of his own college.[66]

Dutch and Walloons looked after their own sick as they did their own poor. There are two references in the 1570s to the city employing Dutch physicians. Second-generation immigrants born in the city would not suffer any restrictions and the names of some Dutch doctors are known. John Cropp came from Flanders as a surgeon in 1567. His son, also called John Cropp, obtained a licence to practise in Norwich in 1602 and is mentioned in the letters of Katherine Paston.[67]

The lazar houses, situated just outside the city gates, were increasingly supervised by the mayor's court. They consisted of one central building and a number of small cottages. Often a husband and wife acted as joint keepers and the woman might carry on as sole keeper after her husband died. The city used the lazar houses for treatment of conditions that affected the ability of the patient to work. The keeper of the lazar house at Magdalen Gate was paid to receive from the Bridewell a 'loathsome boy' who had been sent back to Norwich because he had been born in Ber Street. Most of the lazar houses continued until about 1700. St Augustine's was then used as an infirmary for aged poor people who were unfit for work. It was being used for the same purpose in 1814. 'By the early 19th century, the Magdalen gates lazar house had changed from

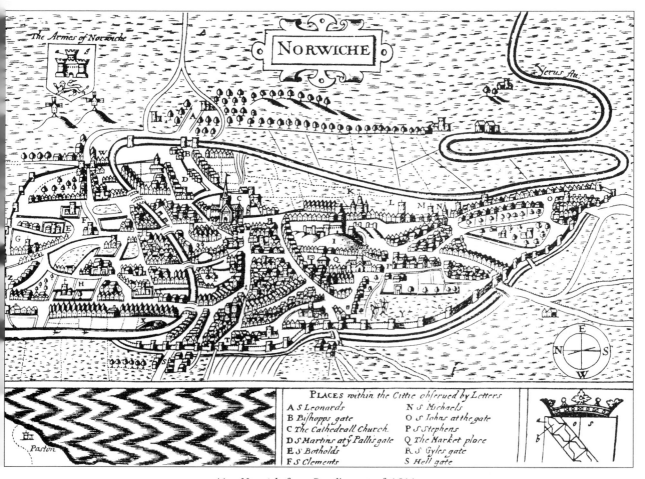

The Armes of Norwiche

NORWICHE

Yerus flu.

PLACES within the Cittie observed by Letters
A S Leonards   N S Michaels
B Bishopps gate   O S Iohns at the gate
C The Cathedrall Church   P S Stephens
D S Martins at ý Palls gate Q The Market place
E S Botholds   R S Gyles gate
F S Clements   S Hell gate

Paston

41 *Norwich from Speed's map of 1611*

leperhouse to "almshouse" to workhouse and finally to alehouse, the last being ... not so far from the first as might be imagined.'[68]

Norwich has weekly reports of the number of burials in the city from 1579 to 1646: they are recorded in the mayor's court books. There is no parallel to this outside London. From these we can trace the waves of plague that hit the city. Plague is related to trade; it probably spread from overseas through Yarmouth. The first wave was in the mayoral year of 1579-1580: 4,831 people died in Norwich, 4,193 of plague—more than 2,000 of these were strangers.[69]

The next major epidemic was from August 1603 to July 1604. In this time 3,841 were buried, almost 3,000 of plague. This means that nearly a quarter of the city's inhabitants died in one year. There were similar rates of death in the waves of plague in 1625-6 and 1665-6. Dogs and other animals were slaughtered *en masse* when plague was feared: they were thought to carry the disease in their hair. In 1630 the Mayor's court ordered that all dogs, hogs, cats and tame doves found loose in the streets should be destroyed.

42   *The Black Tower*

Some of the city's leaders fled the city in plague years, others stayed to issue orders to try to control the spread of the disease. A number of aldermen remained even after most common councillors had fled. The City Assembly met only once during the epidemic of 1579 and not at all during the height of the 1666 outbreak. However the court of aldermen met almost as regularly as at normal times. The Quarter Sessions ordered on 12 July 1666 Norwich market to be transferred to a site outside the city walls during the outbreak of plague. This was to stop country people coming into the city and so 'prevent the scatteringe of that Noysome pestilence'. The Black Tower was used as a pesthouse to isolate the sick. In 1795 over a hundred skeletons were dug up in Lakenham. With them was a Norwich tradesman's token for 1664, so these were probably the bodies of some of the victims of this wave of the plague. Steps taken to control the plague were expensive and not always effective. In Norwich one of those employed as a bearer of the dead stole goods from an infected house and fled to Yarmouth and then to Colchester with a 'lewd woman'. Riots were expected: the town clerk admitted, 'Wee are in greater feare of the poore than the plague, all our monie beinge gone'. The city had to borrow £200 to get through the crisis.[70]

Plague never came back after 1666, and smallpox was the most feared disease of the later 17th and 18th centuries. There was an outbreak in Norwich in 1669-70 when Thomas Browne wrote, 'upwards of 300 families fell down in less than a fortnight'. In January 1670 the town clerk wrote, 'the smallpox rageth still amongst us, and poverty daily invades us like an armed man'. There was another outbreak in 1681-2.[71]

Aspects of popular medicine are summarised by Walter Rye: 'Perhaps, however, the licences to quacks to sell drugs, sometimes on horseback and sometimes on stages, are the most interesting. The stages or booths were sometimes very substantial erections (one in 1680 being 60 ft. long by 30 ft. wide), and were placed near the Guildhall. They were not always well conducted for the servants of one of them, who acted as drolls were complained of for the obscenity of their speeches.'[72]

Before the Reformation, such schools as existed were maintained by monks and nuns. When they disappeared, town authorities had to fill the breach. The statutes of Henry VIII set up a choir school and a grammar school. In 1538 the choir school had eight boys and in 1540 the grammar school had 20 boys. The grammar school moved to Blackfriars in 1541 but was back in the Close by 1546. Norwich secured a grammar school in connection with the Great Hospital under the will of Henry VIII. In 1551 the school made its final move–the former carnary chapel in the Close was bought and the school moved into the building around which it is still centred.

A compulsory rate maintained a few children in St Giles' hospital where they were taught their letters. In each parish select women were provided to supervise up to 12 women and children in the cloth industry: the children were to be taught to read and write as well as to work. When the child was old enough he or she was apprenticed or set to work. There was no set test of eligibility, the deacons deciding off their own bat whether to help families with sick children or with too many children to feed.

In an order of the Assembly of 1592 we read of schools of writing, reading and knitting being closed because of sickness. Presumably these were small schools in private houses while both parents were at work. Several of the 952 children mentioned in the Mayor's Book of the Poor are said to be going to school.

Religion

A very few people–about six–were burnt for heresy at the Lollards' pit in the first quarter of the 16th century, usually for Lollard ideas such as dislike of images and denial of the special role of priests. The most well known was Thomas Bilney who preached against abuses connected with saints' cults. He was convicted of heresy before the Bishop of London in 1527. When he returned to Norwich in 1531 he was burnt as a lapsed heretic.

Mary Tudor became queen in 1553: she tried to undo the Reformation and restore the old religion. She appointed John Hopton as Bishop of Norwich in 1554. Under his rule 48 people in the diocese were burnt for heresy, many at Lollards' Pit. The churches were now expected to have the ritual aids that most had just sold. Eighteen city churches were summoned by the church court and asked

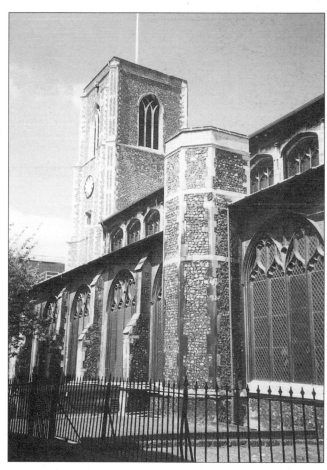

43 *St Andrew's church: the tower is of 1467-98 and the church 1499-1518.*

if they had the neccessary ornaments and if they had removed bible texts painted on the walls. Only five churches were able to say that they had the ornaments.[73]

After Mary's death her Protestant sister Elizabeth became queen and the Reformation in England was assured. Queen Elizabeth relied on her Archbishop of Canterbury Matthew Parker to settle the Reformation. He had been born in Norwich and his father was a worsted weaver. The tomb of Parker's parents can still be seen in the churchyard of St Clement's. Fuller wrote of Parker, 'he was a parker indeed–careful to keep the fences and shut the gates of discipline against all such night-stealers as would invade the same'. Some books claim that the way he poked his nose into the affairs of his clergy gave rise to the phrase 'nosy parker', but this is not the sort of thing that archive evidence can confirm or deny.

The mayor's court kept its ears open and punished words as well as deeds. A wheelwright called Matthew Hamont was convicted at Norwich Guildhall in 1578 for speaking slanderous words against the queen's majesty. He was condemned to pay £100 to the queen or else have his ears cut off. Obviously he could not or would not pay such a vast sum and his ears were indeed removed on the pillory in the Market-Place on 13 May. Clearly thought to be a threat he was returned to prison and tried for heresies including having said that the New Testament was 'but mere foolishness, a story of men, or rather a mere fable'. For this he was burnt in the Castle Ditch on 20 May 1578.[74]

The fabric of the Cathedral suffered less than many others during the Commonwealth. Alderman Christopher Jay had spent nearly £200 of his own money carrying out maintenance. In October 1662 a Dutch tourist reported that the Cathedral and cloisters had been 'restored as new'. By 1670 the chapter had spent £2,800 on repairs apart from what it had received as donations (at least £870) and also spent £1,542 renovating houses in the Close. It raised the money by levying fines on tenants as they gave them new leases. They were even able to pay back to Christopher Jay the money he had spent in the 1650s![75]

The first Norwich man to be converted to the Society of Friends was Thomas Symonds and the earliest Quaker meetings were held from 1654 in his house. Land in Goat Lane was bought for a meeting house in 1676 and in 1678 the Meeting decided 'it shall be 40 foot long and 30 foot wide … and a partition made to run with wheeles to enlarge or lessen the rome as occasion requires'. It opened in 1679 and in 1699 a meeting house at Gildencroft was opened. In 1700 there were about 500 Quakers in Norwich. The legal status of Quaker marriages was sometimes disputed but it was generally held that Quaker marriages and Jewish marriages were the only marriages outside the Church of England that were lawful. The Quakers had bought land in Gildencroft for their graveyard in 1671. At first grave stones were put up but in 1717 the Yearly Meeting decided they should be removed and no more set up.[76]

The Roman Catholic community in Norwich was not large but the faith was never wiped out. Between 1574 and 1616, 49 students from Norfolk were ordained into the Roman Catholic priesthood after studying at seminaries in Europe. The Compton Census of 1676 lists 62 Roman Catholics living in the city with the greatest concentration–of 13 people–living in the Close.[77]

Several cases of supposed witchcraft came before the courts:

> Jane Blogg indicted at Norwich City Quarter Sessions September 1657 not having God before her eyes but being seduced by the instigation of the Devil on 14 Feb. 1652 did devise devillish arts called inchantments witchcrafts charmes and Sorceries in and upon Elizabeth Noblet widow in her body did wickedly divellishly feloniously of her malice before thought did practice by reason of the said arts whereupon the said Elizabeth Noblet was much tormented and did languish from 14 Feb. 1652 until 10 July 1653 and by reason of the aforesaid practice did die and the jurors said she did feloniously do murther against the public peace …

According to Blomefield, a woman called Mary Oliver was executed for witchcraft in 1659 and her goods were ordered to be sold for the benefit of the citizens. We have already mentioned Ann Dant and Margaret Turrell, hanged as witches in 1648 alongside the 'Great Blow' rioters in the castle ditches.[78]

Matthew Hopkins, the self-proclaimed 'Witchfinder-General', worked mainly in Essex and Suffolk. The records of the Norfolk Assizes are lost for the 1640s but he appears to have worked here too. *A Perfect Diurnal* says that 40 witches were tried at Norwich Assizes in July 1645, of whom 20 had already been executed. In 1646 some people put a set of questions to the Assizes in Norwich claiming that Hopkins was himself a witch. We know this because Hopkins published a pamphlet in 1647 defending

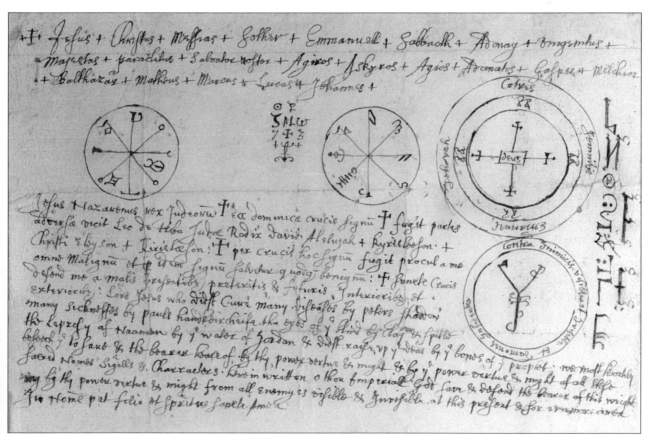

44 *Spell to ward off witchcraft*

himself against the charges. Hopkins' father was vicar of Great Wenham in Suffolk. He died in 1634 and his will is in the Norfolk Record Office; it says he had six children and mentions two by name: Matthew is one of the four not individually named.[79]

The spells of witches were kept at bay by 'witch bottles', jars containing one's own urine together with pins or nails, fragments of cloth (often heart-shaped) and sometimes charms on paper or parchment. This might be buried under the threshold or the hearth of one's house. The Norfolk Record Office has a 17th-century charm that was pinned to the breast to ward off witches' curses–the number of pin holes show that it has been much used.[80]

Housing

The population of Norwich was about 12,000 in 1520, 15,000 in 1600 and had risen to about 30,000 in 1700. There are few records about their houses but some information can be gleaned from the archives.

The effects of the 1507 fire were devastating. The fire may explain why so few medieval buildings survive in the city apart from the stone churches. However, there are some obvious exceptions like the *Britons' Arms* which is reputedly the only building

45   *Weaver's cottage in Lion and Castle Yard*

in Elm Hill not to have burnt down in
1507. The houses built after the fire are
generally built with rubble walls on the
ground floor with timber framing above
and might be of two or three storeys.
Houses like these are shown on the two
earliest maps of the city, the Sanctuary map
of 1541 (which only covers parts of the
city) and William Cunningham's map of
1558. Smaller houses, often off the main
streets, might still be of one ground-floor
room and a single room above. The
thatched cottage in Lion and Castle yard
has been restored by the Norwich Preservation Trust as an example of these tiny
'weavers' cottages'.

The city took steps to prevent a rep-
etition of the 1507 disaster. On 18 May
1509 the Assembly ordered that in future
all new buildings should be roofed with
'thaktyle' and not with 'thakke' under pen-
alty of a fine of 20s.[81] This was renewed
in 1531 but repealed in 1532: people were
now at liberty to roof their buildings with
'slatte, tyle or reeyd'. An Act of Parliament of 1534 ordered the rebuilding of
all 'burnt grounds' or at least their enclo-
sure within stone walls: otherwise the
mayor could enter and seize the property.

46 *The same cottage after restoration by Norwich
Preservation Trust*

Detailed Orders against fire were is-
sued by the city in 1570. All roofs now had to be covered with tile, slate or lead (the
first mention of lead as a roofing material). Buckets and a ladder had to be provided
at every church. Each alderman was also to have buckets and a ladder available at his
house, along with every citizen chosen into the livery. Every great ward was to supply
'one crome of iron with ringes and ropes fixed to the same' and four long ladders.
Every small ward was to have buckets.[82]

The mayor's court books record measures taken against fire. There was one fire
engine and ladders and buckets were kept at St Andrew's Hall and the Guildhall. In
1679 a second engine was ordered from London and Daniel Fromantel was paid £2
a year to keep the two engines in order. Two more engines were ordered in the 1680s.

Probate inventories list the possessions of the dead and those that survive for
Norwich for the period 1580 to 1730 have been analysed.[83] Unfortunately the only
inventories that can definitely be related to a surviving house are two inventories for
the Branthwayt family house in St John Maddermarket and the inside of this house

was altered beyond recognition in the 1920s. Naturally the inventories tend to relate to the houses of the better-off–only 20 per cent relate to houses of three rooms or less. Over the 150 years the number of houses having kitchens increased from 60 per cent to almost 100 per cent.

There was an increase in the number of rooms having hearths but the number remained low, perhaps two hearths in a four- to-six roomed house. An increase in the height of the houses is indicated in the number of inventories mentioning garrets which rose from 10 per cent in 1580-1604 to 60 per cent in 1705-1730; these often had looms or other textile equipment. Priestley adds:

> One other necessary accompaniment to daily life is omitted from the record. Not surprisingly, since they would have been fixtures of no value, the inventories, with one exception, contain no mention of privies. Excavations, however, indicate that they were common in the 17th century city, having superseded 16th century cess pits. Pewter chamber-pots are, however, listed frequently in the inventories, and close stools–i.e. commodes–are also mentioned occasionally.

Sanitary arrangements are occasionally mentioned in archive sources. A messuage with a yard in Ber Street that was sold in 1713 included 'part of jakes' and access to a well. In 1648 Joseph Holback was before the court of Quarter Sessions for owning tenements in St Peter Mancroft 'not having any latrine in English a necessary'. In 1689 little Caroline Body aged two or three was sitting on the seat in 'a house of office' in her father's house by the river in St Andrew's when she fell through and was washed into the river and drowned.[84]

Keeping the city and river clean was a continual pre-occupation of the Mayor's court. In 1675 the keeper of the market cross was paid £5 10s. a year to sweep the market once a week and the city bridges and waste grounds once a fortnight. As always the city was 'careful' with its property. He was allowed a barrow but forbidden to use it for private purposes and had to return it to the Guildhall when he was not using it. Bylaws were passed by the city in 1686:

> to cleanse the Streets and Channels from Dirt, Coulder and other filth lying there, which by sudden Rain is washed into the said River by means whereof laden Keels and Lighters cannot pass as formerly; and the Citizens themselves are no less annoyed, and the said River will be in a short time destroyed if some speedy remedy be not provided.[85]

In 1700 an Act of Parliament was passed for lighting the city streets and Thomas Lombe was appointed to set up the lamps. The Workhouse Act of 1711 included a clause ordering every householder whose property adjoined a public way to set candles or visible lights on the outside walls of their houses from Michaelmas to Lady Day. They were to keep them lit until 11 o'clock at night. Blomefield, writing about 30 years later, was not impressed with the results: 'By virtue of which Act the Streets are enlightened with lamps, which being of the old fashion, and not globular, and standing at a great distance from one another, do not well perform their design'.[86]

Crime

Major crimes such as murder and rape continued to be dealt with by the Court of Assizes, which met twice each year in the county, once in Norwich and once

47   *Thomas Kirkpatrick's 'prospect': the buildings on the Castle Mound*

at Thetford. The royal judges came up from London to hold the court and all its records are at the Public Record Office in London. The Tudor period saw the rise of the Court of Quarter Sessions where local magistrates tried lesser crimes and also dealt with administrative and civil matters, such as disputes about rates, bastardy cases, problems of maintaining roads and bridges. As a borough, Norwich had its own Court of Quarter Sessions, completely separate from that of the county. However both courts were actually held in Norwich. The city court was at the Guildhall, the county one at the Shire Hall on top of the castle mound: this area was still technically part of the county of Norfolk and not of the City of Norwich.

As always there were a few sensational cases. One that reached the Privy Council is described by Ralph Houlbrooke. In 1548, Agnes Randolf claimed that when she was 11 years old she was riding across Mousehold Heath when she was abducted by John Atkinson who forced her to marry him. Atkinson said she had consented and that she was 12 not 11 years old. The exact age is important as 12 was the legal age for a girl to marry. The verdict seems to have been that although she was indeed of age the marriage was not valid as it had not been consummated.[87]

Another notorious Norwich crime is described in the *Pocket County Companion*:

The Hanging Tree formerly stood in the Town Close, and was for some time used as a gallows. On it was hanged Mr. Thomas Burney for the murder of Mr. Bedingfield. These gentlemen were on the Grand Jury in July 1684. Having indulged too freely at the 'Maid's Head' they fought with their swords in the street in St Andrew's, and Mr. Bedingfield was run through the body. Burney was hanged on the 8th of August.'

Ursula Priestley corrects the murderer's name to Berney and quotes the blunt words of a contemporary broadsheet: 'he suffered according to the law, his body was put into a coffin for his friends to inter'. However she suggests he was hanged on the Market Cross (and also gives a wrong date). A chronicle written within a generation of the event tells us that the crime took place at two in the morning of 20 July 1684 and that 'Barney' (yet another variant of the name) 'stabbed him in 4 or 5 places with his rapier, some of which were in his back'. The Assize judge being already in town justice was swift: he was tried the following day and hanged a fortnight later at Town Close. They were both young men: Bedingfield was about 27 and Berney just 21 years old.[88]

The most tragic murder case in this period was probably that of Robert Watts. Watts was a weaver living in the *Old Globe* inn on Botolph Street. He was noted for his jealous behaviour towards his wife. One night in 1701 a man told Mrs. Watts that her husband wanted her wedding ring for a moment to settle a bet about its exact weight. She let him borrow it and he took it to Watts who immediately assumed his wife had cuckolded him. Watts went straight home and murdered his wife: for this he was hanged outside his own door. The inn—not surprisingly—was said to be haunted by the poor woman's ghost. The *Old Globe* was pulled down in 1875 and the site is now a car park next to the Anglia Square shopping centre.[89]

Lesser crimes were punished with the whip, the cage, the pillory and the ducking stool. The pillory was in the Market Place and the ducking stool on Fyebridge. Walter Rye says:

Whipping till the back was bloody was the recognised punishment for vagrants, and the cage was in full use, one woman being sent there for scolding with her neighbours and railing at the magistrates, and was afterwards to be sent to the ducking stool and dipped thrice over her head.

The Norwich Chamberlains' accounts for 25 August 1680 headed, 'A Bout ye duck stule' include payment of 2s. 6d. to watermen for bringing it from Conesford, the purchase of some new pieces of wood and finally 3s. 6d. 'payd to 6 men for gittin of it up'. This last expression is good broad Norfolk vernacular even today.[90]

Many examples of petty crimes can be found in the Mayor's Court books. In September 1561, a widow called Alice Lemon 'was taken upon Sunday night last past in the Cockky Lane with one John Gorney in comyttyng the abhominable act of whoredom'. She was sentenced to be led about the city with a basin tinkled before her (to attract attention) and to be ducked at Fyebridge. Gorney does not appear to have been punished for his part in the act of whoredom. In 1563, Margaret Hare had to ride in a cart to the stool and be ducked: her crimes were scolding and making common bawdy. In the same year Margaret Bundey, as a scold and a bawd, had to spend a morning in the stocks with a paper on her head and then go to the ducking stool.[91]

In 1701 the Norwich Court of Requests (also known as Court of Conscience) was established. It was intended to make easier the recovery of small debts under 40 shillings. It was only the third such court in the country. Before this date the Mayor's Court had handled such cases, and after 1701 both courts continued side by side, ordering debtors to pay their dues in instalments. The Court disappeared in 1846 when it became part of the new County Court.

Leisure and Learning

It has already been noted that the area within the city walls was as large as that of London, which meant that there was plenty of land that was not built on. Norwich was famous for its gardens. Fuller wrote in 1662:

> Norwich is (as you please) either a city in an orchard, or an orchard in a city, so equally are houses and trees blended in it; so that the pleasure and the populousness of the people meet here together. Yet in this mixture the inhabitants participate nothing of the rusticalness of the one but altogether of the urbanity of the other ... The Dutch brought hither with them not only their profitable crafts but pleasurable curiousities. They were the first that advanced the use and reputation of flowers in this city ... the rose of roses (rosa mundi) had its first being in this city.

Nine years later John Evelyn commented, 'The suburbs are large, the prospect sweete, and other amoenities, not omitting the flower gardens, which all the Inhabitans excell in ...'[92]

Walter Rye gives a vivid picture of popular entertainments in the city:

> in 1667 Elizabeth Gillman of St Stephen's had her beer license revoked for allowing unlawful games, and in the same year it was laid down that no beerseller should have a license if he kept nine pins. This game was also specially objected to in 1679 and 1688–in the last named year the marshalls and constables being directed to go and pull them up ... The shows licensed were very numerous: for giants (one woman 7 ft. 6 ins. high), women without arms and hands, monstrous hairy children, a girl 'without bones', a child with six fingers and toes on hands and feet, a monstrous man with two bodies, and so on ... Of the animals shown we hear of lions, camels, tame beavers, dancing bears, dancing mares, dancing dogs, tigers, jackals, elephants, a monkey, a busie (I can't imagine what that was), and an anti-bear, probably an ant-eater. The monstrous man feeding on roots of trees taken amongst the Hills of Carinthia was probably a fraud or a large monkey.[93]

By the end of the period some disapproved of these vulgar pleasures. In 1681 Dean Prideaux wrote, 'The town swarms with alehouses, every other house is almost one, and every one of them they tell us is also a bawdy house'. Alehouses were distrusted by authorities and religious people–drink, gossip and loose women threatened the fabric of society and encouraged apprentices to be insolent to their masters.[94]

On 25 January 1589 (note the date–this was just after the Armada and Drake could do no wrong):

> was read in court a letter sent to Mr. mayor and his brethren from Sir Francis Drake whereby he desired that the waytes of this city may be sent to him to go the new intended voyage. Whereunto the waytes being here called do all assent whereupon it is agreed that they shall have 6 cloaks of Stamell cloth made them ready before go and that a wagon shall be provided to carry them and their instruments. And that they shall have £4 to buy them 3 new howboys and one treble recorder ...

Peter Spratt was to be paid 10 shillings for a new sackbut case.[95]

Drake's expedition was to Spain and Portugal. Three of the waits died on the voyage: the survivors were each paid 50 shillings for the year and the same amount was given to the widows of those who did not return. The Norwich waits were founded in 1408. In Elizabeth I's time they usually lived in the 'Suffragans' Tenements' in Bank Street. These were built by John Underwood, suffragan to Bishop Nykke, and had his badge and initials on the spandrels of the door frame. From the 18th century they were associated with the house on King Street, once Jurnet's, which is why it is commonly known as the Music House.

Norwich had its place in the literary renaissance under Elizabeth I. The Earl of Surrey, discussed later, was known as the 'poet-earl'. His translations of the second and fourth books of the *Aeneid* are the earliest English poems to be published in blank verse.

Robert Greene, born in Norwich in 1560, is most famous for his criticisms of William Shakespeare:

> There is an upstart Crow, beautified with our feathers, that with his Tyger's heart wrapped in a player's hide supposes he is as well able to bumbast out a blank verse as the best of you, and being an absolute Johannes factotum is in his own conceit the only Shake-scene in a country.

Greene went to Norwich Grammar School but spent most of his career in London writing romantic novels, including *Pandosto* from which Shakespeare took the plot for his play *A Winter's Tale*.[96]

Another writer associated with Norwich was Thomas Deloney, who was probably born in the city, although he made his name in London. Thomas Nashe calls him the 'balleting silk-weaver of Norwich'. His ballads earned him disapproval in the 1580s because of the way in which one of them referred to Queen Elizabeth. He turned to novels and published three at the end of the 1590s. They were *Jack of Newbury*, *The Gentle Craft* and *Thomas of Reading*. Although the plots are simple, the dialogue and the background details are very real: they are important because they are almost the only books that describe life among Tudor weavers, clothiers and shoemakers.[97]

Norwich was the first city in England to set up a library. The city library was set up under an Assembly order of 3 May 1608. They decided that three rooms in the house of the sword bearer adjoining St Andrew's Hall should be converted into a library for the use of visiting preachers. It remained a reference library until 1716 when it was decided that books could be borrowed.[98]

Printing was introduced to Norwich by Francis Burges who set up an office near the Red Well in 1700. In September 1701 he published the *Norwich Post*, the first newspaper to be printed outside London. Burges died in 1706 aged only 30: he is buried in St Andrew's church. Henry Crossgrove printed the *Norwich Gazette* at his house near St Giles' Gate in December 1706. Crossgrove became a freeman in 1710, the first printer to be recorded in the Norwich Freeman's lists since Anthony Solempne 140 years earlier.

The Howard Family

Mount Surrey was the house on St Leonard's Hill built by the Earl of Surrey, the poet and son of the 3rd Duke of Norfolk. It was near the site of the former monastic cell of St Leonard's. Surrey began building his new house in 1544: it was of Italian Renaissance design. The house was richly furnished with Turkish tapestries and carpets. He had another palace in Norwich called Surrey Court: this was in Surrey Street. He was charged with using the coat of arms of Edward the Confessor which only the monarch was entitled to use and was beheaded on Tower Hill on 19 January 1547: he was only 30. Mount Surrey was sacked during Kett's rebellion and later fell into ruin: not a stone now remains. Surrey Court was barely finished when he was executed. His father sold the building to the Wodehouse family and the site of the house is now occupied by George Skipper's Norwich Union building.

The Duke of Norfolk set up his town house in Norwich in 1540 on what is now Duke Street. The 4th Duke greatly enlarged the family palace. It was a quadrangle with a court in the centre and an entrance in the middle of the south side.

48 *Naive drawing of the Duke's Palace*

The north and south ranges were three storeys high and the other two ranges four storeys high. It had a bowling alley and a covered tennis court. The Duke is said to have boasted that 'his estate was worth little less than the whole realm of Scotland, in the ill state to which the wars reduced it; and that when he was in his own tennis court at Norwich, he thought himself as great as a king.'[99]

The sixth Duke also spent a lot of money on the Palace. It was during this rebuilding that Charles II stayed there in 1671 as the guest of Lord Henry Howard the duke's brother (the duke himself was insane and lived in retirement in Padua). The tennis court was turned into a kitchen and the bowling alley into five separate dining rooms. There is no known list of the people the king brought with him but the queen's retinue comprised 55 people from her Lord Chamberlain to the laundrymaid.[100]

The Duke's Palace was the largest private house in the city. In the Hearth tax returns of 1666 it was assessed at £2 10s., which equates to 50 hearths.[101] The visitors to Norwich, John Evelyn, Thomas Baskerville and Celia Fiennes all comment on it, Baskerville the most critically. He thought it was 'seated in a dunghole place' and that 'though it has cost the Duke already £30,000 in building … hath but little room for garden and is pent on al sides both on this and the other side of the river with tradesmen's and dyers' houses'.[102]

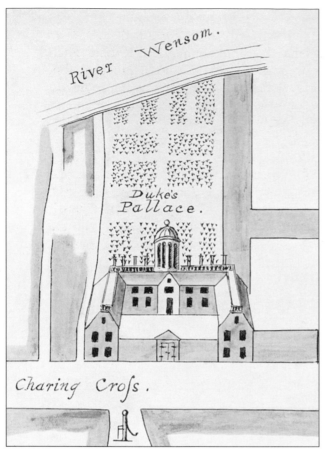

49 *The Duke's Palace, a drawing based on Cleer's map of 1696*

The connection of the Dukes of Norfolk with the city came to a dramatic end. In 1710 the mayor Thomas Havers refused to allow the Duke to enter the city in procession with his private Company of Comedians sounding trumpets and flying banners. Havers may have feared a Jacobite riot (the Dukes were Roman Catholics). The Duke demolished most of his Palace the following year, letting one wing to the Guardians of the Poor who used it as a workhouse. The Roman Catholic chapel survived until the 1960s when it was being used as a billiard room—it was pulled down to make way for a multi-storey car park.

Thomas Browne

Browne was born in 1605. He studied medicine in Montpelier, Padua and Leyden before settling in Norwich in 1637. In 1642 his book *Religio Medici* was published by a London printer without his permission. Browne was a moderate rather than an ardent royalist and included Puritans such as the Hobarts among his friends. He devoted the war years to his enormous work generally known as *Enquiries Into Vulgar Errors*, which contains no reference to the war. He had a great reputation in his own day. Evelyn sought his opinion on gardens and trees, Dugdale about the Fens and about a fossil fish-bone he had found.

When Charles II visited Norwich in 1671 he was entertained with a banquet in St Andrew's Hall and took advantage of the occasion to knight Thomas Browne. John Evelyn, who was with the king, went on to Browne's house: this was in the Haymarket. Evelyn was impressed: 'His whole house and garden being a paradise and cabinet of rarities, and that of the best collection, especially medals, books, plants and natural things'. One thing Evelyn could hardly have missed is the enormous wooden overmantel now in the Castle Museum. This was taken from Browne's house when it was demolished in 1842. It has the arms of King James I on it, so it must have been installed in the house by Browne's predecessor there, Alexander Anguish, who was mayor in 1629.

Sir Thomas Browne died in 1682 and was buried in St Peter Mancroft. In one of his books he had written, 'But who knows the fate of his bones or how often he is to be buried? Who hath the oracle of his ashes or whither they are to be scattered?'

However, he could hardly have foreseen the fate of his own skull. In 1840 the vicar of St Peter Mancroft was digging a grave in the chancel for his wife when he accidentally opened Browne's coffin. It seems that the antiquarian Robert Fitch 'borrowed' Browne's skull and coffin plate to make copies of them. He probably intended to put them back but the tomb was sealed up again before he could do so. After some time both skull and coffin plate wound up in the museum of the Norfolk and Norwich Hospital and in 1901 a silver and glass casket was provided. The church was not happy about this and in 1922 the skull was again buried in the chancel of St Peter Mancroft: that now in the Hospital museum is a replica.[103]

The Stuart period ended on 1 August 1714 with the death of Queen Anne. She was succeeded by the German prince, George of Hanover. Some people preferred the claims of James II and his descendants (or pretended to, as an excuse to attack the established order): these people, known as Jacobites, occur frequently in the many riots that can almost be said to characterise city life in the Georgian period.

4

Georgian Norwich

The Georgian period began in the city in the way it was to continue—with riots in the city streets. George I was crowned on 20 August 1714 and that very day there were attacks on loyalists and their houses. They were followed by Restoration day celebrations on 29 May 1715 and on 10 June (the Pretender's birthday) church bells chimed in the city and many streets were strewn with flowers and oak leaves. A chronicle records that in 1716 'on May Day, at the choice of a New-Elect [mayor] there was such rude and riotous behaviour by the Rabble of the freemen, as the like was never known which caused by fighting many bloody noses, and by throwing of stones and brickbats, many broken Heads'.[1]

In 1720 there was a riot in Pockthorpe, one of the poorest parts of the city. William Massey wrote, 'they armed themselves with whatever weapons came to their hands and fortified themselves in Pockthorpe Street by raising great heaps of stones at proper distance'. According to Blomefield, the mob raided shops selling calicoes and even tore calico dresses off the backs of women in the streets.[2]

All cities were liable to experience unrest and Norwich was seen as especially volatile—Gilbert White referred to Norwich as a 'great factious manufacturing town'. In 1756 when there were rural riots the Government sent soldiers to Norwich; there had not been any riots but because of the city's reputation it was thought there probably would be! Commander Vyse, commanding in the Eastern Counties, did not dare to make Norwich his headquarters in 1792 because of the city's revolutionary reputation.

The 60 common councillors were elected annually in Passion week by the resident freemen of each major ward. Unlike today, every councillor came up for election every year which made for rapid changes of personnel and a rowdy election day every year. A common councillor had to be a freeman living in the ward that elected him. There was a change in 1729 under an Act for better regulating elections in Norwich. The freemen were now to elect only three councillors for each ward, the remainder being chosen by the three and not directly elected. As the three naturally chose men of their own way of thinking this helped towards the two-party system. The system continued until 1835 but was not entirely a success. In 1834 the Municipal Commissioners drew attention to the bribery and corruption to which it led, saying bluntly: 'Bribery in Norwich is as common as the sun at noon'.[3]

Lines through Time 6: 1714 to 1775

George I crowned King	1714	Bethel Hospital built
	1720	Riots in Norwich
Robert Walpole becomes Prime Minister	1721	*Norwich Mercury* started
	1732	Market Cross pulled down
Scots Rebel: The '45	1745	
	1746	Shire House burnt down
	1751	Churchman House built
Lord Hardwicke's Marriage Act	1754	Octagon Chapel begun
	1757	Assembly House & Theatre Royal begun
	1761	*Norfolk Chronicle* starts
	1766	Food riots in Norwich
	1771	Norfolk and Norwich Hospital opened
	1775	

Before 1730 all the Assembly members sat together but in that year they split into two bodies. The aldermen sat in the Aldermen's Chamber and the common councillors in the Council Chamber. They communicated by writing and afterwards met to pass resolutions: any proposal still needed the assent of both bodies. This arrangement also continued until 1835. The aldermen were elected by the freemen of the major wards but, once elected, served for life. Although there were in theory two aldermen for each minor ward, they did not have to live there and tended to live in the richer parts of the city. The mayor was chosen every year by the 24 aldermen: he had to be an alderman and to have served as sheriff.

This period also saw the end of the gild of St George. At the Reformation the gild had not been abolished but it became a secular company responsible for preparing and financing the celebrations that went with the inauguration of the new mayor. The whole street where the new mayor lived was strewn with rushes and the procession of course featured the dragon or 'Snap'–St George himself had long been abolished. By the 1720s prominent citizens were becoming unhappy with the expense and the gild came to an end when one of the aldermen, William Clarke, refused to join. The responsibility for organising Gild-Day passed to a small group of aldermen and common councillors and Mayor's Day–now Lord Mayor's Day–is still celebrated in the city. In 1731 the gild sold all its possessions to the city–including the dragon.[4]

50   *Official pomp, the Norwich Bellman*

Rioting continued to be a feature of urban life. In 1740 there were riots in Norwich and elsewhere because of the scarcity of grain. The mob marched into the countryside demanding money and ale from farmers and treading down the corn of those who refused them. The magistrates called in soldiers who fired on the crowd, killing one of the rioters and seven innocent bystanders.[5] In the same year there was a five-day riot in the city over the price of mackerel.

51 *Triumphal Arch erected in the Market Place, 1745*

The worst of the riots in Norwich was in 1766.[6] On Saturday 27 September, a mob assembled in the market place at about two in the afternoon and began destroying provisions there. After an hour they moved on to the New Mills, partly destroying them. They spent the evening breaking into the houses of various bakers and brewers in the city, finally partly demolishing the *White Horse* alehouse in the Haymarket shortly before midnight. The mob gathered again on the next day and marched to Trowse mills but the miller there appears to have placated them: instead they plundered the house of Mr. Money in Trowse. On their way back to the city they attacked a granary belonging to Margaret Linsey and boarded a boat on the river, throwing its contents overboard. Back in Norwich they attacked the houses of two bakers in Conesford and Tombland.

City authorities seem to have panicked. John Gay wrote to the Earl of Buckinghamshire at Blickling telling him that Mr. Money's house in Trowse had been almost demolished and added a dramatic postscript–'hear a Malthouse by Conisford Gates just now fired'. Lord Barrington wrote from London to the Earl:

> I am at this moment sending by express orders for two Troops of Dragoons to march from Colchester to Norwich to assist the magistrates there. It may be useful to acquaint you, let the call be ever so urgent, I can send no further military aid into Norfolk; for the troops of the whole Kingdom are imploy'd.

The mayor John Patteson had to go out and read the Riot Act to the mob. Before he did, he handed his chain of office to his sister-in-law who acted as mayoress, saying 'Take care of this, little mother, God knows if I shall come back alive.'[7]

In the end the city coped without outside help. The mayor called out the citizens who were armed with staves and who succeeded in making 30 arrests. On 2 October Barrington wrote, 'Norwich has the singular honour of reducing a mob without military aid, an example which I hope other Places will endeavour to imitate'. Two days later he wrote seeking revenge: 'Pray hang as many of your prisoners as possible'. The mayor took a different line. He referred to the prisoners as 'unhappy convicts' and said that troops would be needed in case there were further riots at their execution. The cases were tried before a special commission and eight rioters were sentenced to death but only two, John Hall and David Long, were in fact executed. They were hanged at Norwich Castle on 10 January 1767. Four others were transported for life. Some cases came before other courts: two women were tried at the Norwich Quarter Sessions in connection with the riots, Elizabeth Parr being given three months' imprisonment and Susanna Soons bound over to keep the peace.

Many in Norwich welcomed the French Revolution of 1789.[8] Dissenters, merchants and professional men set up a Revolution Society and Radical Clubs were set up by artisans from 1792; at one time there were more than 40 clubs with 2,000 members. They met in tavern cellars to hear readings from the works of the Thetford-born radical Thomas Paine. They supported *The Cabinet*, a journal strongly in favour of the French Revolution. By 1793 the radical Corresponding Society of London had a link with Norwich.[9] The revolution was warmly greeted at the Baptist chapel of St Paul's. On 29 May 1797 John Thelwall 'the spokesman for English radicalism' came to speak in the city. A party of dragoons went to the lecture room and smashed it up and then attacked and partly destroyed the *Shakespeare* public house next door. Eventually some officers restored order but by then the landlord of the *Shakespeare* had fallen from a garret window and been badly hurt. One man, Luke Rice, was accused at the next assizes of encouraging the soldiers, but he was acquitted on a technicality.

As the Revolution in France became more and more violent, many Dissenters stopped supporting it, especially after war between England and France broke out in 1793. A few Dissenters continued their support, however: in 1795 Mark Wilks

Lines through Time 7: 1775 to 1837

	1775	
America declares independence	1776	
	1783	Chases' *Norwich Directory* published
'First fleet' sails to Australia	1787	
Catholic Relief Act	1791	
	1792	Norwich General Assurance Co. founded
	1794	Chapelfield Reservoir built
	1797	Riots in Norwich
Income tax introduced	1799	
	1800	
	1801	Census: population 36,906
Battle of Trafalgar	1805	
Battle of Waterloo	1815	
	1819	Rosary Cemetery opened
	1821	John Crome dies
	1824	Norwich Music Festival started
	1827	City Gaol at St Giles built
	1828	St Augustine's Asylum built
Parliamentary Reform Act	1832	
Municipal Reform Act	1834	
	1836	Norwich Police Force started
Victoria is crowned Queen	1837	

preached two sermons in Norwich to raise money for defendants accused of treason for their support of the Revolution. The war in France closed the seas to English exports: this spelled disaster to Norwich trade. The city had a direct experience of the war in 1797 when news reached Norwich of Admiral Duncan's naval victory over the Dutch at the Battle of Camperdown. The victorious fleet sailed into Yarmouth and many of the wounded were brought to the new Norfolk and Norwich Hospital in Norwich.

On Valentine's Day 1797 the Norfolk hero Admiral Nelson had a great victory over the Spanish fleet at St Vincent. The Spanish rear-admiral Don Xavier Winthuysen surrendered to Nelson, gave him his sword and died that same night. Nelson presented the sword to the city. On 26 February he wrote, 'I know no place where it would give me or my family more pleasure to have it kept, than in the Capital City of the County in which I had the Honour to be born'. Norwich granted Nelson the freedom of the city. In 1800 they commissioned Sir William Beechey to paint a portrait showing both Nelson and the sword: city accounts show that £210 was paid to Beechey for Nelson's portrait in 1800-1801.[10]

William Windham was MP for the city from 1784. He was a Whig and a friend of Charles James Fox. He was a strong supporter of the war against France and William Pitt made him his Secretary of War in 1794. On taking office he had to stand for re-election and, although he won easily, the election was a rowdy affair. His opponents' supporters carried aloft a loom wreathed in mourning to symbolise the death of the Norwich weaving trade because of the war. Windham's supporters replied with a model guillotine which chopped the head off a female doll and was labelled, 'This is French liberty'.[11] Pitt and Windham both resigned from the government on the issue of Catholic emancipation in 1801. Windham opposed the peace treaty made with France at Amiens in 1802: it was probably because of this that he lost his seat at Norwich.

At the 1801 census, Norwich had 12,267 people engaged in trade, manufacturing and handcrafts—and 408 employed in agriculture. It was noted that the city had furnished at least 4,000 army and navy recruits in the French Wars.

Norwich's 18th-century reputation for radicalism continued into the 19th century. William Smith, MP for the city from 1802 to 1830 (with a short gap in 1806-7) was a dissenter and a radical.[12] He opposed the slave trade and favoured Parliamentary reform. In 1828 he presented Parliament with an anti-slavery petition organised after a meeting at St Andrew's Hall: it had 10,125 signatures and was 150 feet long. In the House of Commons, Smith was notorious for the length of his speeches which gave rise to a sardonic poem:

> At length, when the candles burn low in their sockets,
> Up gets William Smith with both hands in his pockets,
> On a course of morality fearlessly enters,
> With all the opinions of all the Dissenters.

His son Benjamin Smith was MP for Norwich from 1838 to 1847: he was a liberal and supported the repeal of the corn laws.

On 23 June 1815 news of Wellington's victory at Waterloo reached Norwich: the battle had been fought five days before. On 27 June news arrived of Napoleon's abdication and a bonfire was lit in the market place 'with the stalls from the fishmarket and other stolen material'.[13]

Trade and Industry

Georgian Norwich was still the second largest city in England with a population of about 30,000 in 1714. Its wealth was still based on wool—Macaulay called Norwich 'the chief seat of the chief manufacture of the realm'. The records of the freemen of the city show how the weavers dominated. The register for 1714-1752 printed by the Norfolk Record Society runs to 100 pages, of which 40 are filled with the names of worsted weavers. The next largest group are the cordwainers, taking up four pages.[14]

The Norwich worsted trade grew rapidly throughout the early 18th century, outselling Exeter serges because Norwich wages were lower. A range of fabrics were developed, some of pure worsted and some of worsted and silk and, by the end of the century, of worsted and cotton. The first Prime Minister, Robert Walpole, was a Norfolk man and through his influence an Act was passed in 1721 against the wearing of calicoes. Walpole also used his influence to ensure that court mourning dress should consist of Norwich crepes.

Daniel Defoe wrote in 1724: 'If a stranger was only to ride through or view the City of Norwich for a day, he would have much more reason to think there was a town without inhabitants ... but on the contrary, if he was to view the city either on a Sabbath Day, or any public occasion, he would wonder where all the people could dwell, the multitude is so great; but the case is this; the inhabitants being all so busy at their manufactures, dwell in their garrets at their looms and in their combing-shops, so they call them, twisting-mills and other work-houses, almost all the works they are employed on being done within doors.'[15]

By 1750 Norwich had developed a range of high quality fabrics. Regulations protected the textile industry: in 1700 the English were forbidden to import printed cotton cloth and between 1720 and 1774 it was illegal to wear it even if it was made in England. After 1713 exports of worsted and Norwich stuffs captured a world market. The Spanish trade, for example, leapt from £31,000 in 1711 to £112,000 in 1721. An anonymous diary in the Cornwall Record Office describes a visit to Norwich in 1757: 'The Town vastly populous, employing an Infinite Number of Hands in the Manufactory of Crapes and Stuffs, for which Norwich is famous ... You see every woman and child almost with their wool fixt to the top of a stick carried in their Left Hand, which they draw out and twist with their right without the use of a spinning wheel or any other Instrument'.[16]

The Norwich woolcombers showed their muscle in 1752 when they took strike action. The woolcombers objected to the employment of a man named Trye who they said was a *colt* (that is, a man who had not served an apprenticeship) and a thief. Three hundred men left their work and retired to heath land at Rackheath where they camped out, supported by purse clubs, for several weeks, until they had won their point.[17]

The worsted trade declined at the end of the 18th century. Arthur Young noticed the decline in 1771 and blamed the war with the American colonies: however he estimated that there were still 12,000 looms in the city. The outbreak of war with France hit the trade hard and by 1791 William Taylor wrote that the trade was dependent on the orders of the East India Company.[18]

According to the Hammonds, Norwich merchants would not take the risk of introducing machinery to a hostile people, and instead concentrated on making new stuffs, often a mixture of silk and wool.[19] However as soon as a fabric became popular Yorkshire manufacturers copied it and made it cheaper. Mills were not started up in Norwich until 1832. According to the Hand-loom Weavers' Commission report of

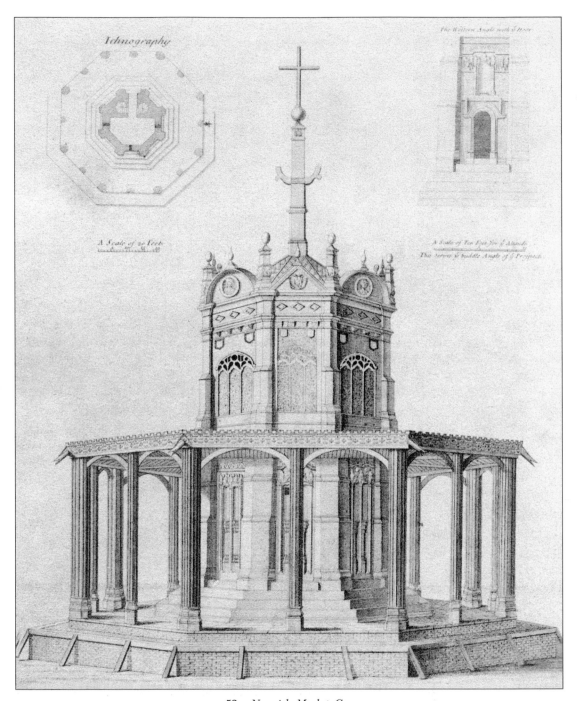

52 *Norwich Market Cross*

1840, weaving was still done at home in the great majority of cases—out of 4,054 looms at work in Norwich 3,398 were in the weavers' own homes.

The well-known Norwich shawl came about because city alderman John Harvey was the only manufacturer who could weave the very fine spinning of Ann Ives of

Spalding. The problem was to make the wool soft enough to be a passable imitation of the shawls of India made from the wool of cashmere goats. The solution was to use a combination of wool and silk. P.J. Knights who originally worked for Harvey soon struck out on his own and brought the art of shawl making to perfection. He worked out how to weave a four-square-yard counterpane for which he won a medal from the Society of Arts.[20]

Joseph Grout introduced crepe making to the city in 1822: this was made from twisted silk yarn and used exclusively for mourning clothes. Grout's crepe factory impressed a visitor from London in 1825:

> The works are in several floors and the winding, twisting, bobbing etc are by Machinery moved by a beautiful 20 Horsepower Engine'. He was not so impressed with the working conditions, however–'These operations are watched and conducted by more than seventy females, some so young as 7 to 8 years of age. These are on foot from seven in the Morning till eight in the Evg watching the thread, repairing the broken and seeing that all go on well–occasionally supplying Oil where wanted to prevent evil from frictions–Only that they have half an hour for breakfast and an hour for dinner–And these little Girls earn some 5/- some 5/6 per week.[21]

By the end of the century boot and shoe making was increasing in importance. James Southall and Co. was established in 1792 and is said to be the oldest shoemaking concern in England. Bally and Haldenstein was founded in 1799. Other factories were also being set up to make a wide range of products: Hills and Underwood, vinegar makers, were established in 1762.

By the 1720's city income was insufficient to maintain its infrastructure and a new source of revenue was needed. In 1725 the commonalty of Norwich put forward a petition to Parliament that the walls, bridges and staithes of the city were ruinous. The city could not afford to repair them, nor maintain 'the great roads to London'. The Tonnage Committee was set up in 1726 to draw up the Tonnage Act by which tolls were paid on goods and merchandise. The money was to be used for maintaining the city walls, gates, bridges, staithes and roads. The journals of the committee survive from 1786 and show the receipts from tolls in the days when Norwich was still an active and important port. As was said at the time, 'It is by water that Norwich receives all its provisions in grain etc and all its coal … in a word all its consumption requirements and all the raw material for its manufactures'.[22]

Norwich market was one of the most profitable of the city's ventures. Money was spent on improving the facilities–the fish market was paved in 1727 and the main market 'new paved' in 1731. In the following year the market cross and the shearing cross were pulled down. The market cross was a major feature as it was between 60 and 70 feet high with a chapel in the middle, which was converted into a storehouse at the Reformation. The cross contained the approved measure for weighing grain and other goods, chained to a pillar for anyone to use. Meat, eggs and cheese were sold by farmers' wives not from stalls but from 'peds', semi-circular baskets, carried one on each side of a packhorse. A well-known painting of Norwich Market Place in 1799 by Robert Dighton shows women selling from baskets or peds and only a few stalls.

The market place in the heart of the city continued to attract the notice of diarists and writers of journals. The diary of Silas Neville for Saturday 19 October 1777 records: 'After breakfast took a walk thro' the Market, it being Market Day. It is

53 *Prince's Street*

certainly one of the largest and best furnished in England, the fowls, turkeys etc. so fat and neatly trussed, the men and women who sell them so clean and neat'. In 1782 William Marshall came to Norwich to see the clover-seed market and was told that the biggest dealer had sold six and a half hundredweight of seed that afternoon. However, Dorothy Wordsworth, the great poet's sister, was not very impressed with Norwich. She visited the city while staying with her aunt and uncle at Forncett St Peter between 1788 and 1794. She wrote: 'It is an immensely large place; but the streets in general are very ugly, and they are all so ill-paved and dirty, as almost entirely to take away the pleasure of walking.'[23]

The Corporation made efforts to regulate trade, often unsuccessful. It occasionally tried to restrict the main Market Place to food stalls, but – as now – sellers of all kinds gathered there, including clothing, soap and books. The city made efforts to make St Andrew's Hall the place of exchange of corn in 1725, 1796 and 1806 but usually corn was sold by sample in the inns. Minor trading offences were punished in the Mayor's court: for example, in 1765 John Dix of Stratton St Mary appeared in the court accused of selling mouldy hay. Tombland was paved in 1733 and the Tombland Horse Fair came to an end in 1744. Hog Hill was paved in 1736. Prince's Street still has a granite sett surface. According to Blomefield, 'In 1738 the ditches on the southern part of the Castle-Hill were levelled and now the market for cattle is kept there'; it had been moved to the castle ditches in 1616.[24]

Gentleman's Walk was laid out at the end of the century. A manuscript *Guide to Norwich* by W.S. Stevenson says that:

> The broad Pavement of Scotch Granite which runs the whole extent of the East Side of the Market Place was erected at the expense of the Owners and occupiers of the respective shops in 179- [*sic*] and will always reflect an honour on their Public Spirit ... This Promenade is on Market Day the rendervaux [*sic*] of the Gentlemen and Farmers and is hence denominated the Gentleman Walk.[25]

The century saw the beginnings of banking and insurance in the city. The first bank in Norwich was that of Charles Weston founded in 1756. Charles Weston's bank

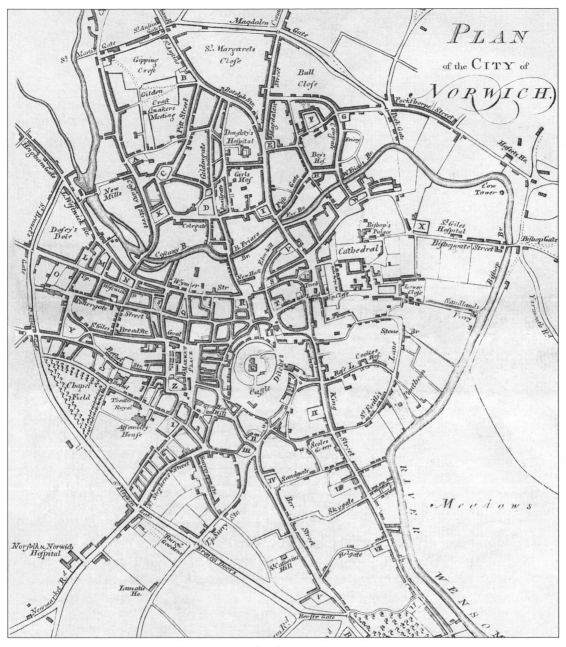

54 *Norwich in 1783: T. Smith's map for W. Chase's* Directory

was on the Market Place. It was one of the first provincial banks in England. Gurney's was founded in 1775 and Richard Gurney married into the London banking family, Barclays. Gurney's was a key element in the growth of Barclays Bank into a nation-wide concern. Peck's *Directory* of 1802 lists five banking firms in Norwich. A branch of the Bank of England opened in Norwich in 1827.[26]

The firm that was to become the Norwich Union originated in 1783 when Thomas Bignold moved to Norwich from Westerham in Kent. According to the traditional story, he tried to insure his luggage for the journey but was told that kind of insurance just did not exist. He replied, 'There is nothing that is uninsurable, the question is merely would those who would fain be insured pay the price?'. The Norwich General Assurance Company was set up in 1792, with Bignold as its secretary. In 1797 he set up the Norwich Union Fire Office. The firm soon extended their business into Europe; in the 1820s they had agencies at Bordeaux and Lisbon.[27]

Norwich continued to supply skills to all of Norfolk. People came from all over the county to shop and, as all the votes for Norfolk county elections were taken at Norwich, so county voters had to travel to the city each time there was an election. The candidates had to supply horses and hotel beds in the city for people coming up to Norwich to vote for them (voting was public, of course, so at least they could be sure their 'guests' did vote for them). The records of Edmond Wodehouse's election expenses for 1817 survive. He provided beds in no less than 50 Norwich inns and the total bill for beds and horses came to £5,408 11s. 4d.[28] Perhaps not surprisingly many county elections were uncontested—between 1714 and 1802 there were only two contested elections, in 1734 and 1768.

Norwich was also becoming more than ever a city of shopkeepers. In the 1783 Directory there are 40 grocers, 30 butchers, 60 bakers, 30 drapers and mercers, 24 hosiers, hatters and milliners, 12 booksellers and 6 chemists. Norwich had 704 tea dealers in 1784 and 938 in 1795-6. Expectations were increasing. In 1793 Edward Leathes wrote home to his mother in Norwich asking for an increase in his clothing allowance:

> I agree with you that Manners make the Man but what are Manners in a ragged coat, dirty waistcoat and threadbare breaches, at the same time I know that a gentleman may appear as well with ten as twenty coats a year, but I by no means wish for either, I shall be content with three.[29]

In the 1820s, gas brought improved lighting to the city. The first gas lamp was the 'Gasolier', a four-branched giant in the centre of the Market Place: this lasted for about 60 years before being replaced with electricity. In 1825 the British Gaslight Company bought a site at World's End Lane for erecting gasworks.

Communications

In 1745 coaches were advertised in the *Norwich Mercury* as running from Norwich to London over the Christmas period, 'to carry Fowles and presents as usual'; these coaches took three days. The Christmas coaches continued to run until coaches were superseded by the railway. A print by Robert Seymour of 1835 shows geese, turkeys and Christmas hampers hanging from every point of the coach. According to the *Norfolk Chronicle* about 6,000 turkeys went to London on the Christmas coaches. In December 1810, 12 carriages were loaded with poultry and game, taking three days to reach London. The first regular coach to the capital was the Norwich Machine from 1762, which took two days. In the summer of 1761 a coach began running from Norwich to London in 20 hours. Previously it had taken two days in summer and three days in winter. The Flying Machine was advertised in 1769 as doing the journey in one day. Mail coaches began to run between Norwich and London in 1785: they did the journey in 15 hours. By 1802 the Norwich Mail Coach Office was running two coaches to London every day, one via Ipswich and one via Newmarket.

In 1707 an Act was passed for continuing the Acts of 1694-5 for making a turnpike road from Norwich to Thetford, the first turnpike in Norfolk and reputedly the first in England. The road only extended from Hethersett to Attleborough, and did not reach Town Close in Norwich until 1767. Norfolk was slow in turnpiking but a clutch of roads were made in 1770, including those from St Stephen's Gate to Trowse and from Bishop Bridge to Caister, the main road to Yarmouth before the Acle straight was built. Between 1766 and 1823 ten of the main roads to the city were taken over by turnpike trustees who were able to spend much more money on improving them than parish highway surveyors could do. Between 1791 and 1801 all the city gates were taken down because they obstructed the flow of traffic. Accidents were common; in August 1776 Raven Hardy, aged nine, wrote in his mother's diary, 'Mamma Pappa Billy Polly and I went to Norwich and as we came back overturned the cart and frightened us all out of our wits. Billy hurt his thigh and we thought it had broke'. Parson Woodforde's sister 'shook like an aspin leave' as she took her first ever coach journey from the *Angel* in Norwich Market Place in 1778.[30]

Various expedients were tried to speed up links between Norwich and Yarmouth. In 1813 a steam barge began to operate between the two towns—it covered the distance in a little over three hours. The service ended tragically on Good Friday 1817 when the steam packet's boiler burst just after the ship had left Foundry Bridge. Eight adults were killed on board and a two-year-old boy was thrown overboard by the force of the explosion: he was drowned. Another person died in hospital later. When Mr. Marten of London visited Norfolk in 1825, he went from London to Yarmouth by paddle steamer: this took 17 hours. From there he took a steam vessel up the river to Norwich and this leg of his journey took five hours. Sail traffic could be even slower, of course. The *Excursions* says that an unladen wherry could do the trip between Norwich and Yarmouth in five hours but a laden one took from 12 to 16 hours.[31]

In 1825 it was proposed to build a horse-drawn tramway from Norwich to Ipswich to transport goods from Norfolk to London. The expense of the scheme put off potential investors. In the same year a road and ship route was established between Norwich and London. This offered fast sailing ships (later a steamship as well) between London and Ipswich to meet goods taken to and from Ipswich by road. However the service was never reliable because the road between Norwich and Ipswich was so bad. As late as 1846 it was said to be at times almost impassable.[32]

Health

Georgian Norwich saw the establishment of two hospitals that served the city well into the present century—the Bethel and the Norfolk and Norwich.

Mary Chapman, the founder of the Bethel, was born in 1647, the daughter of John Mann, an alderman of Norwich. In 1682 she married Samuel Chapman, who became rector of Thorpe in 1670. He died in 1700, leaving £200 each for the support of the Children's and Doughty's hospitals.[33] On 24 February 1712 his widow Mary took a lease from the Corporation of the Committee House and adjoining land for

1,000 years at a peppercorn rent. A very detailed agreement was drawn up with Richard Starling, carpenter, and Edward Freeman, mason, to build the hospital: the total cost of the building was to be £314 2s. 6d.

Mary Chapman died in 1724 and is buried in Thorpe. Her tombstone survives in the chancel of the now ruinous church. It reads, 'She built wholly at her own expence the house in Norwich called bethel for the reception, maintenance and cure of poor lunaticks, to which and other charitable uses she gave all her income while she lived and her estate at her death'.

The hospital was intended for lunatics who were curable, who were citizens of Norwich and who were too poor to pay for their own treatment. The first recorded patient fulfilling these terms was Philip Lewis, who was admitted in 1725: he was a former apprentice with a carpenter in Newgate. He had been disordered in his senses for five years and his brother could not afford to look after him any longer. Those whose family could afford to pay might also be admitted on a scale of charges up to a maximum of 8s. a week. The Hospital had 28 patients in 1753 and 66 in 1833. Of the latter 28 were 'upon the foundation' (that is, paid nothing), 24 paid the full 8s. a week and the others paid something in between.

Many citizens of Norwich gave generously to the Bethel and their names were recorded on donation boards. They included Benjamin Wrench, who was the physician who attended the Hospital for 22 years from 1725: he gave back his entire salary which amounted to £352. The largest donation was £2,733 9s. 2d. by George England in 1897. Three gifts of £1,000 each were by Bartholomew Balderston and Thomas Vere in 1766, and by Robert Denn in 1829.[34]

There were private lunatic asylums for the wealthy. Mary Hardy's diary records that on 30 June 1777 she visited Red House, a private mental home off Queen's Road: 'every patient there cost a 100 guineas a year'.[35]

William Fellowes is regarded as the founder of the Norfolk and Norwich Hospital, but he brought to fruition a scheme which had been long-discussed.[36] The Voluntary Hospital System had begun in 1719 and, by 1750, 11 towns had them. As early as 1744 a letter to the *Norwich Gazette* advocated that Norfolk should follow the example of Devon and set up a county hospital. Thomas Hayter, the Bishop of Norwich between 1749 and 1761, chaired meetings in the city on the subject. In 1758 he asked Benjamin Gooch to examine the hospitals in London with a view to establishing a county hospital and plans were prepared. There was a loss of momentum when Hayter left Norwich but in August 1770 William Fellowes called an open meeting and a subscription fund was opened. Progress then was rapid: the first out-patients were seen in July 1772 and the first in-patients were admitted in November of the same year. The first staff of the hospital consisted of four physicians and four surgeons, all unpaid.

The Norfolk and Norwich was founded as a charity: it received only patients recommended by subscribers as being too poor to pay. Casualties were admitted but, if they were found to be able to, they had to pay one shilling a day subsistence; as early as 1774 the management decided to charge a patient who was, 'above the need of charitable help'. It became famous for its treatment of bladder stone which was unusually common in Norfolk, suggesting that the Norfolk diet was poor and over

55   *The Norfolk and Norwich Hospital*

dependent on cereals. The operations were performed without anaesthetic until the mid-19th century and the Hospital has a unique collection of almost 1,500 stones from operations carried out between 1771 and 1909. William Donne, during 30 years on the Hospital staff, performed 173 operations for the stone: one patient in seven died. His apprentice Philip Meadows Martineau went on to perform 149, gaining a European reputation for his version which became known as 'the Norwich Operation for the stone'.

In 1805 James Neild inspected the Norfolk and Norwich and said, 'It does honour to the county, and is one of the best I have seen'.

Benjamin Gooch was the leading surgeon in East Anglia in the 18th century. He published a textbook of surgery in 1758 and was the innovator of 'Gooch's splints', which were in common use until the 1920s when they were replaced by plaster of Paris. Gooch also played a leading part in the founding of the Norfolk and Norwich Hospital.[37] Another well-known doctor in the city was James Alderson, who prescribed without charge for 400-500 people every week at his house in Colegate. In 1768 Norwich was divided into three districts for medical purposes–the three first district surgeons were William Donne, Joseph Rogers and David Martineau.

Another Hospital that has survived into the 20th century is the hospital and school for the blind in Magdalen Street, founded by Thomas Tawell (who was himself blind) in 1805. It was meant both as an asylum for the old and as a school for the young. Thomas Tawell's monument in the cathedral tells the story:

> In the year 1805 he purchased a spacious dwelling House with extensive garden Grounds in St Paul's in this City and settled them by legal Instruments for a perpetual Hospital and School for Indigent Blind Persons. This magnificent Gift, aided by the Patronage of other benevolent

Characters have secured an Asylum for the pitiable Objects of his Bounty whose melancholy Situation he could but too well estimate having himself passed many Years deprived of the Blessing of Sight.

The old were admitted at the age of 55. Pupils were admitted at the age of 12 and stayed until they had learned a skill or trade. The young girls were employed in knitting and netting, the boys in making rope, twine, sacks, baskets, carpeting and rope mats. Tawell died in 1820 and his monument is within the chantry of Bishop Richard Nykke who was himself 'decrepit and blind' when he died some 400 years earlier.

Inoculation against smallpox by giving the patient a mild attack was practised in England from the 18th century but it was risky—not only might the attack be fatal but the disease might spread to others. Blomefield was an opponent of inoculation and dreaded catching the disease: he stayed away from Norwich several times in the 1740s when smallpox was rampant and this delayed his work on the Norwich section of his *History*, almost allowing his bitter rival Benjamin Mackerell to get his own history of Norwich into print first. Blomefield's father had died of smallpox in 1737 so his fear was understandable. In 1752 he did indeed die from smallpox, at the age of 47.[38] To prevent the spread of smallpox the inoculation was done in special 'inoculation houses'. In 1784 Parson Woodforde visited one near St Stephen's church in Norwich where the four children of Squire Custance of Weston Longville were inoculated.

The early 19th century saw many new private charitable bodies set up in the health field. A Dispensary was opened in Pottergate in 1804 to render medical and surgical help to the poor: 'about 2,000 are relieved yearly'. Norwich Society for Relieving the Sick Poor was founded in 1815 and run by a committee of ladies who visited the poor in their homes, giving money, linen and flannel. The society was funded by donations and by annual sales.

The Norfolk and Norwich Infirmary for the cure of disease of the eye was established in Pottergate in 1822. The Norfolk and Norwich Magdalen was founded on Life's Green in the Close in 1827 'to afford an asylum to females who have deviated from the paths of virtue and may be desirous of being restored to their station in Society. 385 have passed through the house and many are now in respectable situations.' As the Close was increasingly becoming a haven for the 'respectable', some objected to the Magdalen being there. Dean Pellew moved a chestnut tree in the Deanery garden so he would not have the House in view from his back windows. In the 1840s the Magdalen was moved to Chapelfield.[40]

One of the great risks to health was the water supply. Most of the poor got their water from wells or from the river. William Arderon was appointed clerk and manager at the New Mills in about 1729, at a salary of £60 a year. He wrote of 'the too frequent practice in Norwich of turning their Old Wells into Boghouses, this undoubtedly mixes with the waters that supply other wells and makes them vastly unwholesome as well as intollerably disagreeable'. Apart from the quality of the water, it was dangerous enough just to fetch it: in 1760 Sarah Batcheler, aged 10, drowned falling off a defective staithe in St Martin at Oak while fetching a pitcher of water. In 1784 an old man fell into the river and drowned while fetching water at St Anne's staithe. Conditions were even more difficult in winter: in December

1784, 11-year-old John Miller, when fetching water, slipped on the icy staithe, fell in to the river and drowned.[41]

According to the city assembly books, Robert Mylne was commissioned in 1788 to report on the waterworks. On the expiry of the current lease on the New Mills in 1793, the Corporation advertised for proposals to improve the water supply and in 1794 they accepted those of William White and Robert Crane. Their plan included building a reservoir on Chapelfield. They appointed Joseph Bramah as their engineer. Mylne was asked to report on the progress of the works and his highly critical report appeared in 1798, followed by Bramah's equally spirited defence. The corporation must have been convinced, as in 1803 they extended White and Crane's lease for a further 99 years. The copy of this lease in the Norfolk Record Office has a plan showing the waterworks connecting New Mills with the Chapelfield reservoir. The reservoir was an added city attraction but also an added danger–Charles Stiles aged 13 (January 1808) and James Nudds also 13 (December 1813) both died after falling through the ice when playing on Chapelfield reservoir.

Industrial accidents were common. In 1820 Stephen Sutton, aged 18, while working at his master's mill in Pockthorpe was struck on the head by a sail. He was taken to the Norfolk and Norwich Hospital where he died. In 1824 Edmond Hurne aged 56 and Noah Larter aged 64 were at work with four other men at their master's marl pit in Thorpe. They were barrowing away earth and sand to get at the chalk when the earth collapsed on them–they fell 60 or 70 feet and were buried under 30 or 40 cartloads of earth. It took half an hour to dig them out by which time both men were dead. Their inquest was held at the *King's Arms*, Thorpe on 24 February 1824.

The Poor

In the 1770s Norwich workhouse had an average of 1,200 inmates in winter: 600 were able bodied and the rest were children or 'impotent' poor. The population of the city was between 20,000 and 30,000 and so perhaps one person in 20 or 30 was living in the workhouse. For some the workhouse conditions proved unbearable: William Priest aged 32 threw himself from a window in Duke's Palace workhouse in 1798. On 8 May 1827 an inquest held at the *Trowel and Hammer* heard that on 2 May Francis Clark, aged 11, and another boy called John Smith, being 'Paupers in the Workhouse in the parish of St Andrew', tried to escape from the workhouse through the privy. Smith climbed on to the privy roof with a muck fork to try to raise the spars of the roof. Unfortunately he dropped the fork which fell striking Clark on the head. He was taken to the Norfolk and Norwich Hospital where he lingered until 7 May when he died.[43]

Conditions in the Bridewell also proved intolerable to some. In June 1801 Benjamin Pygall, aged 24, slit his throat with a pruning knife while he was being held at the Bridewell. The inquest verdict was suicide and the return is endorsed 'Paid for burial of Benjamin Pygall in the public Highway £1 1s. 0d.' It is not said in which highway he was buried; he must have been one of the last people in England to suffer this fate. His clothes and possessions passed to the authorities and were listed. He had eight shillings and a halfpenny in cash and an 'old silver watch' which was sold for 18s. The clothes he was wearing were: one twill slop, one fustian jacket, one linen waistcoat, one pair fustian breeches, one shirt, one pair worsted stockings, one silk handkerchief. He had no other possessions.[44]

For the Guardians the problem was always to provide a subsistence allowance for the poor without alienating the rate-payers. Maximilian de Lazowski wrote about his visit to Norwich in 1784: 'The Poor Tax is enormous. It is 8s. 4d. in the pound sterling on the rent of each house. There are surely very few examples of a tax as high as this. It amounts in all to £18,000 sterling (last year, but it is not usually so much)'. The Guardians were always looking for economies they could make. They decided it was cheaper to buy bread from the baker than make it themselves because the workhouse inmates did not have the skills–'a great waste of flour had been made, an extravagant quantity of yeast had been used, and the dough so improperly compounded and so imperfectly fermented as not to admit of the due increase'. In the same way, they decided in 1788 that it was cheaper to buy beer than to make it themselves.[45]

In February 1802 the Guardians said that the average number of people maintained in the two workhouses was 1,282. It was proposed to build a single house to take 1,300 and a site near Chapel Field was bought, but the plan fell through. In April 1802 it was announced that 300 paupers had been discharged from the workhouse, leaving only 550 inmates. The poor rate was reduced to 4s. 3d. in the pound.

In October 1805 James Neild wrote to the *Gentleman's Magazine* on the terrible conditions in the Duke's Palace workhouse:

> The building is old. The average number in the house about five hundred and fifty. In the first room I visited there were forty two beds, ten of them cribs for single persons, and the others had two in each, there being seventy-four persons in this room. At the entrance, and in the room, is a most offensive and indecent privy, something like a watchman's box, and so much out of repair, and so situated, that the sexes cannot be separated when decency most requires it. The paupers ate, drank and slept on their beds, having no other room to live in ... In the boys' room were offensive tubs as urinals; these are emptied daily into a sink in the room, and it did not appear to have been lately washed. One bed in the room was particularly offensive; from an infirmity of the boy who slept in it, his urine passed completely through the bedding, and was suffered to accumulate on the floor to a very putrid degree.

However Norwich did not allow this savage indictment to go unchallenged. John Gurney wrote a long reply to the *Gentleman's Magazine* in December 1805. He claimed that the privy Neild objected to was in fact 'a night-stool, enclosed in a box as described applied to the use of those whose age or infirmity disqualified them from going downstairs'. He said Neild was wrong to say it was used by both sexes–the room was a male ward and the only female there was a wife of one of the paupers who acted as a nurse. Gurney admitted that the inmates had no other room to go to but denied totally the criticism of the boys' ward: 'I am well assured the vessels described were every morning emptied and cleaned, and that the floor under the particular bed described was so frequently washed as to render a putrid accumulation impossible'.[46]

In 1827 the Whigs won the city election by attacking corruption and they sponsored an Act which restricted the nominees of the Corporation to one-third of the Guardians, and from 1831 all the Guardians were elected by the ratepayers and the officials they chose depended on party allegiance.

Private citizens continued to leave bequests to the less well off in their city. Peter Seaman, mayor in 1709, left the thatched house in St Swithin's Alley and land in St Julian's parish, the profits from the properties to be used to pay for apprenticing poor boys. John Norman was mayor in 1714: he died in 1724 and is buried in Catton church. He left his estate for educating and apprenticing sons of his relatives and of his first wife, and 60 years after his death for erecting a hospital for boys.[47] Norman's charity still helps fund the education of the alderman's descendants. A very different bequest was that of John Spurrell who in 1762 left money for specified poor people to have on each 1 August 'a pint of strong beer and veal of the best hand to be that day roasted and boiled for the dinner of the said poor and for a proper quantity of butter to be eaten thereof.'

Penny Corfield says that Norwich must have had at least 400 'incomers' every year in the 1670s and 1680s to explain the population growth: no records were kept of people's movements within England so there is no archive evidence, but a similar sort of figure must have applied throughout the 18th century. Because the authorities tried to send the destitute back to where they came from, records of examinations of the poor provide details of the lives of a class of people otherwise poorly recorded. Two examples are given here. Between 1742 and 1762, 433 paupers and vagrants were removed from the city to their place of origin. Of these 40 per cent came from East Anglia but the others came from further afield: 33 from Scotland and 16 from Ireland. Sixty years later, patterns of movement were much the same. Between January and September 1828, Norwich magistrates examined 269 people applying for relief. Of this group, 79 claimed to have legal settlement in the city, 132 came from elsewhere in Norfolk, 25 from Suffolk and 22 from elsewhere in England. Five came from further afield: three from Ireland, one from Scotland and one from Guernsey.[48]

Poor people were not always sent back home. Susan Spooner and her bedridden sister were living in Norwich but their place of settlement was Braintree in Essex; there was a whole group of Braintree paupers living in Norwich. They received a regular allowance from the overseers of the poor of Braintree parish. They were even visited several times by representatives of the Braintree select vestry to see if their allowances should be continued. In 1831 the representatives said of the Spooner sisters, 'both weave Silk but can get very little to do–a complaint general throughout the trade'. Each of the poor people in the group received a weekly allowance of two shillings which was sent by bank order to the overseers of Norwich who then handed it out to them.[49]

The lives of many of the poor can be typified by two entries in the St Mary in the Marsh overseers' book: 'October the 14th 1792–Frances Lillaway was delivered of a Male Bastard Child in the Parish of St Michael Coslany; March 27th 1794–John Lillaway the abovesaid child taken by order to St Andrew's workhouse, The Mother Run Away.'[50]

Some people came from still further afield and again are only recorded because they needed money from the authorities. The Norfolk Record Office has a certificate to beg and subscription book of James Cordeney. The certificate says that Cordeney and two other men were homeward bound from the West Indies in a ship laden with coffee, rum and sugar but were shipwrecked on the Lizard. They took to the ship's boat and drifted until they were rescued and brought into Dartmouth. Devon magistrates issued the certificate to beg and the supporting subscription book contains 36 names donating sums between 6d. and a guinea. However the certificate was in the hands of one James Nash who confessed that he had bought it 'of a man for a pot of beer'. The affair came to light when Nash used the certificate to beg in the cathedral close.[51]

A rather different case is that of three African youths taken out of a Portuguese slave ship by Captain Irby of the frigate *Amelia* who were sent by him to Norwich for education. They were baptised at St Peter Mancroft on 30 May 1813.[52]

Housing

Norwich had many fine houses, some of which are shown around Corbridge's map of 1724. However, there were slum areas, especially along the river where the poor people were crowded together in alleys and yards. One of the poorest parishes was St Peter Parmountergate where W. Hudson analysed the people who voted in 1768: 114 people cast their votes and their names are recorded. Hudson compared the names with those who paid church rates—only 27 of them did so. All the others were presumably in holdings of rentals of less than 40 shillings' value.[53]

Incidental details of poor quality housing show up in the records. A Sun Insurance Policy Register of 1730 mentions a house in St Giles occupied by a worsted weaver as of part brick, hair, plaster and tiled. A lease of a messuage in a yard off Needham Street in 1788 is taken out 'with use of well, necessary and muckbing'. Forty years later a messuage in Squirrel Yard, St John Timberhill was leased to John Howard

> together with the right for John Howard to use the privy and bin belonging to Samuel Clay and to take spring and river water from a certain well and cock in the which the river water is conveyed, John Howard paying a proportion of the expenses of keeping privy, bin, well and cock and pipes and tackle therefor according to regulations made by proprietors of Norwich water works in 1826.[54]

There were still no sewers in the modern sense, of course, and toilets were in outside sheds from which the night soil had to be removed. In 1749 Daniel Steward 'whilst in the privy house belonging to the house of John Thaxter, the boards at the back being old and decayed, fell into the receptacle and suffocated'. The inquest jury, on hearing this, tried to fine the owner of the house 40 shillings for his negligence but the coroner appears to have been unsure if they had the power to do this.[55] Many people naturally used the river as a public convenience and there are several inquests on people who drowned when they fell from staithes while relieving themselves.

Fire remained a constant danger. Ann, Bartholomew and Susanna Ward, Elizabeth Garrod and Elizabeth Fooley all died when Mr. Ward's house on Ber Street burnt down on Christmas Day 1766. The inquests survive in the city records: the inquest jury decided that the cause was 'a linen sheet hanging near a fire in the parlour catching fire'.[56] On 30 September 1746 the Shire House on Castle Hill was completely destroyed by fire and in February 1773 two felons died in a blaze at the county gaol.

In October 1751 a fire broke out which destroyed the Bridewell. A local newpaper records 'that extraordinary and well-known man Peter the Wild Youth was confined here at this time'. Peter had been found in the woods near Hamelin in Germany in 1726 'walking on his hands and feet, climbing trees like a squirrel, and feeding on grass and moss'. He appeared to be about 14 years old. He was brought to London by George I and became the sensation of the season in fashionable society and is mentioned by Swift and Defoe. However, his moment of fame soon passed and he was boarded out at the King's expense. He was of low intelligence and became an alcoholic but lived to a good age, dying in 1785. It is not known how long he was in Norwich as the records of the Bridewell do not survive for the period.[57]

The population of Norwich in 1714 was about 30,000 and in the 1790s was just below 40,000. There was still plenty of space within the walls: Lord Bradford's house in Magdalen Street had four acres

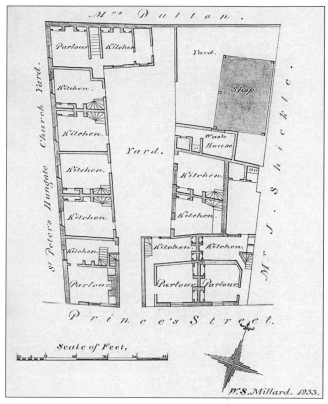

56   *A Norwich Yard. The houses in the yard have a single room ('kitchen') with a single bedroom above. The wash house is shared by all.*

of garden (this was the site later used for the Blind Institution). The present bus station is on the garden of the Wodehouse town house in Surrey Street. Many of the richer citizens were already living in the 'suburbs' outside the walls, such as Jeremiah Ives at Town Close House and Joseph Gurney at The Lodge, whose grounds are now occupied by City College.

Lazowski was not impressed when he visited the city in 1784: 'Norwich, like all ancient cities, is badly planned and built. It is not that there are no good or beautiful houses, but a well built house on a bad site or in a narrow street can never appear more than mediocre.' However, there are many fine Georgian houses in the city. They include Churchman House built of red brick in about 1730 and described as 'one of the finest in Norwich'. There are several good houses in Magdalen Street and Colegate including 20 Colegate, with a fireplace with two cherubs on the pediment said to have come from the Duke's Palace. Some of the most ornate Georgian houses in Norwich are in King Street and in the Surrey Street and All Saints' Green areas.[58]

Some of the Norwich architects of this time are nationally famous. Matthew Brettingham worked at Holkham Hall and built the Shire Hall to replace the one that burnt down in 1746—his has now gone, too. The leading Norwich architect was Thomas Ivory, who became carpenter for the Great Hospital in 1751 and held this job

57   *Churchman House*

until his death in 1779. His best surviving buildings are the Assembly Rooms, the Octagon Chapel and the block of large terraced houses on Surrey Street. Pevsner and Wilson say: 'Norwich can be proud of its Assembly House. No other town of its size in England has anything like it except of course for a spa like Bath.' However, an anonymous diarist called it 'a very large, tall, grand affair, by far the tallest in the city. I have not mentioned these things to our honour but rather to our shame, and must also add to our madness too, seeing trade is so very sickly and nobody knows when it will recover'. The Octagon is discussed later in this chapter.[59]

The two blocks of huge terraced houses in Surrey Street of about 1760-1769 were built as a form of speculative housing and are unique in Norwich, although common in London and elsewhere. Wearing says that 29-35 Surrey Street were built on a site bought by Ivory from Dr Peck for £262 10s. 0d. and that the site of 25-27 Surrey Street was leased to Ivory in 1769 for 200 years by the churchwardens of St Stephen's. It then had six cottages and he agreed to rebuild the site so that it could be let for £50 a year.[60] Another Norwich architect was William Wilkins who adapted the castle for the county gaol–which had been rebuilt only three years earlier by John Soane–in 1792-3. His son, William Wilkins junior, went on to build the National Gallery in London.

Arderon wrote about Norwich buildings:

The Houses and other Buildings in Norwich have formerly been constructed for the most part of flintstone and lime. Some of the flints being cut exactly square, and so curiously perform'd as not to admit of a Knife's Blade between them ... A remarkable example of this is to be seen at Bridewell, St Andrews ... A great many of the Cellars are arched and very strong and capable of preserving goods from fire [the undercrofts referred to in the chapter on the Middle Ages] ... The modern manner of building is now with Bricke, tho' of very bad soft sort, composed of a little Clay and a great deal of sand.[61]

Older buildings had to be maintained or allowed to fall into ruin. Parts of the deserted Duke's Palace became ruinous; on 24 September 1739 three children were killed when a wall in Duke's Palace Yard fell on them.[62] The tower of St Andrew's Hall fell down in 1712 but the building was still used for Corporation banquets and for the Assize Courts. On the advice of the Tonnage Committee the market cross was pulled down in 1732. Benjamin Mackerell was one of the first to disapprove of this act of destruction. He wrote: 'Market cross pulled down which in all probability with a little repairing would have stood many ages, for the mortar with which it was built was as hard as the flints themselves and broke several of the workmens' tools in battering it down.' The gate on Bishop's bridge was pulled down in 1791 and the other gates in the city walls soon followed; they had all gone by 1810. They were pulled down because they impeded traffic and also because they were thought to restrict the flow of air and thus encourage the spread of diseases. We know what the gates looked like because drawings survive by John Kirkpatrick and paintings by Henry Ninham.

Schools

The 18th century was the age of the charity school and the Norwich schools were described proudly by Mackerell:

> The first charity schools in this city were begun on the 24th June 1700 viz. one in the parish of St Ethelred [sic], a second in St Benedicts, a third in St Mary's, the fourth in St James's, in each of which twenty five poor children are taught to read, write and cypher, and some of them at proper ages are bound out apprentices. These are under the tuition of four masters, when any of them have finished their learning they have a new Bible given to them gratis.[63]

In 1707 Bishop Trimnell and other Anglican clergymen raised money to set up more charity schools

> for poor children of both sexes to be taught reading, writing and arithmatick, the boys cloathed with coats, capps and bands, the girls with gowns ... the girls are also taught use of their needles so far as is necessary for them in order to their being serviceable in the necessary affairs of a family.

The schools were funded by sermons and by private contributions.

The first Sunday School in Norwich was set up in 1785 in St Stephen's and many other parishes followed suit. The first Nonconformist Sunday School was opened by the Methodists in 1808: by 1835, 5,861 children attended Sunday School, of whom 3,327 attended Nonconformist schools. By 1877 there were over 7,000 'on the books' in Nonconformist schools alone. The chief aim of Anglican schools was to provide religious instruction to poorer children, often to supplement that taught at day schools. Nonconformists, in contrast, saw their schools as the spearheads of conversion. The first and main objective was to teach reading and also writing (which often was not taught in Anglican Sunday Schools: many thought it would give children ideas beyond their station in life). Sunday Schools also provided other social amenities, such as excursions to the seaside at Yarmouth: one of these, in 1846, involved 1,600 children and 500 teachers.[64]

The general development of day schools in the early 19th century also came from the churches. The British and Foreign School Society was founded on the basis of work by Joseph Lancaster who visited Norwich in 1810 and gave lectures on his system of education. In 1811 a free school for boys on his plan was established by public subscription and with the support of leading Nonconformists like Joseph Gurney and Jeremiah Colman. No less than 537 pupils enrolled during the first year, but a large number of them stayed for only a week or so. The school was intended to be non-denominational but Anglicans preferred to start their own schools with specifically Church of England teaching. They combined with the Charity Schools to buy land in Aldred's Court in St Peter Hungate to establish a large school to replace all their small scattered ones. However, many small schools continued to be founded and by 1839 there were 28 day schools in the city with 2,632 children on their books.

There was a growth in the education of adults as well–in 1815 Norwich was one of 14 towns in England that had a school for adults. With the increasing literacy came a growing demand for cheap and educational literature such as the *Penny Encyclopedia*. The Corresponding Society contributed by lending out books and pamphlets.

Religion

Apart from its support of charity schools, the 18th century was not a time of great achievement in the Church of England. Many of the 18th-century bishops hardly ever came to Norwich and one, Robert Butts, was known mainly for his fondness of the bowling green. Silas Neville was unimpressed with Bishop Yonge's preaching. He wrote in his diary on 21 August 1772: 'Heard an inanimate sermon at the Cathedral by Dr Philip Yonge, Bishop of this Diocese for the benefit of the Norfolk Hospital. This fat blown-up fellow is said to be one of the best preachers in the Establishment. But it is low in preachers if that is the case.' John Wesley was in Norwich on Sunday 17 October 1790 and noted that only two sermons were preached that day in the city's 36 churches; they were at the cathedral and at St Peter Mancroft.[65]

Of the cathedral deans only Prideaux and Bullock spent much money on the building; Bullock repaired the west end, spire and the cloisters where nearly 6,000 feet of Pirbeck paving were laid down. The gentrification of the Close continued; the canal was filled in around 1780 and laid out as 'Prebend's Walk'. The Lower Close was laid out as a private garden. There were still five public houses within the Close but they were all 'respectable'.

The Cathedral was becoming a tourist attraction, though many people found it a disappointment. Marchioness Gray wrote in 1760, 'the cathedral itself is large but not I think fine' and her husband thought the Bishop's Palace 'a rambling unpleasant house'. Seventy years later, William Cobbett wrote of the 'offensive and corroding matter, which is so disgusting to the sight round the magnificent pile at Norwich'.[66]

No new Anglican churches were built in the city in the Georgian period. St George Colegate has fine Georgian fittings–a west gallery on Tuscan columns, a reredos of dark wood with columns and pilasters, and a pulpit with back panel and tester. The

58   *Gentrification of the Close*

tower of St Augustine's church was rebuilt in red brick in 1687 and the worshippers became known as the 'red steeplers'. The church contains a memorial to the architect Matthew Brettingham who died in 1769.

From the middle of the century the Methodists were influential in Norwich. The first preacher John Wesley sent to Norwich was Samuel Larwood, but he only stayed two weeks. John and Charles Wesley themselves came in July 1754 and Charles stayed on. James Wheatley had arrived in Norwich in 1751 but he was not sent by Wesley; he had been expelled from Methodism two months earlier.

After about six weeks riots began occurring at his meetings. Details are given in a contemporary diary for 1752, 3 February:

> This morning poor Mr. Wheatly preached at the Tabernacle, but was invested by the mob upon the Castle Ditches: fifty or more of Mr. Wheatly's friends undertook to surround and protect him. The mob (some think) was from nine to ten thousand strong; neither side had stayes, but drums, clapboards, and all instruments of noise; there was dreadful fighting on both sides, for the mob obliged the others to dispute every inch of ground—some who saw it said they had fought like furies on both sides. Mr. W. could not get away, he was shamefully handled, his hat and wig lost, his head broken in several places, his clothes rent, and himself all over mire and dirt; at length he was driven through the Griffin yard and took sanctuary in a house hard by, till the mayor sent his officers to release and guard him.

However, he persisted and the diary records similar riots on 11 and 14 March and again in August. Wheatley obtained a preaching licence in December 1752. His

59   *St Augustine's church, with its tower of red brick*

triumph was shortlived. He was accused before the Norwich Consistory Court in 1756 of misappropriating funds and of adultery with several young ladies. He lost the case and also lost appeals in 1757 and 1759. He then gave up preaching but still came to Norwich practising 'physick'.[67]

The most important Dissenter church was the Octagon Chapel attended by William Taylor, the Aldersons, the Martineaus and James Smith. The Octagon Chapel was built in 1754-6 by Thomas Ivory. It is of brick and the interior has eight giant Corinthian columns with wooden galleries between them. The single storey portico has four unfluted Ionic columns. There is a wrought iron pinnacle on the roof. John Wesley wrote, 'I was shown Dr Taylor's new Meeting House, perhaps the most elegant one in Norfolk ... the Communion Table is fine mahogany, the very latches of the pew doors are polished brass. How can it be thought that the old coarse gospel should find admission here?' However, he recommended the design as one Methodist churches could follow.[68] Some Anglicans took against it, calling it 'the Devil's cucumber frame'.

The Rosary cemetery was the first private cemetery in England. It was established in 1819 by Thomas Drummond, a Presbyterian minister, and his wife was the first burial, being reinterred here from the Octagon Chapel. In the next 80 years some 18,000 burials took place. It was naturally favoured by Nonconformists but many Anglican families used it too and, with its hillside site and its trees, it is the most atmospheric burial place in the city.

Roman Catholics were forbidden public worship until 1778. The Catholic Relief Act of 1791 allowed building of Roman Catholic places of worship and they bought a plot of land in St John's Alley which was formerly part of the garden of Strangers' Hall. The chapel opened in 1794 and in 1797 they bought Strangers' Hall itself for use as their Presbytery: it served this purpose until 1880. By 1801 the Jesuits had a chapel in St Swithin's Lane: this became a school after the Willow Lane chapel opened in 1828.[69]

Prominent members of the Roman Catholic community included the surgeon and botanist John Pitchford. His son proposed to Rachel Gurney (Elizabeth Fry's sister) but Mr. Gurney refused to allow his daughter to marry a Catholic. The Roman Catholic chapel in Willow Lane was built in 1827 following the Catholic Emancipation Act of the previous year. The architect was J.T. Patience who had designed the

60   *The Octagon Chapel*

Friends' Meeting House in Upper Goat Lane: this replaced the one in which Elizabeth Fry was married.

Popular superstitions are reflected in an advertisement of 11 February 1725 in the *Norwich Gazette*:

> Whereas I, Hester Brown Percy, of St Augustine's, have falsely and indifferently charged one Mary Parker, of St Martin at Oak, with being a witch and in great measure the author of the pains and afflictions I have for some years laboured under, which charge I now believe to be absolutely groundless and may be prejudicial to the said Mary Parker: therefore I do here publicly declare that I am fully satisfied that the said Mary Parker is perfectly innocent of the charge I have made against her ...

Crime

Hanging was still the most common punishment for most types of crime but it no longer took place at the scene of the crime, the market cross or the 'hanging tree' at

Town Close. All hangings were now conducted outside the castle, where they attracted large and boisterous crowds. In 1805 Martha Alden murdered her husband Samuel while he was asleep, striking him repeatedly with a billhook. For this she was executed on Castle Hill on 31 July 1807. Her ghost was supposed to walk on the Hill; in December of that year a party of drunken men attempted to invoke the ghost and they were kept in prison for two days to sober up.[70] Perhaps her ghost was still haunting the castle 15 years later: an official report for the castle gaol in 1820 said that three men waiting in the cells to be transported were driven out of their minds by the sight of a ghost.

Some executions were especially gruesome. John Pycroft was executed on Castle Hill on 16 August 1819 for poisoning his infant child. 'The culprit had a diminutive form and decrepit figure; when the platform fell his chest expanded at intervals during the space of 7 or 8 minutes although every precaution was taken to shorten his sufferings by the addition of some heavy appendages.' After he finally died his body was dissected by surgeons and then displayed to public view at the Shirehouse. However, in the case of Richard Nockolds it was his own family who displayed the body. Nockolds was found guilty of setting fire to straw stacks at Wood Dalling and was executed at Castle Hill on 9 April 1831. The body was handed over to his widow. Apparently because of her poverty she displayed his body at their cottage outside the Barrack gates in Pockthorpe, charging a penny for a view; 'a considerable sum was in this way raised for the widow'. Nockolds was eventually buried at St James Pockthorpe church on 13 April.[71]

In 1821, John Thurtell advertised that he had been in Chapelfield at 9 pm one January night when three men had knocked him down and robbed him of £1,508 in cash that he had on him: he offered a £100 reward for information. It sounds an incredible sum of money to be carrying and indeed it was a scam: within a week Thurtell's bombazine firm was declared bankrupt and Thurtell himself had absconded. He was in worse trouble in 1823 when he was accused of a murder in Hertford. Thurtell's father, Thomas, was a Norwich alderman and created a local scandal by refusing to pay for a lawyer to cross examine the prosecution witnesses in the case (there was no legal aid in those times). Thurtell junior was hanged for the murder in 1824 but the career of Thurtell senior was not permanently blighted–he became mayor of Norwich in 1828.[72]

Criminals were occasionally transported to the American colonies in the 18th century. This came to an end with the American War of Independence but from 1788 many convicted prisoners were transported to Australia instead. In 1783, at the age of 20, Henry Cabell was condemned to death with his father and brother for breaking into a house at Alburgh. All three were sentenced to hanging but Cabell's sentence was commuted to 14 years' transportation to the American colonies. However, America had declared independence and could no longer be used as a dumping ground for convicts and Cabell stayed in Norwich Castle awaiting his fate. While there he fell in love with a girl also waiting to be transported, Susannah Holmes. They asked permission to marry but this was denied and in 1785 she bore him a son, also called Henry.

In 1786 Susannah with her baby and two other woman prisoners was taken by coach to Plymouth under the guard of John Simpson: they were to be put on a boat bound for New South Wales. Henry had begged to be allowed to go with them but he was refused. There was drama in Plymouth when the captain of the ship refused to take the baby as it had no papers. Simpson had no choice but to bring Susannah and the baby back to Norwich. On his own initiative he took them to London first and forced his way into the house of the Home Secretary, Lord Sydney. Sydney agreed that the family should be transported together and they landed at Port Jackson on 26 January 1788. Cabell is supposed to have carried the new governor ashore on his shoulders and thus to be the first person on the fleet actually to set foot on the land. Two weeks later five couples on the fleet were married, the first Christian marriages in Australia: they included Henry and Susannah. They stayed in Australia for the rest of their lives. Henry later became a merchant and trader in Adelaide and lived to be 84. He and many of his family are buried at Old St Matthew's church in Windsor, Australia.[73]

£100 REWARD.

WHEREAS

AT about Nine o'Clock on the Evening of MONDAY, the 22nd of January inst. Mr. JOHN THURTELL was attacked in Chapel Field, Norwich, by three Men, knocked down, and ROBBED of a Pocket Book, containing £1508 in Notes, 13 of which were of the Bank of England, value £100 each, and the Name " JOHN THURTELL" is indorsed on them.

Notice is hereby Given,

That whoever will give information which may lead to the apprehension and conviction of the Persons concerned in this Robbery, shall be paid the above Reward, on applying to Mr. THURTELL—and any Person concerned in the Robbery, who will give information of his Accomplices will receive the Reward, and a FREE PARDON.

Norwich, January 23rd, 1821.

John Berry, Printer, Norwich.

61 *John Thurtell claims to have been robbed of £1500*

Although a sentence for transportation might be for seven or 14 years, most probably stayed on in Australia. One person who did come back was Thomas Sutton. He was only 16 when he was sentenced to seven years' transportation in 1800 for stealing a pony from General Money at Trowse. He must have had a grudge against the General: seven years later he was back in Norwich and set fire to his barn and barley stack. This time he was hanged. His father had also been hanged for horse-stealing.[74]

Treatment of the convicted could be very harsh. In 1830 a 19-year-old youth, William Brooks, was being held in Norwich Castle awaiting trial for highway robbery. He tried to escape, fell 70 feet and was permanently crippled. He was tried and sentenced to transportation anyway.[75]

Both the prisons in the city were rebuilt in the 1820s to take account of rising demand. The city gaol on the Earlham Road—where the Roman Catholic cathedral now is—was built in 1827. It cost £30,000 and had eight wards and 69 dormitories. The county gaol on the castle mound opened the following year at a cost of £50,000 and with 240 cells.

62   *Elizabeth Fry*

Body-snatching was a crime brought about by the demand for bodies for medical reseach and Norwich had its share of cases. In 1815 the stables of the *Duke's Palace Inn* were used by resurrection men pretending to be apple merchants: one night the ostler found three sacks that contained corpses which turned out to have recently been buried at Hainford. The body-snatchers were never caught. At the *Rampant Horse* inn in February 1823 suspicion was aroused by the frequency with which trunks were sent from the inn to London by the 'Telegraph' coach: on investigation they turned out to be bodies. An inquest among the Norwich city archives on an unknown man records: 'his body was found in a box in a coach offices occupied by the proprietors of the Telegraph Coach … with a direction To Be Conveyed To London'. There were no marks of violence on the body–these were body snatchers but not murderers. Two men were eventually tried and sentenced to three months' imprisonment and fined £50.[76]

The state of English prisons was to be transformed by one of the most famous people to have been born in Norwich, Elizabeth Fry.[77] She was born Elizabeth Gurney at Gurney's Court off Magdalen Street in 1780. She was the fourth of 12 children of the banker John Gurney and his wife Catherine Bell. Only one of this large family died as a baby, an unusually low death rate for the time. The family were Quakers but not the strict or 'plain Quakers' who said 'thee' and 'thou' and wore a Quaker cap. They were wealthy and when Elizabeth was six they moved out of the city and rented Earlham Hall, now part of the University of East Anglia. She married Joseph Fry in the Goat Lane chapel in Norwich in 1810 and moved with him to London. Soon after this she became an active Quaker and she was formerly acknowledged a minister in 1811.

The work for which she is justly famous is prison reform. She visited Newgate Prison in London for the first time in January 1813 and was appalled by the conditions in which the female prisoners lived. She wrote to her small children, 'I have lately been twice to Newgate to see the poor prisoners who had poor little infants without clothing, or with very little and I think if you saw how small a piece of bread they are allowed you would be very sorry'. Conditions for poor women in gaol were awful:

prisoners whose relatives had money could buy food, drink, clothes and privacy but those with nothing were herded together in large rooms, with no clothing apart from what they arrived in, no access to basins or towels and a bare survival ration of meat and bread. It was Elizabeth Fry who spent 30 years making people aware of these conditions and led the way in suggesting changes. She was also active in making sure that prisoners should be kept busy: the Norfolk Record Office has a letter from her asking that women prisoners in the Bridewell in Tothill Fields in London should be allowed to work at the needlework she had arranged for them. She was well in advance of her time in her view that the Government should provide work for prisoners and should pay them for it.

She became famous as an inspiration to many. An American minister visiting England wrote:

> Two days ago I saw the greatest curiousity in London, aye and in England too, compared to which Westminster Abbey, the Tower, Somerset House, the British Museum, nay Parliament itself, sink into insignificance. I have seen Elizabeth Fry in Newgate, and I have witnessed there the most miraculous effect of true Christianity upon the most depraved of human beings.[78]

Later she visited other countries and her ideas improved the conditions of female prisoners all the way across Europe and as far as Russia.

Elizabeth Fry took up other causes too. She regularly inspected the ships of female prisoners being transported to Australia and made suggestions to improve their lot on board and when they arrived in Australia. Finding the body of a dead boy on a frozen winter night in London led her to set up a group of ladies to run a night shelter, providing soup and bread as well as a bed for the night.

Elizabeth kept a Journal for most of her life describing her prison work and her spiritual development.[79] As well as her reform work, she was also the mother of five sons and six daughters: fellow Quakers alleged she did not bring them up strictly enough and almost all of them did in fact leave the church. Elizabeth died in 1845 and is buried in the Quaker burial ground in Barking.

Leisure and Art

The 18th century saw a flowering of culture in the city, including its first purpose-built theatre. In the Georgian period the city boasted the most famous botanist in the country, its own school of art and some of the leading thinkers, writers and musicians in England.

The Theatre Royal was designed by the Norwich architect Thomas Ivory: it was built in 1758 and was only the second purpose built theatre in England. It was very small and 40 years later another Norwich architect, William Wilkins, was complaining that 'a lady must be separated from the Arm of her protector both on entering, and on leaving the lobby … it really is otherwise impossible that ladies can reach their carriages without danger of spoiling their Dresses and being squeezed perhaps between Doorkeepers, Porters and prostitutes'.[80]

There was a slump in theatre-going in the early 1820s but a new Theatre Royal was built a few yards from the old building at a cost of £6,000 and opened in 1826. Edmund Kean was in Norwich in 1830, playing Lear. In the 1850s Edward Fitzball

63 *The first Theatre Royal*

declared that in Norwich plays were 'much better performed than they are at the present day in any theatre in London'.

The Theatre Royal's company had from the start toured their productions throughout the market towns of East Anglia: this came to an end in 1852 and from then on there was no stock company and the theatre became just a host for touring shows. From the late 1800s variety shows were put on as well as 'serious' theatre.

Before the theatre the *White Swan* inn had been the centre of acting in Norwich. On the Millennium Library site, the inn was associated with the Norwich Company of Comedians from at least 1727 when it advertised in the *Norwich Mercury* a 'Tragedy call'd the Fall of Saguntum, With Entertainments of Singing and Dancing'. The Comedians made it their permanent home in 1731. Charles Macklin played Macbeth here in 1747. The *White Swan* declined as a centre of drama when the new theatre opened in 1758 but still held variety shows and also more popular entertainments: it was one of the centres of cock-fighting in the city.

The pubs and inns provided a huge variety of entertainments The quack doctor Graham advertised his show at the *Maid's Head*–'he will deliver his very celebrated Lecture to Gentleman, on the Propagation of the Human Species, and on the Arts of exalting and rendering permanent the Joys of the Marriage Bed'. Graham had been a sensation in London where his lectures on 'The Female' were animated by a lightly clad model called Emma Hart, who was later Lady Hamilton and the lover of Norfolk hero Lord Nelson. Parson Woodforde visited the *Rampant Horse* inn in 1785 to see the 'learned pig' which could spell words and numbers from letters and figures put in front of it. Woodforde noted in his diary, 'Paid for seeing the Pigg 1s.' The *Bell Hotel* was a centre of clubs including the Tory Hell-Fire club, a gang of ruffians who attacked John and Charles Wesley when they visited Norwich in 1754. This was a terminus for local coaches including those to Yarmouth.[81]

In 1788 a large tiger worth 200 guineas was exhibited at the *Bear* inn. It broke loose and devoured two monkeys. It was caught but died soon after 'from a brass collar and chain, which he had swallowed [was one of the poor monkeys wearing it?] having gangrened within him'. In December 1816, George Wombwell was in Norwich exhibiting his 'Royal Menagerie' at the Castle Ditches over Christmas. The star attraction was a rhinoceros which was claimed to be the only one in Europe. It was actually auctioned at Norwich Cattle Market and fetched £300.[82]

The earliest Freemasons' lodge in Norwich met at the *Maid's Head* from 1724. The list of its first 23 members includes Edmund Prideaux, son of the Dean of Norwich, and four future sheriffs of the city, two of whom also became mayor. Other early lodges included the Union Lodge meeting at the *King's Head* from 1736 and the Unity meeting at the *Bear* from 1747: both these inns were in the Market Place.[83]

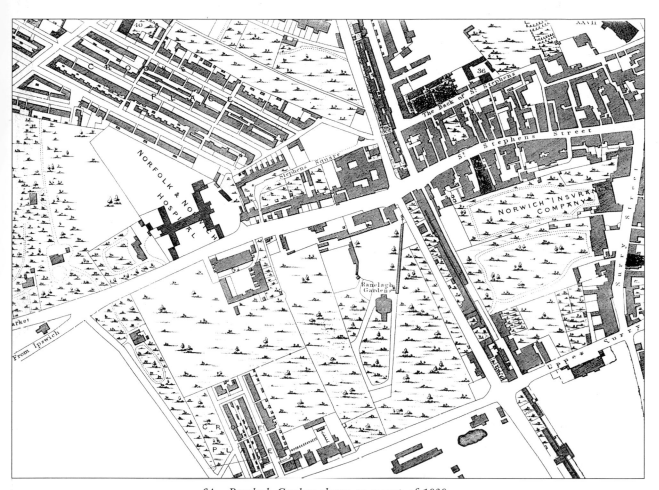

64   *Ranelagh Gardens shown on a map of 1830*

Mackerell was proud of the city's inns.

For good-fellow-ship perhaps not one city in England can match us. The gentlemen and better sort of tradesmen keep their clubs constantly every night in the week some at one tavern some at another, neither are the alehouses empty, for their are many persons of good fashion and credit that meet every night at one or other of these houses besides great numbers that are filled with poor labouring working men who go to these houses to refresh themselves after they have left work.

However, Arderon was not so impressed. He describes what he calls a:

particular custom in Norwich—Both rich and poor when they meet in Taverns or Alehouses, pis into a large pewter Chamber pot (when they have occasion) wch stands in the Corner of every Publick Room, and there it stands stinking till it is full and often it runs about the Room, in a very nasty manner ... [84]

A sign of increasing leisure—for some classes at least—was the Pleasure Gardens in the city.[85] The New Spring Gardens between St Faiths Lane and the river was founded in 1739; the Wilderness begun in 1748 and was illuminated by 1768; Ranelagh Gardens outside St Stephen's gates had fireworks and an illuminated Grand Walk by 1768. All the gardens had fireworks displays; in 1782 a man was killed at Bunn's Gardens while the fireworks were being prepared. There were Public Baths at Chapelfield: charges in 1789 were 5s. for a hot bath, 2s. 6d. for tepid and 1s. for cold.

The Gardens were the centre of the late 18th-century craze of ballooning. James Deeker, who sold experimental balloons in London, announced that on 1 June 1785 he would make a balloon ascent from Quantrell's Gardens in Norwich. A violent storm damaged the balloon but Deeker tried to ascend anyway: unfortunately the fabric had torn and he fell rapidly, landing unharmed at Sisland. On 23 June he tried again and in a flight of 45 minutes reached Topcroft.

On 23 July Major John Money of Trowse had a try. He also started from Quantrell's Gardens: his was a charity event and the money raised from the 700 fee-paying spectators went in aid of the Norfolk and Norwich Hospital. The balloon rose and was in sight for 45 minutes as it drifted slowly to the south east. Money tried to let out gas but the valve would not open and he eventually came down in the sea about 20 miles off Southwold. A Dutch boat which passed did not stop, apparently mistaking the balloon for a sea monster but, after clinging to the balloon for five hours, Money was spotted by the Harwich revenue cutter which pulled him aboard. He was put ashore at Lowestoft next morning and arrived at his home in Crown Point in a post-chaise.[86]

Norwich Public Library was founded in 1784, a private venture, funded by subscriptions. Norwich Literary Institution followed in 1822: they combined to form the Norfolk and Norwich Library in 1886. The library was built on the site of the old city gaol on Guildhall Hill in 1837. The architect was J.T. Patience; the facade was rebuilt at the end of the 19th century after a fire. The library closed in 1977 and many of its books passed to the Norwich School.

Boating was becoming more popular as a leisure activity but was not without its dangers. In 1754 a boat being sailed by five young men overturned in the Wensum off King Street and four of them were drowned. Four people out of six travelling in a boat from Conesford Gates to Yarmouth in December 1763 were drowned when their boat 'overset' near Whitlingham ditch.[87]

In 1820 the famous 'pugilist' Ned Painter moved to Norwich, taking over the *Sun and Anchor Inn* in Lobster Lane. Born near Manchester, he had lost to Tom Oliver ('the Chelsea gardener') in 1814 and fought Thomas Winter ('Tom Spring') twice in 1818. Painter was defeated in the first fight but gained his revenge in the second. Painter planned to retire from the ring when he moved to Norwich but he was persuaded to fight Oliver once more. The contest took place at North Walsham before a crowd of about 20,000: it is described by George Borrow in *Lavengro*. Painter won after 12 rounds and announced his final retirement at a dinner held in his honour after the fight. In 1843 he was found guilty of thrashing a corn merchant called Jeremiah Cross at the *Rising Sun Inn* in Norwich. After this he passed into obscurity; his death in Lakenham in 1852 is not even noted in Mackie's *Annals*.

These fights were of course savage affairs compared with modern contests. In 1820 a prize fight at St Faith's lasted 65 rounds. Three years later a man named Purdy died after a fight near Bishop Bridge. The courts were in sympathy with the pugilists;

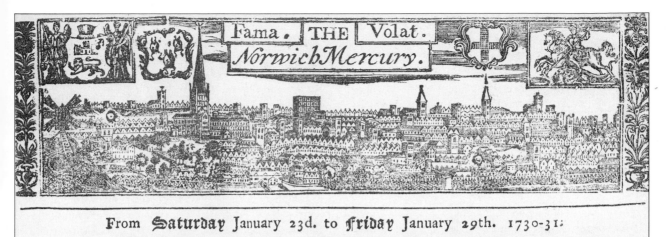

Fama. THE Volat.
Norwich Mercury.

From **Saturday** January 23d. to **Friday** January 29th. 1730-31.

65   *The Norwich Mercury Mast Head*

Painter was fined a mere shilling even though Cross was hospitalised after the assault. Purdy's opponent, Grint, received only three months' imprisonment.[88]

Until 1752, the New Year officially began not on 1 January but on 25 March. This has caused confusion to many people using parish records and other documents. For example, all the 300 people sworn in as city freemen in January 1678 (by modern reckoning) are entered in the Freeman's register under the date January 1677. As Millican's transcript of the register simply copies the original document, many people using his book are a year out in their calculations.[89] Popular celebrations of the New Year, however, always took place on 1 January.

Sir James Edward Smith

Smith was born in Norwich in 1759, the son of a wealthy wool merchant. He studied medicine and botany in Edinburgh and London. When in London in 1784 he bought the whole collection of books, manuscripts and natural history specimens of the great Swedish botanist Linnaeus for a bargain one thousand guineas. They consisted of 19,000 pages of pressed flowers and the descriptive volumes. When the King of Sweden heard of the sale he sent a ship to intercept the one carrying the collection but it was just too late and the precious cargo arrived safely in England. Smith moved back to Norwich in 1796, bringing the collection with him to his house at 29 Surrey Street, where it was kept for 20 years. When he returned to this city, the Bishop of Carlisle wrote to him, 'at the distance of Norwich you will be quite buried alive' but it was here that he wrote his most famous works including the text of *Sowerby's Botany* and *The English Flora*. Smith also founded the Linnaean Society which bought the collection (for 3,000 guineas!) on Smith's death in 1828. They are now at Burlington House in London.[90]

One of James Smith's students was William Hooker, born in Norwich in 1785. Hooker founded the Royal Botanical Gardens at Kew in 1841 and was its director until his death in 1865. He was followed in the post by his son Joseph Hooker.

Literary Life

A *Lecture on Art and Letters in Georgian Norwich* describes literary life in the city: 'Norwich like one of its neighbouring broads forms a sort of literary backwater wherein were hatched many of the young fry of letters, several of whom escaping later into the mainstream of English literature became comparatively big fish.'[91]

William Taylor was born in 1765 of Norwich parents. He travelled widely and met Goethe at Weimar in 1782. He was one of the leaders of political, philosophical and debating societies in Norwich. He was known as a translator of German poetry. Mrs. Barbauld wrote to Taylor: 'Do you know that you made Walter Scott a poet? So he told me the other day. It was, he says, your ballad of Lenore that inspired him.' William Taylor tried to enrich the literary life of the city by inviting the poet Robert Southey to live here. Southey replied that the letter excited a half desire to diet for life upon Norfolk puddings, turnips and turkeys. However he moved to Italy instead.[92]

Harriet Martineau, who disliked Taylor, admired 'his tenderness in guiding his blind mother every Sunday to the Octagon Chapel, getting her there with her shoes as clean as if she had crossed no gutters in those flat paved streets'. Taylor took to drink after his mother died. Martineau says that 'at supper parties William Taylor was managed by a regular process–first, of feeding, then of wine bibbing, and immediately after that of poking to make him talk: and then came his sayings, devoured by the gentlemen and making ladies and children aghast'. He died in 1836.

Amelia Opie was born in Calvert Street in 1769. She lost her mother early and lived as companion to her father Dr. Alderson, becoming hostess to her father's friends. She married the artist John Opie in 1798 and the couple lived in London. In 1801 she published her novel *Father and Daughter*. John Opie died in 1807. After his death, Amelia came back to Norwich and became increasingly involved with the Society of Friends. Harriet Martineau thought she did this in an attempt to gain a second husband in the person of the philanthropist, Joseph John Gurney. She published her last novel in 1822 and was formally received into the Society in 1825. She died in 1853 and is buried in the Society of Friends' graveyard in Gildencroft.

Harriet Martineau was the sixth child of Thomas and Harriet Martineau and was born in 1802 in Gurney's Court off Magdalen Street, in the same room as Elizabeth Gurney, later famous as Elizabeth Fry. She was a sickly, introverted child who was almost deaf in adolescence. She wrote essays and stories in the 1820s and later, travelling widely including America and the Middle East. She cured herself of illness through Mesmerism, a popular form of hypnosis. Her autobiography is probably her best-known work. Harriet's brother James Martineau became the most eminent Unitarian divine of his generation.

Another Norwich woman to achieve a certain literary fame was Elizabeth Bentley. She was born in All Saints Norwich in 1767, the only child of a cordwainer. She published two volumes of verse: *Genuine Poetical Compositions on Various Subjects* in 1791 and *Poems: Being the Genuine Compositions of Elizabeth Bentley of Norwich* in 1821. She spent the last years of her life in Doughty's Hospital and died in 1839 aged 72.

Andy Warhol famously said that everybody is famous for 15 minutes but not many people reach the height of their fame when they are three years old. This was

the fate of William Crotch, born in Norwich on 5 July 1775. His father was a
carpenter and built an organ for his own
use. William was able to play 'God Save
Great George Our King' on this when he
was two years and three weeks old. He
was an instant sensation and became 'a
child prodigy without parallel in the history of music'. He played before a large
crowd at Norwich in February 1778 and
his mother then took him on tour: he
played before the King and Queen at
Buckingham Palace on 1 January 1779,
appeared in London again in October
1779 and then 'toured' throughout the
country. He went on to write three orato-
rios and a good deal of church music. The
Pocket County Companion calls his oratorio
Palestine 'the finest work of the kind ever
produced by an Englishman up to that
time'. He was the first principal of the
Royal Academy of Music in London from
1822 to 1832 and wrote books on the
theory of musical composition. His last
public performance was at the Handel
festival in Westminster Abbey in 1834. He
died in 1847 on a visit to his son, who was
master of Taunton Grammar School, and
is buried at Bishop's Hull in Somerset.[93]

Perhaps the fame of William Crotch
contributed to the success of the first Norwich Music Festival which was held in

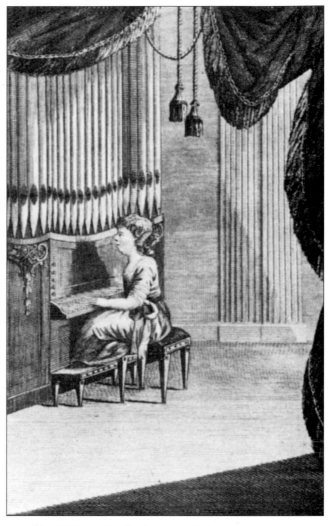

66   *William Crotch, the musical phenomenon*

1824. It was organised by Richard Mackenzie Bacon, the editor of the *Norwich Mercury*,
to raise funds for the Norfolk and Norwich Hospital. The first festival raised £2,400
and it became a triennial event. It is the second oldest music festival in England (the
oldest being the Three Choirs Festival in Hereford, Worcester and Gloucester).

Another Norwich resident who has contributed to the musical life of England is
Sarah Ann Glover. She developed the 'do-re-mi' system of learning musical notes (the
Tonic Sol-fa system). She taught this to children in her school in Black Boy Yard,
Colegate, and it has since spread across much of the world.[94]

The turn of the century saw a flourishing of painting in the City leading to the
group of artists known as the Norwich School of Artists—Norwich is the only city in
Britain to have a school named after it. The name is given to three generations of
Norwich based landscape painters who were linked together by master-pupil

relationships and by family ties. The Norwich Society of Artists was founded in 1803 and held yearly exhibitions from 1805 to 1833. The most important artists were John Crome, John Sell Cotman and Joseph Stannard.[95]

John Crome was born in a public house in 1768: some books say this was in the castle ditches, others that it was the 'King and Miller' in St George Tombland. At the age of 12 he was errand boy to Dr. Edward Rigby and in 1783 he became apprentice to a coach painter. Thomas Harvey introduced him to the famous artist William Beechey who wrote later: 'Crome when I first knew him must have been about 20 years old and was a very awkward misinformed country lad but extremely shrewd in all his remarks upon art although he wanted words and terms to express his meaning'.

Crome painted signs for several Norwich inns including for the *Three Cranes* in the Lower Close. This sign is now in the Castle Museum as are many of the urban and rural landscapes for which the School is famous. Crome became a full time artist and drawing master with the support of local gentry like Harvey, the Gurneys of Earlham and Dawson Turner of Yarmouth. Although most of his landscapes are of Norfolk scenes, he did paint in the Lake District and elsewhere and once visited the Continent. Crome died in April 1821 and is buried in St George Colegate where there is a plaque to his memory. He had married Phoebe Berney in 1792 and they had 11 children, some of whom also became artists. They lived all their married life in Gildengate but the house no longer survives.

George Borrow wrote expressively of Crome in *Lavengro*:

> he has painted not pictures of the world but English pictures such as Gainsborough might have done; beautiful rural pieces … with trees which might well tempt the wild birds to perch upon them. The little dark man with the brown coat and the top-boots, whose name will one day be considered the chief ornament of the old town, and whose works will at no distant period rank among the proudest pictures of England.

Borrow was right. After Crome's death his reputation grew and eventually he came to rank with Turner and Constable as one of the three major English landscape painters of the century.

John Sell Cotman was born in St Mary Coslany Norwich in 1782 and was a pupil at Norwich Grammar School. He trained in London, moving back to Norwich in 1806. He published etchings of antiquarian scenes and worked in Yarmouth for 12 years under the patronage of Dawson Turner. He made three visits to Europe and after a further 10-year spell in Norwich he went back to London in 1834 to be Teacher of Drawing in the newly founded King's College school. He was not fully recognised in his own time because of his forward-looking style. Cotman died in 1842. From 1823 to 1834 he lived in St Martin at Palace Plain and had a drawing school there. Two of his sons later lived in the same fine Georgian house which is now called Cotman House.

Joseph Stannard was born in 1797. He was never a formal member of the Norwich School but his paintings of the coast and rivers of Norfolk were immediately popular and have had a high reputation ever since. In 1824 he painted the 'Thorpe Water Frolic'. This was commissioned by Colonel John Harvey of Thorpe and he and Stannard are both shown in the painting. The colonel is in the centre directing proceedings and

Stannard is the figure on the extreme right shielding his eyes. Harvey refused to buy the painting at first; either he did not like it or Stannard was charging more than he had expected. He changed his mind a couple of years later. Stannard's later years were severely restricted by tuberculosis and he died in 1830. The 'Water Frolic' was one of the first Norwich School paintings to be acquired by Norwich Castle Museum. It was bought by J.J. Colman in 1894 for 110 guineas. He presented it to the museum when it moved to the castle later in the same year.

The first printed trade directory for Norwich was published in 1783 by William Chase. He gives a long list of proposed improvements to the city: every street should have its correct name painted up; every house should be numbered; the city gates and walls should be pulled down, and he had many other suggestions designed to 'gentrify' parts of the city (but not improve the living conditions of the poor). Some of Chase's schemes were achieved after the Norwich Paving Commissioners were set up in 1806 under an Act for better Paving, Lighting, Cleansing, Watching and otherwise improving the City of Norwich. They levied a rate to raise £5,000 a year and paved the main streets including St Stephen's, St. Giles and what is now London Street. Davey Place, between the market and the castle ditches, was cut through in 1812 at the personal expense of Alderman Davey who pulled down the *King's Head* hotel to make the space. He is supposed to have caused a sensation by announcing 'Gentlemen I intend to put a hole in the King's Head!'[96] People thought he planned to kill George III and a guard was placed on his house. The city already had 900 oil lamps, some put up by the Corporation and others by individual citizens. The Board increased the number of lamps to 1,200. However, it was in the age of Queen Victoria that the infrastructure of the city was to be revolutionised.

5

Victorian Norwich

The age of Queen Victoria was the time when Norwich finally lost the tag of being the 'second city' of England. Although its population continued to grow, it was outstripped by the huge growth in population in the industrial towns of the Midlands and the North. It was also the time when both local and national authorities began to exercise powers to bring about drastic changes in the city's infrastructure which transformed people's lives. These include the supply of water, the provision of sewers, the beginnings of slum clearance, the introduction of minimum standards of housing and the start of a system of free education for all.

The population of Norwich rose throughout the 19th century but not at the speed of the cities of the North. The census figures for the city are 36,909 in 1801; 68,195 in 1851; 80,386 in 1871 and 100,964 in 1891.

In the 1830s the Parliamentary Reform Act and the Municipal Reform Act changed the face of government in England. The Parliamentary Reform Act extended the number of people who were entitled to vote. It made little difference in Norwich: the franchise was very wide already as all freemen were entitled to vote. Two members were still elected for the city and all voters still had two votes. The number of people voting in the first election under the new rules went up by about seven hundred.

The Municipal Reform Act had a much more drastic effect. It extended the franchise in the elections for the City Council from all freemen to all male ratepayers. This quadrupled the franchise but paradoxically those few women who had a corporation vote as 'freemen' lost it. In 1869 women ratepayers were given the same right to vote in City Council elections as male ratepayers and in 1885 Norwich had 2,600 female voters to 14,000 male voters. These women were all single women or widows; married women were held not to have property of their own and therefore not entitled to vote.

The Act altered the four great wards of the 1404 charter into eight wards. The ratepayers elected councillors who in turn chose aldermen and also the sheriff and the mayor. The title 'Corporation' was changed to 'Council'. The council was given the power of raising money by imposing a general rate; before this all rates had been raised by *ad hoc* bodies for particular purposes. In 1892, 16 wards were established, each with as near the same population as possible. As W. Hudson pointed out at the

Lines through Time 8: 1837 to 1900

Victoria is crowned Queen	1837	
	1841	Census: population 62,344
	1844	Norwich/Yarmouth Railway opened
	1845	Elizabeth Fry dies
	1849	Jenny Lind sings in Norwich Fire-fighting Force set up
	1851	George Borrow's *Lavengro* published
	1852	Norwich Boys Home started
Crimean War begins	1853	Amelia Opie dies
	1856	Earlham Road Cemetery opened
	1859	Norwich Workhouse erected
	1867	Last public hanging in Norwich
Transportation abolished	1868	
Secret Ballot Act 1872	1872	
	1877	*Black Beauty* published
	1880	City Asylum opened at Hellesdon; Mousehold Heath given to the City
	1881	Census: population 87,842
	1882	St John's Catholic Church begun
	1887	Mousehold Prison opened
	1894	Castle becomes a museum
	1898	Jenny Lind Hospital moved to Unthank Road
	1899	Royal Arcade built
	1900	Trams come to Norwich

time, each of these new wards had roughly the same population as the whole city 700 years earlier.

The first police force was set up in the city in 1836, on the model of that founded in London seven years earlier. The force consisted of 18 men and one superintendent. In 1840 the night watch became night constables and they were soon incorporated into the police force proper which by 1851 numbered 80 men. In November 1846 the Corporation delegated the Watch Committee to:

> appoint a fire brigade of six men, whose business it will be to attend all fires in Norwich ... The men in the daytime are to act as common policemen, and to sleep near the station house, where the engine is kept, each night, that they may be ready in case of alarm.[1]

Norwich continued to embrace radical causes. Daniel O'Connell, 'the famous Irish agitator', was in Norwich in November 1837 and addressed a large meeting at St Andrew's Hall. The city also played a part in Chartist activities in the 1830s and 1840s. Chartism was a movement in which the working classes demanded universal adult suffrage and changes in the Poor Law of 1834. The movement began in Norwich in 1838 when J.R. Stephens from Ashton spoke to rallies in the market place. He told the crowds: 'England stands on a mine; a volcano is beneath her ... Hitherto the people have been held in leash; they can be held back no longer'.[2] The first Chartist leader in Norwich was John Love, treasurer to the Norwich Weavers' Society and a Primitive Methodist lay preacher. He attacked the new workhouses for the way married couples were separated inside them.

Love was committed to non-violent protest and condemned the abortive rising in 1839, the year in which Chartism reached its peak. Violence was expected in the city. On 5 March 1839 a Charles Loftus wrote to Lord Wodehouse, the Lord Lieutenant of the county. He said that a man named Land who lived in Graham's Court in St Peter Mancroft parish was making pikes for chartists. Radical clubs with supplies of pikes were being held at the *Cottage* behind Patteson's Brew Office in Pockthorpe, the *Angell* in St Martin at Oak, the *Roebuck* in Peafield, Lakenham, and the *Shuttle* in St Augustine's. These were public houses in some of the poorest areas of the city.[3]

In the event there was no violence in Norwich in 1839. After a great meeting on Mousehold Heath, led by Love, the Chartists turned on the churches. They would attend a church in large numbers and sometimes disrupt the proceedings. About 5,000 turned up at St Stephen's one Sunday and heckled the vicar when he preached on man's duty to be content with his lot in life, shouting, 'You get £200 a year! Come and weave bombazines!'.[4]

Love was rivalled and soon eclipsed in popularity by the orator, John Dover. John Ward says that the Norwich chartists 'drove out their early bourgeois leaders, preferring the heady oratory of the promiscuous and rascally publican John Dover— at least until 1841'. Dover was not against violence and when he was arrested in 1839 pikes, guns and bullets were found in his house. Like any mob orator he ran the risk of angering them too—once he was suspected by the crowd of taking a bribe and they dragged him to the river intending to throw him in. He had to be rescued by the newly formed police force. However his career came to a sudden end in 1845 when he was sentenced to transportation on a charge of receiving stolen goods. Dover's family were reduced to poverty after his transportation: his wife Martha is described in the 1851 census as a pauper, formerly a silk weaver.[5]

Love also left Norwich in 1845, going to work for the chartist cause in the north of England. He came back to Norwich in 1848 and spoke to large crowds as the final petition to Parliament was being organised. After the petition had failed Chartism died out and Love became destitute: he was forced into the workhouse against which he had preached so strongly.

There was a great increase in the number of men entitled to vote after the Act of 1868. In 1867 there were 1,981 registered as freemen, 2,607 as occupiers, 1,324 as freeholders. In 1868 there were 1,984 freemen, 9,798 occupiers, 1,488 freeholders and also 26 lodgers.

Elections to Parliament in the Victorian age were the source of endless disputes, petitions and counter-petitions. In the 1868 election Sir Henry Stracey and Sir William Russell were elected. After an enquiry it was found that Stracey had offered bribes and he was therefore not legally elected. In May 1870 Jacob Henry Tillett was elected to the vacant seat. After a petition this election was also declared invalid and Tillett was unseated. At the subsequent by-election in 1871 Jeremiah James Colman was elected in his place. Both Tillett and Colman were Liberals but in the next election of 1874 the voting was so close that one Liberal and one Conservative were elected. Despite being so close the election was not disputed but after Tillett was elected in a by-election in the following year there was another petition against him: once again Tillett was thrown out. This time no by-election was held and the second Norwich seat remained vacant until the 1880 general election. At this election two Liberals—Colman and Tillett—were elected and they actually held their seats undisputed for the

252. What is the principal public house in the seventh ward?—The principal public house is a smaller house kept by Mr. Minns, the brother of the Jesse Minns that I spoke of; another is where the seventh ward association used to meet, and a third one is kept by Mackley, called "The Marquis of Granby." Of course it is very difficult to recollect all the signs of these public houses, but I am reminded that Minns keeps "The Queen's Arms;" that is the house where the seventh ward association used to meet. "The Marquis of Granby" is a house kept by Mackley, a man who always supported the Liberals.

253. What other public houses were there in the ward which the late men would be at?—The public houses in that ward are of a lower class, and any public house tolerably within reach of the polling place, I should say, would have a few voters drinking their glasses; but I cannot mention any one in particular.

254. What streets are they in?—Pockthorpe, St. James' Street, St. Paul's Plain, St. Paul's Opening; those are places where the lowest class of voters in the city live.

255. And the public houses in those streets would be close to the polling places of that district?—Yes, there are four or five polling places in the ward, and there would be one in St. Paul's Plain. Pockthorpe, St. James', and St. Paul's are in, I regret to say, the poorest district in the city, and undoubtedly if men are corruptly influenced that is the ward in which the corruption more especially takes place.

256. That is one of the poorest wards?—Yes; the seventh ward is most undoubtedly the most corrupt ward in the city.

257. Now will you go on to the eighth ward, and give me first the managers?—The manager of the eighth ward for Sir William Russell was another of my clerks, A. J. Berry, the brother of my cashier, and Mr. Abel Tillett, a nephew of Mr. Tillett's, for Mr. Tillett.

258. What gentlemen were there working with them?—It is rather difficult in the eighth ward to find any; the eighth ward is essentially a working man's ward, and we have always regarded it as one of the strongholds of liberalism. There are some very active men. One of the most active men there was a Mr. Harper. Mr. Samuel Spinks is a very active man. There is a Mr. Lofty, Mr. Cossey, Mr. Gilbert; in fact one or two of the Gilberts are very active indeed.

67 *Evidence before the Bribery Commission 1869: Isaac Coaks names the poorest parts of the City*

full five-year term. There was a further dispute after the 1885 election and this time it was the Conservative Harry Bullard who was unseated. J.J. Colman finally retired as MP in 1895 and in that year the city elected two Conservatives for the first time for 60 years.

Leglislation of the later 19th century gave the city all sorts of powers of regulation and control. These were pulled together in the Local Government Act and the Norwich Corporation Act both of 1889.

Trade and Industry

The weaving industry declined greatly in the 19th century and the city faced a crisis. It was saved by an increase in a wide range of manufacturing and above all by the rapid growth in boot and shoe making which became the leading occupation in Norwich by the end of the century.

There were several reasons for the decline of weaving in Norwich. As soon as Norwich manufacturers invented new fabrics they were copied more cheaply in Yorkshire. At the end of the 18th century Norwich depended on producing worsted camlets for the East India Company. Yorkshire flooded the Eastern markets with cheap imitations after the Company lost the monopoly on trade with India in 1813 and with China in 1833. When the company stopped exporting Norwich cloth it was 'a blow as serious as any [the city] had suffered since the Black Death ... Disastrous unemployment, semi-unemployment and rioting followed'. By 1845 it could be said of the city, 'It was formerly a great manufacturing city; but it has declined much of late'.[6]

The industry also declined because Norwich manufacturers failed to invest in machinery and large-scale factory-type production. In 1835 Yorkshire had 2,856 worsted power looms: as late as 1839 Norwich had only a handful in one mill. Norwich failed to introduce machinery into spinning too. In 1850 Yorkshire had 746,000 spindles, 40 times the number in Norfolk.

Some efforts *were* made to keep up with rivals. The jacquard loom was a French invention using punched cards. It was introduced in about 1833; 'by this ingenious contrivance, the most complicate patterns can be introduced upon the different fabrics, with the same ease as the plainest'. Mills intended to match those in the North were introduced to Norwich in the 1830s. The city's weavers had received their yarn from Yorkshire and elsewhere until 1834 when the Norwich Yarn Company (founded by Samuel Bignold) built their mill for spinning yarn by the river in

68   *St James's Mill, built for the Norwich Yarn Company*

St Edmund's. This employed 400 people. A second mill was built in 1836. They followed this with the St James' mill for weaving. It was built by Richard Parkinson (some books say John Brown) and had two steam engines. The rooms in the factory were let out to different manufacturers who ran about 600 power looms there.

The mills were still going in 1850 when Hunt's *Directory* wrote:

> The Yarn Co. formed in 1835 has 2 factories, the silk yarn mill on Cowgate employing 400 in spinning worsted yarn, the other in Whitefriars, built by Richard Parkinson, was worked by a steam engine and let out to various manufacturers who together employ about 1,000.

The building contained 65 spinning frames and 500 power looms. However Norwich just could not compete with Yorkshire and the Yarn Company had to admit defeat: it was wound up later in the year. The Whitefriars' mill survives, one of the most spectacular industrial monuments in the city.

In spite of the mills, the handloom worked in the weaver's own home still dominated the city scene. The loom was a large piece of furniture, as can be seen from the one on display in the Bridewell Museum. This explains a feature typical of many older Norwich houses–the unusually tall attics with dormer windows the full height of the roof. By 1900 only about 2,000 people were engaged in the textile industry and in the 1901 census there were no worsted weavers at all in the city.

Other parts of the industry did continue to flourish. Printed shawls were made in the city from the 1840s and were widely exported. One won a first-class medal at the International Exhibition in Paris in 1855. Whereas the number of worsted weavers fell from 800 in the 1851 census to about 80 in 1891, the decline in silk workers was not so drastic falling from 4,000 in 1851 to just over 1,000 in 1891. In 1849, Charles Dickens wrote to his wife Kate: 'I bought you a shawl in Norwich–I don't think much of it. It's Norwich manufacture. That's all I can say. But it's bright and cheery besides–I forgot that'.

It was the great growth in boot and shoe making that compensated for the collapse of the weaving industry. The trade employed 1,913 people in 1841 and this had increased to 6,278 in 1861 and to over 7,500 by the end of the century. Successful firms included Howlett and White, founded in 1846, Sexton, Son and Everard in about 1886 and Edwards and Holmes in 1891. The making of clothes also flourished, led by Rivett and Harmer founded in 1826 which became F. W. Harmer and Co. in 1851, setting up a new factory using sewing machines. Their factory, built in Exchange Street in 1891, was praised for its 'light and airy' conditions. The site of Hills and Underwood's was said in 1879 to occupy 10 acres; the factory obtained water from an artesian well 700 feet deep.

In the later 19th century, Norwich also became a major centre for engineering. Charles Barnard established an ironmonger's business in Norwich market place in 1826 and built the first patented wire-netting machine in 1844: the firm of Barnard, Bishop and Barnards sold this all over the world. The machines were similar to those used in the city for weaving cloth. The foundry was in Pottergate. They also made wrought-iron gates. A pair sent to an exhibition in Vienna in 1873 is now in a Vienna museum and the well-known Norwich Gates made for the entrance to Sandringham are still to be seen there. The firm also made the Slow Combustion or Norwich Stove, known as the Country Parson's Fire Grate.[8]

69   *Boulton and Paul*

William Boulton introduced wire netting machines at his Rose Lane factory in
1868. The firm became Boulton and Paul in 1869. The firm built their new office in
Rose Lane in 1899 incorporating timber from a merchant's hall discovered when slum
properties in King Street were being pulled down. They moved to a larger site across
the river in the 1920s.

William Scott began to make dynamos in 1883 and was joined in 1888 by Reginald
Laurence. The firm was a great success: new works were built in 1896 and a second
factory in 1900.

The timber merchants Jewson's were founded at Earith in Huntingdonshire in
1836 and John Jewson moved to Colegate in 1868. The firm imported timber into the
city by boat, offloading at Yarmouth. The first cargo steamer to come to Norwich was
the *Saxon Prince* carrying timber from Viburg for Jewson's.

J. & J. Colman were established as a milling firm at Stoke Holy Cross in 1804.
They moved to Norwich in 1856 and by 1900 had 2,000 employees. Colman's won
medals for their mustard and starch at Dublin in 1865 and Paris in 1868. They led the
way in good treatment of the work force and their efforts in this field are referred to
later in this chapter.

70 *Industrial Norwich, 1868 print*

A.J. Caley and Son was established as a chemist in London Street in 1860. In 1863 they started making mineral water in the back of their shop. The firm moved to Chapel Field Road in 1883 and started making cocoa, followed by chocolate in 1886. In 1898 they began making crackers but they continued to make mineral water using water drawn from two artesian wells on the site 400 feet and 500 feet deep. Coleman's began making tonic wine in the 1880s and was later famous for its tonic wine Wincarnis.

Norwich continued to be a major brewing centre in the 19th century. Because of the predominance of the large brewers, Norwich had a lower proportion of pubs brewing their own beer than anywhere else in England. The 1830 Excise Returns show that in the country as a whole one public house in three was brewing its own beer but in Norwich there were only 37 brewing victuallers and 1,070 victuallers.

The Anchor Brewery was founded beside Coslany Bridge by Richard Bullard and James Watts in 1837. Ten years later the partnership was dissolved and Bullard carried on alone. His son Harry Bullard joined the family business and by the end of the century the site covered seven acres. The brewery used water drawn from an artesian well dug into the chalk beneath the brewery site.

71   *Norwich Market Place in the later 19th century*

The other big breweries were Steward and Patteson in Barrack Street, Youngs, Crawshay and Youngs in King Street and Morgan's also in King Street. The last developed from tragic beginnings; in May 1845 Walter Morgan who, with his brother, had just bought Thompson's Brewery in King Street was found drowned in the fermenting vat there–he was only 23 years old.[9]

There was a wide range of other trades of the kind to be found in any large county town. To take just one example, in 1845 Norwich soap makers made over one and a half million tons of soap. Newspaper printing continued and expanded–the *Norfolk Chronicle* and the *Norwich Mercury* were both published once a week. They included international, national and county news: sensational local murder cases like the Yarham and Rush cases described below took up many pages including special supplements. They featured local advertising too. In December 1843 Mr. Beard of the Royal Bazaar was the first person in Norwich to advertise photographic portraits. Each paper had its own political viewpoint and the *Norfolk News* was founded in 1845 by a group of Liberal Nonconformists dissatisfied with the views of the *Norwich Mercury*.

Printing and publishing was boosted when Jarrold and Sons moved to Norwich from Suffolk in 1823. Their most successful book was *Black Beauty* by Norwich writer Anna Sewell, discussed later in this chapter.

72 *The Crown Bank, later the Post Office*

The Provision and Cattle Markets continued to be the heart of Norwich. Orders for the Markets issued in 1872 show that the provision market was normally open every day including Sunday from dawn until very late. In 1882 it was ordered to close at 10 p.m. instead of 11.30 p.m. on Saturdays. Market tolls were 3d 'for every Stall Ped or other Standing' which was not to exceed three feet in width without special permission of the Collector.[10]

Ber Street was known as 'Blood and Guts Street' in the 19th century because of all the butchers–hence the pub name *The Jolly Butchers*. Cows were driven along the Street from Trowse to the cattle market. Once the railway was opened the main traffic came by train–Trowse station had a huge area of animal holding pens.

Fire was an ever-present danger in the city. In October 1822 the chandling office of Staff and Chamberlin in St Martin at Palace burnt down. The tallow ran into the river and more than ten cartloads of it were skimmed off the surface of the water by people in boats. On 26 June 1839, the factory of a cabinet maker Mr. Bush of Roach's Court, Fisher's Lane was destroyed by fire together with the adjoining house of a silk weaver who lost his machinery and his stock of silk. 'The fire engines were not in a state for such an emergency and many of the leather pipes had to be tied together with handkerchiefs.'[11]

On 20 December 1806 the Norwich Fire Office announced that its travelling fire engine was to be kept at St Peter Mancroft church, from where it could be obtained by sending a man and two horses. In 1808 Thomas Bignold set up a separate office for life insurance: the total funds of the life office were £1 million in 1830 and £2 million by 1890. He was followed by his son Samuel Bignold who was secretary of both the Fire and Life Insurance Societies for nearly 60 years. In 1864 the Norwich Union took over the Amicable Society which was the world's first life insurance society founded in 1706 by Samuel Talbot, Bishop of Oxford: his statue now graces one wing of Skipper's Norwich Union building. An office to cover insurance of accidents was set up in Norwich in 1856 and merged with the Fire Office in 1908.

Harvey and Hudson's Bank was founded in 1792 by James Hudson and Robert Harvey: its offices were in King Street. Hudson had previously been in the banking partnership of Hudson and Hatfield who had run a bank in Haymarket from at least 1783. The bank descended through several generations of the Harvey family to Robert Harvey, who built the Crown Bank premises at the top of Prince of Wales Road in 1866. The new bank was praised by the 1868 *Directory*: 'The building altogether is very handsome, stands in a fine position, and is a great ornament to the city'. Safety considerations were not forgotten; 'the whole building is also as fire-proof as it is possible to make it'. Two years later the Bank came to a dramatic end when Harvey shot himself in the grounds of his house at Crown Point on 15 July 1870, dying three days later. The Bank never reopened its doors and it emerged that Harvey had been using bank money for years to speculate on the Stock Exchange. The fall in prices following the outbreak of the Franco-Prussian War had ruined him.

Housing and Health

The Victorian period saw a massive increase in the city's housing stock, mainly in terraced housing in the suburbs. In 1821 there were 10,833 houses in Norwich, an increase of 2,300 in the previous ten years. The 1881 census records 19,777 inhabited houses with 1,011 uninhabited and 246 being built.

Squalor and overcrowding were common in all major cities in England and Norwich was no exception, especially as the weaving trade declined. The Health of Towns Commissioners reported:

> Norwich, it is feared, has seen its best days as a place of commerce, and would appear to be in that painful state of transition from once flourishing manufacturing prosperity to its entire decline, and must, ere long, revert to its original condition as a capital of an extensive agricultural district. A large portion of its inhabitants are therefore poor, their labour becoming daily lowered in amount and recompense ... Neglect and decay are now conspicuous in the streets and quarters occupied by the working classes, so as to render them places of the most dismal aspect.[12]

73   *Working-class housing near to St Peter Mancroft church*

Working-class people lived mainly in courts or yards housing anything up to 40 families and with a single doorway leading into the street. These yards often had a single pump for water and unbelievably primitive toilet arrangements. In 1900 there were over 700 yards; their houses often backed onto those of the next yard, so that the only windows were in the front wall of the house. Some yards which were below the level of the main streets were known as 'holes' and where they were near the river these were always wet. Such houses would be let out for £3 to £5 a year, with some single room properties at £2 or £3 a year. Terraced housing was developing outside the city walls from the early 19th century, starting with the very low quality speculative housing at Peafield in Lakenham. Small houses could be rented for £5 to £7 a year: these houses usually had four rooms but often they were shared by more than one family to save expense. By the 1820s larger estates were built at Crook's Place and Union Place. Railway cottages in Thorpe built in the 1840s still survive with their triangular communal court.

Fire was a killer in these crowded houses with open hearths and the inquest papers record many deaths, especially among the very young and the very old. A typical example from 1817 is Maria Beales aged nine, whose clothes caught alight when she went to take a boiling kettle off the fire in her father's house.[13] She was taken to the Norfolk and Norwich Hospital where she died of her injuries.

Of course, not all housing was poor quality. The city had no control over houses already built but it owned much of the land within the city walls and could control the quality of new houses built on its land by stipulating the minimum annual rents and sanitary requirements. Some of the high quality housing put up from the 1820s onwards survives at the Crescent, the Town Close estate and Victoria Street. By the beginning of the 19th century the richest families like the Harveys, the Gurneys and the Custances had moved out of the city and their places were taken by managers and clerks. By the middle of the century the better paid artisans were moving out too–into newly built houses in the suburbs. The population of Heigham rose from 842 in 1811 to 5,932 in 1841.

The 1851 Census is the first to give exact ages and places of birth.[14] It shows that, although there was a considerable movement of people into Norwich, it was not nearly so great as into the cities of the North. The census shows that the great part of the city's population still lived in crowded streets and yards. In tiny Flower Pot Yard, off Oak Street, there were seven households. Five of the householders were weavers. There were 22 children living in the yard and out of all its inhabitants, young and old, only one had not been born in Norfolk. The wealthy lived in streets like Bank Plain, where the eight households employed between them 15 live-in servants (there were none in Flower Pot Yard). The people of Bank Plain were small businessmen. Their origins were different too–half the Bank Plain householders were born outside the county.

The movements of a more migratory population can be picked up from the census as well. In three inns on Ber Street–the *Fox and Hounds*, the *Jolly Butchers* and the *Bull's Head*–there were 34 lodgers born in all parts of Britain, including one each from Scotland and Ireland. The impact of the railway on jobs is shown in that five of these lodgers (all under 30) were railway workers. Older ways were represented by the Scotsman James Briggs, a 50-year-old drover.

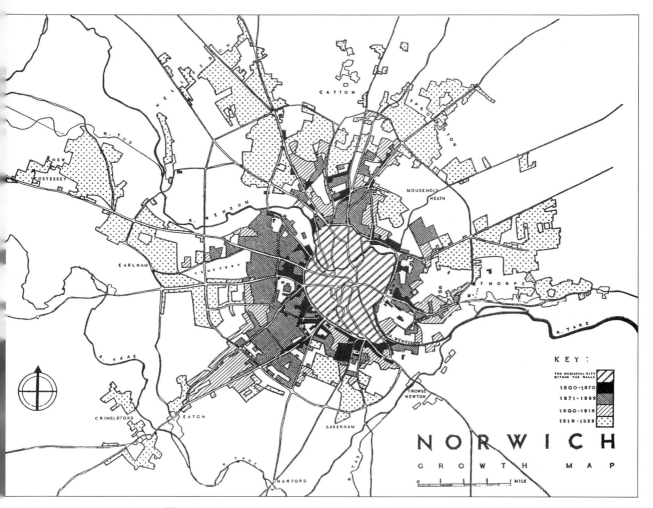

74   The growth of the city suburbs, taken from *The Norwich Plan*

Norwich's first housing by laws followed the Local Government Act of 1858. New regulations came in from 1889; the minimum room height was to be eight feet, and there had to be 150 feet of open space at the rear. Plans for new houses had to be submitted to the City Council and from 1877 these plans survive as a complete record of new building in the city.

The years after 1877 saw the development of the terraced house in the suburbs, especially off the Earlham, Dereham and Unthank Roads. The process took several stages. The owners of farm land outside the city sold it to developers who undertook the layout of streets and sewers. They might build the houses themselves or, more commonly, divide them into plots for small firms to do the actual building work.

The houses were then bought in blocks by landlords who rented them out. Standards were enforced by the original ground landlords who put covenants into the title deeds which the builders and later inhabitants had to obey. This might dictate the minimum rent to ensure that only the desired class of person could afford the house,

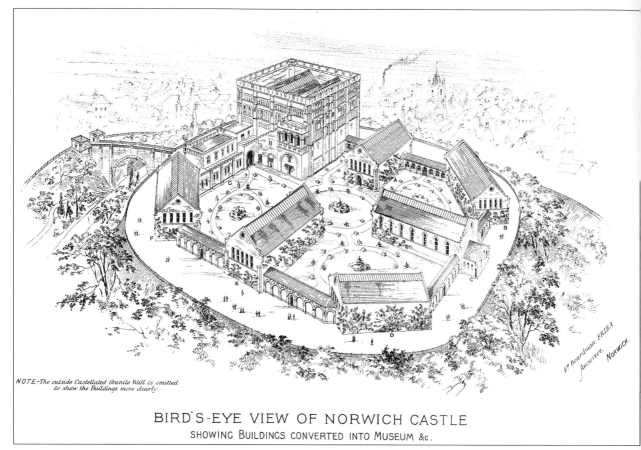

NOTE:-The outside Castellated Granite Wall is omitted
to shew the Buildings more clearly.

BIRD'S-EYE VIEW OF NORWICH CASTLE
SHOWING BUILDINGS CONVERTED INTO MUSEUM &c.

75 *Edward Boardman's plan to convert the castle into a museum*

or it might stipulate that any building be used as a house and nothing else–this is why shops and public houses are usually found on corners. Because the development was later than in the industrial cities, the Corporation was able to enforce building regulations and the horrors of back to back houses were avoided. Characteristic Norwich terraced houses have a small front garden (only a few streets do not have this) and a yard at the back with a toilet, rear access and often a small garden. Few have basements or third storeys.

Most smaller houses were still rented rather than purchased but there was a growth in the owner-occupier market and its development can be traced through local records. In 1865 a dwelling-house facing Chapel Field Road, containing an Entrance-hall, front Sitting-room, Kitchen, Scullery, Pantry, and Cellar, and four bedrooms occupied at the yearly rent of £16, was purchased for £195. In 1899, 4 Eastbourne Place, with five bedrooms on two floors, was bought by Walter Morris, a Norwich cycle manufacturer, for £410.[15] Co-operation between private enterprise and the City is illustrated by Isaac Coaks, who laid out the streets of terraced houses on the Hill in Thorpe Hamlet and who gave land to the council for a school. The names of his six daughters are recorded in the names of the roads–Ethel, Ella, Florence, Marion, Beatrice and Primrose.

The first slum clearance programme began in 1877. In 1899 the City Council acquired the power to compel the owners of courts and yards to clear them.

Edward Boardman, founder of the firm Boardman and Son, practised in the city from 1860 to 1900. He was the architect of some of the most important buildings in Victorian Norwich. They include the rebuilding of the Norfolk and Norwich Hospital, the conversion of the

76   *The Royal Arcade, the east window*

castle from a prison to a museum, the *Royal Hotel*, the London Street Improvement Scheme of 1876-1880, and a large number of 'villas' on the Unthank, Newmarket and Ipswich Roads. He also designed the Alexandra Mansions on the Prince of Wales Road, perhaps the first residential flats in Norwich and now part-occupied by a cinema. His work on the Norfolk and Norwich Hospital is discussed later in the chapter. Three successive generations of the Boardman family were to be prominent architects in the city, spanning a period from the 1860s to 1968. Some 20,000 of the firm's plans are held at the Norfolk Record Office.

The other famous Norwich architect was George Skipper, who built the Royal Arcade in art nouveau style with glazed Doulton tiles decorated with peacocks. It was

77   *The Agricultural Hall*

78   *The* Royal Hotel

opened in 1899 on the site of the *Royal Hotel.* A local newspaper said, 'it is as if a
fragment of the Arabian nights had been dropped into the heart of the old City'.[16]

The City also committed itself to improvements in its infrastructure. The building
of Thorpe station led to a new main route developing along London Street, Castle
Ditches and Rose Lane but this route soon became choked with wagons. Small schemes
for widening London Street were put into practice. The London Street Improvement
Committee was set up in 1876 and the street and nearby roads were widened over the
next few years. The architect was Edward Boardman: the Venetian-style buildings at
the Market Place end of London Street are a legacy of this scheme.

Prince of Wales Road was built in the 1860s to provide a wide direct route to the
station and it was taken over by the council in 1865. They pulled down part of the old
city wall at Chapelfield and used it as rubble for the new road: obviously they had not
yet begun to think about preserving the city's historic heritage. A new and much wider
Foundry bridge was built, the old one being taken down and re-erected at Heigham.

The Foundry bridge built then is the present bridge—Pevsner and Wilson are wrong to say it has been removed.[17]

Some of the finest large buildings of Victorian Norwich are on Agricultural Hall Plain. The Crown Bank has already been mentioned. After the bank collapsed it became a post office. Next door is the red brick Agricultural Hall designed by J.B. Pearse and built in 1882. The building was still new when Oscar Wilde visited Norwich in 1884 and lectured here: his subject was 'The House Beautiful'. Opposite is the *Royal Hotel*, designed by Edward Boardman in a very different style from his heavy Nonconformist chapels: no doubt there was plenty of money to be put into Norwich's most prestigious hotel, with its easy access to the railway. The date is 1896-7. All three of these buildings are now used by Anglia Television who have preserved all the frontages.

In the 1870s wood paving was introduced to London Street and by 1883 most of the city centre streets had been paved with wood—over 17,000 square yards in all. Main roads like Newmarket Road, St Stephen's and Ipswich Road had macadamised all-weather surfaces as early as

79   *St John Maddermarket parish pump*

1835. In 1881 the City Council decided to extend its scheme of electric lights from the two it had put up in the Market Place to the principal streets: however, this was discontinued in 1883. In 1891 the prospectus of the Norwich Electricity Company was published and capital of £50,000 was raised in 5,000 shares of £10 each.

It was in the second half of the century that the twin problems of supply of fresh water and disposal of sewage were solved. As we saw in the last chapter, the Norwich Water Company took water from the river at New Mills to its reservoir at Chapelfield. However, it supplied only the houses of those willing and able to pay, and even these could only have water for a few hours each day. The water was unfiltered. As late as 1849, only 3,000 of the 15,000 or so houses in the city had access to this supply.

Most people were still using wells or the river. There were 10 public pumps in the city but unfortunately five of them adjoined churchyards, like the pump at the bottom of St John Maddermarket churchyard which survives to this day. The 2,000 people in Peafield had eight pumps and two wells between them. Supply from the river was also extremely unhealthy. Two of the worst cases are quoted in the *Mercury* report of 1850. In Water Lane people were taking their water from directly below the dye works and the water was coloured according to the dye being used. People found brown coloured water the best–'the black spoiled the tea and so did the scarlet'. The worst situation of all was Crown Court Yard in St Benedict's where 200 people had no water at all except what they fetched from the staithe. There was only one privy in the Yard and that emptied into the river just three feet upstream from the staithe; 'parties fetching water first tried the [privy] door to see if anyone was inside. If so, they waited'.[18]

In May 1850 William Lee, a government health inspector, visited the city. He noted that the city graveyards were full and were scattered with fragments of bones. He said of the city water supply, 'bad in quality and bad in everything that should constitute a water supply'.[19]

The water supply was revolutionised in the 1850s. In 1854 the city drew up an agreement with Foster and Peale, plumbers of London, to supply water to the City of Norwich in lead pipes. A new Water Company was set up and this successfully improved the water quality which was described as 'very good indeed' by the Norwich Sanitary Inspector in 1869.

The polluted state of the Wensum got worse as the population grew and as more factories were set up. In 1866 the parish of Thorpe threatened to obtain an injunction against the city for the polluted state of the river. (Thorpe is the next place downstream and depended on the river for its own water.) Steps were taken by the city after an *Act for the Better Sewering of Norwich* had been passed in 1867. Two sewers were built, one on each side of the Wensum, running down to Whitlingham where a sewage farm was opened. The total cost of the scheme was £120,000. The first sewers were badly built and had to be repaired in 1887: many of the drains built by these Victorian engineers are still in use today.

As the century passed there were rising expectations in hygiene among the middle classes. The Social Science Association held an exhibition of 'sanitary appliances' in Norwich in 1873: it was so popular it had to be extended by public demand. Lambert comments: 'That so many should flock to examine water-closets, stink-pipes and the like indicates not only the widespread interest in sanitary affairs, but the recreational poverty of much mid-Victorian town life.'[20] However, the process of connecting all the poorer houses in the city to the sewers was a fairly gradual one–as late as 1893 there were 20,000 houses still without water closets. They were still using privies or a midden–these were emptied at the city's expense but they were never cleaned.

The diseases most characteristic of the 19th century were smallpox, cholera and typhus. In the 19th century vaccination slowly replaced inoculation in the fight against smallpox. In 1805 it was announced that nearly 400 of the poor in the city had been vaccinated. In 1812 Edward Rigby persuaded the Guardians of the Poor to pay 2s. 6d. to any of the poor who produced a certificate of vaccination and the scheme made Rigby nationally famous. However, smallpox broke out in 1813 with 65 deaths in the city and again in 1819 when there were over 500 deaths from smallpox in Norwich between January and September, nearly all of children. There were several other outbreaks later in the century with an epidemic in the spring of 1872: at its height 30 people a week were dying of smallpox in the city. The Roman Catholic priest Edmund Costello died at the Willow Lane presbytery on 2 July 1872, his death hastened by his work among the poor during the smallpox epidemic.[21]

Cholera reached England in 1831 and the Corporation prepared for it by issuing orders for cleaning the city in the same year. They were not successful; cholera reached Norwich the following year. There were 320 cases of the disease in the city between August and October 1832: 128 people died.

The Board of Health issued advice to avoid getting cholera:

1. Above all things be strictly temperate: for drunkards and persons of loose irregular habits, are among its first and most hopeless victims.

2. Avoid food which is difficult of digestion, such as uncooked fruit and vegetables, pickled fish, hard, salted and pickled meat, heavy dumplings and stale or sour beer. The best diet is stale bread, milk, mealy potatoes in moderation, and rice or bread puddings, with the addition of plain roast and boiled meat, if it be within your reach. Carefully avoid heavy suppers.

3. Keep your persons, your clothes, bedding, house and furniture clean; sweep up your house and put everything into its proper place at least once daily; and suffer no filth of any kind to remain near your house. Allow fresh air freely to enter your house; but be careful to keep it dry.

4. Go to bed early–avoid loitering about in the evening, or in low damp places, or near water;–if you become wet do not sit in your wet clothes; and especially keep your feet warm and dry;–avoid as much as possible great fatigue; and if you are tired and hot, by no means expose yourself to currents of cold air.

5. Guard against anger and other violent passions, and endeavour to keep your mind tranquil and your temper even.[22]

The outbreaks of cholera led to a concern for health in cities. From the 1850s it was forbidden to bury people in the overcrowded city churchyards and municipal cemeteries were set up. At one time the Corporation intended to put a cemetery on Mousehold Heath but in the end land in Earlham was purchased from John Cater in 1855: the Earlham Road cemetery is still in use. As late as March 1893 an outbreak of cholera was feared in the city and preventive measures were announced.

Typhoid was endemic throughout the century: there were 98 deaths in 1898.

The charity hospitals developed throughout the century. The Bethel Hospital had several unfortunate incidents. In 1813 the Master, James Bullard, was murdered by a patient. In 1833 a patient called Elizabeth Westbury hanged herself with her pocket handkerchief which she had fastened with wire to a beam: it was ordered that all the clothing of patients be removed from their cells at night. In 1899 a female criminal lunatic escaped by jumping through a window. She was recaptured at Lewes in Sussex and brought back but it was decided not to accept criminal lunatics in future, except in very special circumstances.[23]

However the general tone at the Bethel continued to be one of charity and concern. In 1832 the Master was authorised to procure a person to sit up at night with any patient who appeared to need it. In 1897 a grateful patient who had experienced cruelty in five other asylums wanted Mary Chapman's tomb at Thorpe renovated and

80   *Norfolk and Norwich Hospital as rebuilt in the 19th century*

this was done at the Governors' expense. The usual 19th-century improvements were made. Gas was introduced in the winter of 1848-1849 and 'proper washing places' for the patients in that of 1851-1852. The Victorian religious revival was embraced: in 1860, after a letter from Lord Shaftesbury, the Master and Matron began to read prayers to the patients each day after breakfast. Electric light was introduced in 1896.

There was an innovation of great importance to the patients of the Norfolk and Norwich Hospital in 1847: chloroform was used there for the first time. The *Norfolk Chronicle* described the occasion:

> A young woman had her leg amputated after having inhaled the fumes from a convenient apparatus. She became perfectly insensible to pain, and continued so throughout the operation. Her sensations were apparently of a very happy description, as she partly amused herself by singing psalms in a very clear and distinct voice, and partly by holding lively conversations with imaginary persons during the performance of this painful operation.[24]

One of the leading doctors at the Hospital was John Green Crosse, who wrote an account of the Norwich smallpox outbreak of 1819. He died in 1850 and is buried in the cathedral cloister green, which was then the parish graveyard for St Mary in the

Marsh and was crowded with tombstones: his is one of the few that have not been removed. His daughter Lavinia Crosse founded the Anglican community of All Hallows, Ditchingham in 1854.

The Norfolk and Norwich Hospital was almost completely rebuilt by Boardman and Wyatt in 1879-1883. At one stage it was proposed to pull down all of the old building but in the end one wing was kept: this saved about £2,000. Sir Thomas Wyatt was a famous London architect who had designed Knightsbridge Barracks and the Adelphi Theatre. Later, Boardman complained that Wyatt took the credit while Boardman did the work. Wyatt was already very ill even before he undertook the commission. He died on 5 August 1880, and Boardman continued alone: the first stage of the work was opened on 30 June 1881. His achievement was acknowledged in an anonymous booklet: 'Mr. Boardman's name must ever be associated with a structure which is hardly less admirable for the soundness and just proportions of the fabric, than sacred and venerable for the ends which in time to come it is intended to subserve'.[25]

A new children's hospital in Norwich was built after Jenny Lind, the singer known as the 'Swedish Nightingale', gave two charity concerts at St Andrew's Hall in

1849. Jenny Lind's two concerts raised just over £1,250 and with the proceeds land was bought in Pottergate and a hospital for sick children was built, with 12 beds and an out-patients department. The Jenny Lind had high standards–no nurse was to be engaged who could not read and write. In 1897 a new hospital was begun on Colman Road, using money from the Queen Victoria diamond jubilee fund. This hospital opened in 1900 but the out-patients department in Pottergate continued until 1929. In 1898 James Jeremiah Colman bought the old hospital site in Pottergate and gave it to the city as a park in memory of his son Alan who had died the previous year. The park had an imposing gateway. By 1970 there were few children living in the Pottergate area so the park, with the gateway, was transferred to its present site near the Norfolk and Norwich Hospital.

Slow steps were taken to improve care of the mentally ill. The county led the way; the Norfolk County Lunatic Asylum was built at Thorpe in 1814. In 1828 the city built 'a new Bethel at the Infirmary without St Augustine's Gates' on the site of the pest house there which had become an asylum for aged and infirm paupers: it was capable of holding only 19 lunatics. This was not big enough for its purpose and from the 1840s the Commissioners in Lunacy criticised Norwich's provision for the insane. Under an Act of 1863 the city was ordered to make proper provision for its lunatics. The hospital was transferred from the Board of Guardians to the city. A report of 1865 found the place unsuitable for expansion: 'the whole place is hopelessly bad, and it would be a disgrace to the City of Norwich to attempt to apply it to the permanent use of an asylum'.[26]

After 40 years of pressure the city opened a new asylum at Hellesdon in 1880. It was designed to house 311 patients and was jointly funded by the councils of Norwich, Yarmouth, Thetford, Lynn and Bury St Edmunds. The hospital passed to the state in 1948. There were also private madhouses in the city for those whose relatives could afford them; that at Heigham Hall opened in 1833 and did not close until 1960. The private madhouses were supervised by the city magistrates. A supposed scandal at Heigham Hall came before Quarter Sessions in 1854. It appears that a clergyman called Edmund Holmes had raped a girl in Hethersett in 1852: the girl was under 12 years old. Holmes had then had himself admitted to the asylum in order to avoid being charged with the rape. By 1854 he had become the asylum's chaplain. He appears never to have been charged with the crime, although the magistrates did decide he was not a fit person to be chaplain.[27]

In one way Norwich (together with Sheffield) led the way in its treatment of the sick poor. The Guardians of the Poor in these two towns provided medicines. A separate apothecary was employed to dispense the drugs: this meant the doctor could order what he thought the patient needed, without having to consider the cost to himself. The dispensary was at the workhouse and the doctors gave the sick prescription notes to take there–or the doctor would visit if the patient was too ill to get up. The doctors were under strict instructions to give treatment only to the destitute.[28] During the cholera outbreak of 1832, the Workhouse Committee was instructed 'that strong neat soup, and boiled down rice, and well spiced, be prepared and kept in the Workhouse, ready for the paupers attacked with Diarrhoea or Cholera'. This was not just for inmates; poor people living in their own homes could also partake, provided they produced a doctor's certificate.

Small private charities continued. A free hospital for incurables was established in 1852 by William Webber in Willow Lane and, according to the 1854 *Directory*, 'is chiefly supported by that gentleman'.

During the 19th century many bodies were set up with responsibility for health matters such as local health boards, highway boards, school boards, sanitary boards and poor law unions. The Public Health Act of 1872 pulled them together under the control of the Urban Sanitary Authority. The first Medical Officer for Health for the City was appointed in 1873. In his first report he noted that more than a quarter of the deaths in the city were of children under five. He blamed bad diet, bad housing and the use of opiates. He found that many parents did not want their children vaccinated against smallpox and some did not register their children's births in order to avoid this.

The Lancet reported that in the period 1870 to 1878 Norwich had the highest mortality rate of 20 large towns that it surveyed. The birth rate was also very high at 32 per thousand—about ten per cent were illegitimate. The Norwich Improvement Act of 1879 gave the city power to enforce the notification of infectious diseases and this led to the detection of many sources of impure water. In 1878 Colman's appointed the first known industrial nurse in the world, Philippa Flowerday.[29]

Giving birth continued to be a home event with the aid of a city midwife. These included Phoebe Crew who died in 1817: according to her tombstone in St Helen's church she had brought into the world 9,730 children in 40 years' practice. A stone in St Etheldreda churchyard commemorated Elizabeth Elvin, who died in 1849 and 'during 30 years practice as a midwife in this city brought into the world 8529 children'.

Although the first year of life and childbirth were dangerous, people who survived them might live longer than is often thought. The 1854 *Directory* cites seven Norwich people who had lived to be over 100 in the 19th century: only one was male.

Crime and Punishment

There was a gradual liberalisation of the treatment of criminals through the century. Hangings continued to be a popular public spectacle outside the castle until 1867 and transportation to the colonies was abolished the following year. Charles Dickens, who was fascinated by public hangings, wrote to a friend in 1849, 'Norwich, a disappointment, all save its place of execution, which is fit for a gigantic scoundrel's exit'.[30]

Samuel Yarham, who murdered Harriet Candler at Yarmouth, was executed outside the castle on 11 April 1846. This was the same day as Tombland Fair and, according to the *Norfolk Chronicle*,

> 800 persons came from Wymondham in one train; it was found necessary to use bullock-trucks to convey the people, there not being a sufficient number of regular carriages ... After the execution, gongs, drums and other instruments commenced their uproar, mountebanks and clowns their antics, the vendors of wares and exhibitors of prodigies their cries, while the whirligigs and ups-and-downs were soon in full swing. The public-houses round the Hill were crowded, and hundreds finished the day in riot and intoxication.

A total of 30,000 spectators watched the hanging.[31]

There were similar huge crowds three years later when the double murderer James Blomfield Rush was hanged. Cheap return tickets were issued to Norwich from London, with police boarding the trains at Attleborough to turn off known trouble-makers. Many people were disgusted at the revelry and when Hubbard Lingley was hanged in August 1867 it was done at eight o'clock on a Monday morning to discourage crowds. This turned out to be the last public execution in Norwich: later hangings were held in the castle in private.

The first private hanging in fact involved a sensational case. In June 1851 the hand of a woman was found in Miss Martineau's Plantation in Martineau Lane by a boy called Charles Johnson. Other pieces of the woman turned up, scattered throughout the suburbs of the city. They were kept in spirits of wine in the Guildhall, but the victim could not be identified.

Nearly 20 years later, on 1 January 1869, a man called William Sheward walked in to the Carter Street police station in London and said, 'I have killed my wife. I have kept the secret for years, but I can keep it no longer'. Sheward was living in Tabernacle Street in Norwich when his wife suddenly disappeared in June 1851: at the time he said she had gone away in search of a former lover. In fact he had cut her throat during an argument. He kept her body until it started to smell and then dismembered it, boiling arms and feet on his stove in the hope they would dissolve. Sheward was hanged in the city gaol on 20 April 1869. (Sheward may have been inspired by James Greenacre, a Norfolk-born man who, when he was living in London, killed his mistress, dismembered her body and scattered it across the capital. The case created a great sensation and over 16,000 people watched Greenacre's execution at Newgate on 2 May 1837.)[32]

Sheward was a pawn-broker and is supposed by some to have cut his wife to pieces on the pledging counter in his shop on Orford Hill. This counter was still in use in 1982 and the founder of the firm of W. and G. Boston recalled that he used to sleep on it when he was an apprentice.

A macabre event occurred at the hanging of Robert Goodale at Norwich Castle in 1885. The *Norfolk Chronicle* reported:

> The lever was pulled, the trap-door fell, and the prisoner who weighed 15 stone and was 5ft. 11ins. in height, and was allowed a drop just short of 6 feet, disappeared from view. To the horror of the bystanders the rope rebounded, and it was thought that by some means it had become unfastened. On looking into the pit below the scaffold the spectators observed the body lying on the ground, with the head still enveloped in the white cap, completely severed from the trunk.[33]

On 13 December 1875 Robert Edwards, a 42-year-old weaver from Marsham, ran amok in the children's ward in the Norfolk and Norwich Hospital. He grabbed a pair of tongs from the fireplace and attacked the young patients killing four boys–William Martin aged 14, John Lacey aged 10, Joseph Colman aged 11 and Alfred Clarke aged nine. The last lingered of his wounds for two months before he died. Edwards was disarmed by the bravery of the house surgeon, Mr. Baumgartner, and sent to Broadmoor, a hospital for the criminally insane. Edwards had been admitted to the Hospital with psychiatric problems on the recommendation of his local clergyman.[34]

In 1898 questions were asked in Parliament about a boy called Robert Cooper, who was put to work at the treadmill in the castle even though he said he was ill. He was kept at work for several days and his bed was taken from him as a punishment: after a few days he was found dead in his cell. Perhaps it is his ghost that now haunts the loading bays of Castle Mall.

Just over 500 people are recorded in the Norwich Quarter Sessions records as being sentenced to transportation between 1788 and 1856. After 1856 there were no more transportation sentences from this court although the system was not abolished until 1868. The convicts all went to Australia. The peak decades were the 1820s to the 1840s with an average of about fifteen people a year being transported. Their crimes were almost always stealing or receiving stolen goods. More serious crimes like murder and rape were dealt with at the Assize Courts and might lead to transportation (often an original sentence of death was on appeal commuted to transportation). As might be expected, it was a mainly young and male population that was being excluded from society. The youngest was William Tuck, who was only eight years old when he was sentenced to transportation in 1839 for stealing two bottles from doorsteps.[35]

Although the length of sentence of transportation was fixed, the crown did not pay for a passage home so it was in effect for many a life sentence. The end of transportation meant that more prison accommodation was needed. The efforts of Elizabeth Fry, John Howard and other prison reformers resulted in higher standards of prison accommodation. Norwich's new prison at Mousehold was completed in 1887. Prisoners were moved there from the castle which had served as a county prison since 1345 and from the city gaol on Earlham Road. The Castle was bought by the City Council and opened as a museum in 1894.

Religion

The 1851 Religious census asked people what church they had attended the previous Sunday. The people of Norwich divided into three almost equal groups. One third had been to an Anglican church, one third to a Nonconformist place of worship and one third had not been to any place of worship. The Nonconformists were divided into many groups, of course. Even the Methodists (by far the largest group) were split into four movements each with their own chapels: the Wesleyan Methodists, the Primitive Methodists, Wesleyan Reform and the Countess of Huntingdon's Connexion.[36]

Several Nonconformist chapels were put up in the 19th century, such as the massive block making up the Prince's Street Congregational church and associated buildings. This was built by Edward Boardman between 1869 and 1879. He worshipped there himself and it is now called Boardman House. Boardman built the Methodist Chapel at Chapelfield too and worked at St Mary's Baptist chapel: this was destroyed in the last war but has since been rebuilt. The fine 1810 Calvert Street chapel belonging to the Methodists was pulled down by the City Council and the Congregational chapel of 1858 at Chapelfield has also gone. Other faiths were also building; the Jewish synagogue in St Faith's Lane was opened in 1849. This too was destroyed by bombs in the Second World War.

81   *St Matthew, Thorpe Hamlet, by local architect John Brown*

The Salvation Army came to the city in 1882. The Norwich Skating Rink between Bethel Street and St Giles had opened for roller skating in 1876 but folded for lack of support in less than four years. The Salvation Army bought the building in 1882, converted it at a cost of £290, and it was open shortly before General Booth made his first visit to Norwich on 9 September 1882. Booth urged his followers to 'Get a drum and arouse Norwich from end to end'. The first leader in Norwich was a woman, Captain Harkey. The present St Giles citadel was opened in 1892 and the Skating Rink later became a builders' store. (The building still stands, now being used as a shop.)

In 1870 the Roman Catholic community in Norwich amounted to about 1,200 people with 215 children at Catholic schools. In 1869 six sisters of the teaching order of Notre Dame arrived at the Catholic school in Ten Bell Lane and in 1870 they opened a boarding and day school for girls. The end of the century saw the building of St John's Catholic church, 'an amazing church, proof of Victorian generosity and optimism' according to Pevsner.[37] It was built by the Duke of Norfolk, thus renewing the connection between the Dukes and the city that had been severed in 1708. It was begun in 1884 on the site of the city prison and was not finished until 1910. The architects were George Gilbert Scott junior and his brother John Oldrid Scott. The church has some fine stained glass by John and Dunstan Powell. After it was opened, the former Willow Lane church became a school.

The Church of England had a revival too, some clergymen doing vital work among the poor of the slum parishes. One of them was Samuel Stone of St John de Sepulchre who died in 1848 and is commemorated in the east window there. In the 19th century, Anglican churches were built for the expanding population of the sub-urbs, including Christ Church, New Catton (1841-2); St Mark, Hall Road (1844); St Matthew, Thorpe Hamlet (1851); Holy Trinity, Essex Street (1860-1); Christ Church, Eaton (1873); St Philip, Heigham Road (1868); St Thomas, Earlham Road (1886).

Several of the city centre churches were neglected for much of the century. A late 19th-century newspaper article says:

> It is fourteen years ago and more now since matins and evensong were said or sung in St Mary's Coslany. St Mary's indeed has long been an eye-sorrow and is now rapidly becoming a nuisance and a source of positive danger to those who live near it ... if among those who live in that neighbourhood of yards and slums there is one who has a dead cat or dog for which he can find no place of burial, in the carcase goes, through the fine old traceried windows, every pane of which has long been smashed out.[38]

There was a growing interest in the buildings, however, and by the end of the century every Anglican church had been restored except St Helen and St Simon and St Jude.

Norwich led the way in a revival of Anglican monasticism. Joseph Leycester Lyne was an Anglican who had become convinced it was his calling to restore to England the monastic life lost when Henry VIII dissolved the monasteries. He gathered together a few followers in Claydon, Suffolk, and in January 1846 they moved to Norwich, taking over a rag merchant's house in Elm Hill. The vicar of St Lawrence, Mr. Hillyard, offered to give them daily communion so the 'monks' would walk there in their robes each morning. They were shouted at and sometimes assaulted and Lyne had to ask for police protection. Lyne now started calling himself Father Ignatius.

Lyne built himself a church behind Elm Hill which still exists and is now used by the Art School. The building is still recognisably a church although its entrance has been altered. This must have been put up in about 1868 as the *Norfolk Chronicle* of 16 January 1869 mentions the 'so-called monastic chapel newly erected at Elm Hill'. Lyne's monastery dissolved when he had a nervous breakdown—he later founded one at Llanthony in Wales.

Popular superstitions had not changed much through the centuries, however. The *Norfolk Chronicle* reported a case in 1843 when a Mrs. Kedge complained to the magistrates that a Mrs. Clarke had bewitched her 'by sending her and her children a vast number of vermin'. Two months later the city magistrates had another witchcraft case to deal with. Mr. and Mrs. Curtis claimed to have been bewitched by a Mrs. Bell:

> Mrs. Curtis saw Mrs. Bell light a candle and fill it with pins. She then put some red dragon's blood, with some water, into an oyster-shell, and having repeated a form of words over it, her husband's arms and legs were set fast, and when he lay down he could not get up again without somebody helping him.

Transport

Pull's Ferry was known for most of its life as Sandling's. Sandling, who had been a chorister at the cathedral in the reign of Queen Elizabeth, kept the ferry in the early 17th century: according to Sir Thomas Browne he lived to be 89. The ferry was named after him until the death of John Pull, who kept the ferry and the adjoining inn from 1796 to 1841, when the licence for the inn lapsed. In 1881 it was planned to extend the railway from City station along the river edge of the Close to a point opposite Thorpe station. This would of course have meant destroying Pull's Ferry. The plan was strongly opposed by Dean Goulburn, whose efforts earned him the nickname 'the fighting dean', an allusion to the 'fighting bishop' of 500 years earlier. The ferry continued until 1943.

The most important trade route to Norwich before the railway was the river. In the 1820s coal was the chief import in Norwich being unloaded at Yarmouth into barges which could each carry 28 tons up the river. The shipping interests of Norwich and Yarmouth had combined to form the Norwich and Yarmouth Navigation in 1682: the original Act had to be renewed every year. Because Breydon Water is very shallow, boats coming up the river had to draw less than three feet. To allow larger ships, drawing up to ten feet, to reach Norwich it was proposed to build a new canal to Lowestoft. As this would cut out Yarmouth, Yarmouth Corporation were naturally against the new canal: they spent £8,000 opposing it in Parliament but to no avail.

The 'New Cut' across the marshes at Reedham to Lowestoft opened in 1833 when the first two ships—the *Squire* and the *City of Norwich* arrived in the city. The celebrations were muted as the son of the master of the *City of Norwich* had fallen overboard in Surlingham Reach and drowned. The new waterway was put to good use in April 1834 when the *Sarah* took 54 convicts directly from Norwich to Australia, saving the county the expense of taking them to London overland. There were plans for a large new harbour in Norwich but the arrival of the railway killed river transport: the scheme now only survives in the public house name *Clarence Harbour*.

Trade on the Norfolk rivers was mainly by wherry. The 1854 *Trade Directory* says:

> The general navigation from Norwich to Yarmouth is by keels and wherries. The latter are peculiar to the rivers of Norfolk and Suffolk; and those used in the Wensum carry from 15 to 40 tons, and draw from three to four feet of water; the mast is at the head, and so balanced by means of lead, that the strength of one man is sufficient to raise or lower it in the event of passing bridges.

Wherries can be seen picking up cargo from warehouses by the river in Norwich in Henry Ninham's painting, 'The River Wensum, Norwich'.

The Bridges

The first cast-iron bridge in Norwich was that at Coslany, built by James Frost and opened in 1804: it is still in use but now only for foot traffic. (Sir John Soane's bridge at St George's is earlier—1783/4—but only the railings are cast-iron, the bridge itself is of stone.) Carrow Bridge was built in 1810 as a private toll bridge, mainly used by cows going between Trowse marshes and the cattle market. The bridge was rebuilt in 1833 and continued to charge tolls until 1900. The present bridge was built in 1923

82   *Coslany bridge, built by James Frost in 1804*

on a site slightly further south of the old one. Duke's Palace Bridge was opened in 1822. This was also of cast-iron. It was a private money-making venture. Tolls were charged until 1855 when the Corporation took over the bridge. This bridge is now part of the entrance to the Castle Mall car park.

The first Foundry Bridge was opened in 1811: a ten-year-old boy drowned after falling off the structure when it was being built.[39] The bridge is shown in Robert Ladbrooke's painting 'Foundry Bridge' (1822-3). This shows the hill up to the castle covered in trees and the castle itself has many more battlements than now—this was before Salvin's 'restoration' work.

Foundry Bridge was also built as a toll bridge. On the opening of the railway a new bridge was built at a cost of £6,000, of which the railway company paid half. The new bridge was toll free and was itself replaced by the present bridge in 1888—it is 50 feet wide and cost £12,000. St Martin's Bridge in Coslany was built by the Eastern and Midlands Railway Company when their line was extended to Norwich.

The Coach and the Railway

In 1816 there were four coaches a day from Norwich to London. Two Royal Mail coaches left the *Angel* inn at 3.45p.m., one going via Newmarket and the other via Ipswich. The London Day Coach left the *Rampant Horse* inn at 6a.m. and took 14 hours. The Telegraph London coach left the *Norfolk Hotel* at 7a.m. taking 13 hours. These coaches were in competition and the owners of the Day coach announced that they would 'not risk the lives of their passengers by racing against time'.[40] In 1844 there were seven coaches a day from Norwich to London but they were doomed. The first through train to London ran on 30 July 1845 and by January 1846 the coaching trade was dead.

On 7 February 1835 a 'moveable panorama' of the Liverpool and Manchester Railway was exhibited in the Theatre Royal in Norwich. Two companies put schemes before Parliament in 1836 to connect Norwich to London by railway, but both ran into money problems. In 1841 George and Robert Stephenson decided upon Yarmouth as the starting point of a great east to west trunk route across England. The first stage was to be the 20-mile route between Norwich and Yarmouth via Reedham. Work started in 1843 and no tunnels were needed but the river was diverted into a new channel between Trowse Hythe and Wensum Reach as this was cheaper than building swing bridges. The contractor was Samuel Morton Peto, now commemorated by a bust at Norwich railway station.[41]

The Norwich and Yarmouth Railway was formally opened on 30 April 1844. The first public traffic was on 1 May when 1,015 passengers were carried, in the case of the third-class passengers in some discomfort: 'The third class are six-wheeled carriages, open, and at present without seats. We trust they will not continue so; the inconvenience of standing, especially to females, during a journey in a cold weather, will be very great'.[42] The fare for third class was 1s. 3d. for one way, compared to 2s. 6d. for second class and 3s. 6d. for first class. By means of the railway, passengers and freight could be carried between Norwich and Yarmouth in 50 minutes.

The Norfolk Railway's line to Cambridge opened in 1845 and the first through train to London ran on 30 July, starting at Trowse as the swing bridge over the river was not finished. The bridge was finished in December 1845: the engineer was George Parker Bidder. On Christmas Eve in the same year, the engine of a train to Norwich left the line at Thetford and the driver and stoker were killed; 'the accident was supposed to be due to the excessive speed at which the train was travelling–fifty-five miles an hour'.[43]

The effects of the railway were dramatic. The *Norfolk Chronicle* said on 25 April 1845: 'During the droving season last year 9,300 beasts were housed at the *Bird in Hand* public house Tasburgh ... but so great is the diminution of traffic occasioned by the Norfolk Railway, that during the present season only twelve beasts have been taken in'. On 17 January 1846 the same paper said starkly: 'All the coaches between Norwich and London have ceased to run'. In fact, because Norwich was the last major city to be connected to the main railway system, its mail coaches had survived longer than any others: the last run was on 8 January 1846. The news was not all bad for horse transport; the same newspaper acknowledged that there had been a great increase in horse carriages connecting towns without stations to the railway.[44]

The line to London via Ipswich was opened in 1849 by the Eastern Union Railway which built its own station out of an old circus building in a pleasure ground off Queen's Road. This was Norwich Victoria and it became something of a white elephant as early as 1851 when the line was linked to Thorpe station. However the city was reluctant to see it closed and it remained open to passenger traffic until 1916. The railway continued to be used for freight traffic, mainly coal, until the 1980s: part of the line is now a road.

The Norwich and Yarmouth line was one of the first to introduce the 'block' system whereby only one train was allowed at a time on each section of line. Even so there was a disaster in 1874 when a train from Yarmouth crashed into the mail from Norwich on the single-line track in Thorpe. Both drivers and firemen were killed and 23 passengers also died. The fault was with the staff at Brundall who had let the train from Yarmouth through. It was unclear whether the night inspector Alfred Cooper or the telegraph clerk John Robson was responsible; in the end Cooper was jailed for eight months.[45]

The swing bridge proved to be something of a bottleneck. It was single track and by 1905 was carrying 170 services a day. In August 1905 it was replaced with the present double-track structure. The present Thorpe station of red brick with stone dressings and a zinc-covered dome was opened on 3 May 1886. One major piece of early railway engineering to survive is the Lakenham viaduct: this was financed by Samuel Bignold. The drum of Bidder's swing bridge also survives, beneath the more recent superstructure.[46]

The third station in Norwich was City station, off what is now Barker Street. This opened in 1882 and was the terminus of a line from Melton Constable. Later it became part of the Midland and Great Northern Railway Company, offering services to the North Norfolk coast and through trains to Birmingham. This station closed to passengers in 1959 and to freight in 1969. It was originally planned to run the railway from City station right through the centre of Norwich to join the Thorpe line and end in a new station in front of the cattle market. The failure of the scheme meant that all the stations were on the edge of Norwich and there was never a line through the city. The result is, as Arthur Ransome says, that 'Thorpe Station at Norwich is a terminus. Trains from the middle of England and the south run in there, and if they are going on east and north by way of Wroxham, they run out of the station by the way they came in'.[47]

The most profitable route was always that to London. In 1846 trains ran from Shoreditch to Norwich in 260 minutes, making four stops. Just as there had been two coach routes to London so there were two train routes—one via Colchester, the other via Cambridge. Both routes had about the same number of trains until after the Second World War when the Colchester route became the only main line between Norwich and the capital. In the 1960s many of the branch lines disappeared and even more drastic proposals would have left only the line to London open. These came to nothing, but evening and winter trains on the Cromer and Yarmouth lines have had to be subsidised by the County Council.

Communications

In August 1808 a shutter telegraph system between London and Yarmouth via Norwich began to operate. It had 19 stations including one at Thorpe Hill from which the road name Telegraph Lane is taken. In good visibility a message could travel from London to Yarmouth in 17 minutes. The system was really for military purposes and it closed down in 1815 after the defeat of Napoleon.

The electric telegraph service came in with the railways; telegraph companies rented the wires used for railway signals and by 1854 Norwich was provided with services along the lines to Ely, Yarmouth and Fakenham. For the first time communication became almost instantaneous. In November 1846 the London stock market prices were conveyed to Norwich by telegraph. When Isaac Jermy, the recorder of Norwich, and his son were murdered at the isolated Stanfield Hall in 1848, a servant swam the moat and ran the three miles to the police station at Wymondham. The police telegraphed Norwich and reinforcements were sent in carriages: they surrounded the house of the suspect James Blomfield Rush and arrested him there.

In 1881 the United Telephone Company ran a line from Morgan's Brewery in King Street to Mousehold House, where one of the directors lived. This is the first record of a telephone in Norwich. The first telephone exchange was set up in Exchange Street in 1883 (the street name refers to the earlier Corn Exchange and not to the telephone exchange). A larger one opened in Haymarket in 1894 with 200 subscribers. At first they could only telephone each other and people in Yarmouth and Lowestoft, but the system was extended over the next few years.[48]

Gentleman's Walk letter box is a rare example of a surviving 'Penfold' box, hexagonal with a highly decorated roof. This type of box was in use between 1866 and 1879. It is not mentioned in the 1877 *Trade Directory* but it does appear on the 1883 Ordnance Survey map.

Poverty

The treatment of the poor in most of England was run under the New Poor Law Act of 1834, which grouped country parishes into unions with a workhouse. However, the parishes of Norwich were already in a union and already had a workhouse so it did not come under the Act. The poor law administration established in the city in 1712 lasted until 1863. The Norwich Poor Act of that year made the electoral districts for the guardians the same as the city wards: it also brought the parish of St Mary in the Marsh into the city system for the first time.

There was no drastic change in policy in 1863, however: as always it was a question of looking after the poor while spending as little ratepayers' money as possible. Poverty was probably at its peak in the middle of the century. In 1845 the *Norfolk Chronicle* said that 2,000-2,500 were unemployed in the city and 75 per cent of these were weavers. They were costing Norwich ratepayers over £300 each week. By 1848, one in five of the city's population were paupers—in 1847, 35,596 were excused payment of poor rates because of their own poverty.

The Committee of Guardians in 1834 ordered that all able-bodied applicants for relief should be put to work (this was to stop them claiming benefit while they were working). They worked alongside the indoor paupers in the workhouse in the weaving, hosiery and shoemaking factories there. This system lasted until 1857 when it was stopped because of the cost.

The capacity of the workhouse at St Andrew's was only 380 but the conditions were good. A poor law commissioner wrote: 'I have never seen bread of such fine quality in any other workhouse, it is equal to any provided for my family'.[49] In 1848 the Poor Law Commissioners enforced the regulation for the separation of married men from their wives in workhouses. This led to riots in the workhouse in May and June and a policeman trying to move some of the paupers was hit on the head with a stone and killed.

A new workhouse opened in 1859 on Bowthorpe Road with room for 900 paupers. On an average day there were about 300 people in the workhouse, rising to almost 600 in the 1860s. The number of poor being relieved in their own homes rose from about 1,600 to 4,600 in the same period as unemployment rose with the collapse of the weaving industry.

Norwich guardians paid professionals to train poor boys in a craft, usually shoemaking. They also continued to bind out boys as apprentices. In 1847 a Boys' Home was opened and selected boys went there from the workhouse school, staying on for two or three years after they had found a job. Of the 67 boys sent out from the home between 1847 and 1854 only eight failed to make a living for themselves. A Girls' Home was set up in 1850 where poor girls were trained as domestic servants. In 1880 the Guardians proposed to save money by closing the Boys' Home and sending the boys back to the workhouse. This was opposed by Canon Copeman and his amendment was carried. In the event both homes continued into the 20th century. The Boys' Home was at St Faith's Lane until 1932 when it moved to 58 Earlham Road.

Norwich Infirmary had 139 inmates in 1844. The infirmary, in St Augustine's, was designed especially for the old and only those of good character were allowed in. They were paupers over 65 of good character and who had been on poor relief for at least six months. They were transferred from the out-relief lists or from the workhouse. Inmates wore a uniform but could come and go freely, and could wear their own clothes when they went out. It was much preferred to the workhouse which the aged regarded as a prison. The downside was that they had to share it with dangerous lunatics, as Norwich had failed to provide adequate accommodation for its insane. The Infirmary closed in 1859 as part of an economy drive and the inmates went to the new workhouse. Even here there was a row of cottages set aside for deserving old people.

Under the Municipal Reform Act the management of municipal charities passed from the Corporation to trustees appointed by the Lord Chancellor. There were over 70 charities involved. The Master in Chancery divided them into Church Charities (the Great Hospital and others with church connections) and the General List (all the others including Doughty's and the Boys' and Girls' Hospitals). A new hospital for girls was opened in 1864 and was enlarged in 1908 to take 48 girls. The Boys' Hospital site in Fishergate was sold for £550 in 1885. In 1896 a scheme was set up by which each boy was given a set of clothes and two pairs of boots a year.

By 1830 the inmates of Doughty's were receiving 5s. 6d. a week and in 1840 two extra cottages were built for women. Between 1867 and 1869, the Hospital was improved: the small rooms of adjoining cottages were knocked into one larger room and another storey was built over the existing buildings. The south side of the square was removed and the west and east sides extended. Due to lack of money, many cottages were left empty in the later years of the century as the Hospital could not afford to pay the pensions. It 1892 it was agreed to set aside six cottages for freemen and their

widows, whose maintenance was paid by the Town Close Charity. Cook's Hospital
site in Rose Lane was sold in 1892 and eight new almshouses built at Gildencroft. In
1899 the hospital was merged with Doughty's. Pye's Almshouses moved from St
Gregory's parish to West Pottergate in Heigham in 1827.

On a more local scale Norwich residents were to be found all over the world. John King, son of a
Norwich miller, was sent by the London Police Commission in 1840 to launch the
Cape Town police force. There is a grave in Sparta Diggings California recording the
death there of Norwich-born John Smith. It was written by a mourner who could get
his message across despite a lack of spelling skills:

> IN MEMORY OV JOHN SMITH WHO MET
> WIERLENT DEATH NEER THIS SPOT
> 18 hundred and 40 too. He was shot
> By his own pistill;
> It was not one of the new find
> But an ole fashioned brass barrel kind
> Such is the Kingdom ov He'ven[50]

On a more local scale Middlesbrough census returns for 1851 include names like
John Patton and Robert Spinks both born in Norwich and working on the railway.

Schools

The education reformer James Kay-Shuttleworth wrote his *Report on the Training of
Pauper Children* in Norwich in 1838. He said that classrooms should be full of maps,
drawings and blackboards and fitted up on the plan used in Dutch schools with all
the pupils facing the teacher. The monitorial system should be replaced with the
Continental system or the teaching of the children in classes of reasonable size. The
curriculum should embrace the three 'Rs', geography, religious instruction and also
include vocal music as taught in Dutch and German schools.

The sons of richer parents would attend academies such as that of Charles
Turner on Pottergate. Boarders paid fees of 20 guineas if under 10 years old and
25 guineas for older pupils. For this they were taught English, arithmetic, history
and book-keeping. Everything else was extra. If they paid they could have lessons
in classics, astronomy, drawing, dancing and music and mathematics and natural
philosophy.

In 1838 new district schools were opened at St Augustine's Gates by the Bishop
of Norwich. They were supported by voluntary contributions and intended to accommodate 450 children, but demand was growing and by 1854 about 700 were attending
the school. There were similar but smaller district schools in Surrey Street and Upper
Westwick Street.

The Norwich Charity Schools were smaller institutions. In 1854 there were nine
schools with a total of 750 boys and 500 girls. The Central or Model schools were in
Prince's Street for boys and in Broad Street for girls. Although largely funded by
subscription, each pupil did have to pay 1d. or 2d. a week.

In 1854 there were National schools at Pockthorpe, Lakenham and Heigham and
British schools in the city mission room in Julian Place and in Lakenham. The Dissenters ran their own school in St James' Road with about 200 pupils and also supported

the Lancastrian school in College Court. Dissenters' Sunday schools were attended by about 4,000 children in 1854.

Following the formation of the Ragged School Union in 1844, a Ragged School was set up in Norwich in 1848. This functioned on Sundays and two evenings in the week and was supported by Nonconformists and radicals. However, following rioting and disorder in 1857, the school closed down.

The new Norman school, 'a neat Gothic building with a residence for the master', was opened in Cowgate in 1839.[51] Thirty boys were instructed as free scholars and their parents were given £10 a year for their maintenance. When a boy reached 14 he was apprenticed with a premium of £15 and a further £10 if he reached 21 with no complaints about his apprenticeship. Norman's School also took in fee-paying pupils.

The 1851 Census shows up many small schools in the city. On Bracondale, William Paul with three live-in teachers (all young men between 18 and 21) looked after 37 boys aged between nine and seventeen. Most came from Norfolk or Suffolk but two had been born in India, where their parents were no doubt on Colonial Service. In Pottergate Anna Barnsdale looked after nine girls between four and twelve all described as orphans: this was the Girls' Orphan Home and School, supported by voluntary subscriptions. A 17-year-old female lodger, described as a shoe binder, was probably a former pupil.

In 1856 Jeremiah James Colman and his wife started a school for the children of their employees. Parents paid a penny a week for one child and a halfpenny for any others: the money went entirely to school prizes. The school began with 22 pupils and had 324 by 1870.

Under the Education Act of 1870 School Boards were set up. These were intended to supplement the church schools and not to replace them. The Norwich Board estimated that the existing schools provided 8,674 places but that over 5,000 more places were needed and they began building schools to fill this gap. The School Boards were elected bodies and women could stand for election. The first two women to obtain seats on the Norwich Board were Charlotte Bignold and Mary Anne Birkbeck, both elected in 1881. In 1893 Margaret Pillow ran for the Board as the first woman representative of the National Union of Teachers. She was elected and fought hard for teachers' salaries but was defeated at the next election three years later.

The Socialist League was active in Norwich from 1886. In 1899 a Social Democratic Federation candidate was elected to the Norwich School Board with a five-point programme described by *Justice* magazine as being 'as definitely and outspokenly socialist as any of us could wish'. The five points were:

1. Raising the school leaving age to sixteen.
2. Total abolition of the half-time system (under which children worked half the day and went to school the other half).
3. No fees.
4. A purely secular education.
5. Class sizes to be limited to 30.

How many of these aims have been achieved in the last hundred years?

Many dioceses established colleges for the training of teachers. In Norwich the first college to train elementary school teachers was set up in a house in the Close in 1839. In 1853 a building on St George's Plain was bought and adapted for 40 trainee teachers. A purpose-built college was built at a cost of £15,000 and opened in 1892. Most of the students at the college were pupils from elementary schools who had been awarded Queen's scholarships.

The Technical Institute was built in 1899 on St George's Street with its long face rising directly from the river and with a dome at the corner: it is now the College of Art and Design.

Leisure

In the Victorian period Norwich saw the establishment of two of its best known public parks–Chapelfield and Mousehold Heath. The College of St Mary in the Fields, from which Chapelfield takes its name, was founded as a hospital before 1250 but very soon became a college for secular priests. At the Reformation the site was granted to the last dean, Miles Spencer, and the college and chapel buildings were destroyed. Chapelfield House built on the site was later owned by the Hobart family. Two wings of the house were incorporated into Thomas Ivory's Assembly House. The adjacent Chapelfield Gardens, then called Chapelfield Croft, was granted to the city by John Worseley in 1569 and has been city property ever since. In Elizabethan times it was used for archery practice and Braun and Hogenberg's map of about 1581 shows archers there.

Chapelfield was leased out on condition that the people of Norwich should be free to use the grounds for walking or recreation, and that the city chamberlain should be able to dig and take away sand and clay for the repair of the city walls between St Giles' and St Stephen's gates. A reservoir was built in Chapelfield under the waterworks system started in 1794. After the reservoir was no longer needed it was at first intended to keep it as a lake but it was filled in after 1854. In 1866, the field was enclosed with iron palisading with four gates opened at daylight and closed at sunset.

Soon after his conversion to the Japanese vogue, Thomas Jeckyll was employed by Barnard, Bishop and Barnard to design for them a great cast-iron pavilion to be shown at the Philadelphia Centennial exhibition of 1876. Two years later it appeared at the Paris exhibition where it was admired as a technical *tour de force* and a perfect example of the application of Japanese design to contemporary use. The pavilion was bought by the city for about £500–its original cost had been £2,000. It was set up in Chapelfield but it was taken down in 1949: parts of it can still be seen in some Norwich public parks.

Most of the vast area of Mousehold Heath lay outside the city; over 1,000 acres of it was enclosed under Parliamentary Acts for Sprowston and Thorpe in 1801. Only the part within the city boundary (about 184 acres) survived as common land. It was owned by the cathedral who gave it to the city in 1880 on condition that the Corporation tried 'all lawful measures to prevent the continuance of trespasses nuisances and unlawful acts and to hold the heath for the advantage of lawful recreation'. Due to lack of grazing, oak and birch trees have reclaimed much of it in the 20th century.[52]

83 *Jeckyll's Pavilion in Chapelfield Gardens*

Norwich was still a city of gardens. In 1845, Thomas Dugdale wrote, 'the houses being generally furnished with gardens, it [the city] occupies more ground in proportion to its population than any other city in England'.[53]

Thorpe was a popular excursion, whether by foot or by train. As early as 1819 the *Excursions* had said of the views from the meadows leading to Thorpe and from Mousehold, 'the prospects just mentioned are far superior to anything of the kind in England, perhaps equal to any in Europe'. Bayne wrote in 1869: 'The road from the Foundry Bridge to Thorpe village is a favourite walk of the citizens'. Twenty-five years earlier Dean Pellew had opposed the running of excursion trains to Thorpe on Sundays. In 1844 (the first year of the railway) he wrote about working men going to Thorpe by train

his seat could only be paid by the sacrifice of him and his family's Sunday dinner or of some other item equally essential to their well-being—to say nothing of the temptation to drinking and to excesses of even worse kinds to which the directors expose numbers unnecessarily every Sunday by taking them to such sinks of iniquity.[54]

The kind of costumes worn for a promenade in Thorpe or in Chapelfield can be imagined from a *Norfolk Chronicle* report of a gale in Norwich in February 1860:

locomotion was extremely difficult and laborious, and, indeed, quite out of the question to those of the fair sex whose fashionable expanded dresses, assuming the properties of parachutes, compelled them to undertake a species of aerial voyage for a distance of a few yards, or exposed them to the still more unpleasant predicament of having their parachute garments inverted.

The Theatre Royal may have undergone something of a decline in popularity in the middle of the century. Bayne wrote sardonically, 'the interior is quite commodious enough for the limited number of patrons which Norwich furnishes to the drama'.[55] One successful performer there was the actor Walter Montgomery. He was born in Norwich and made his first stage appearances in the city. He was at the height of his fame when he recited from Othello at the Assembly Rooms in 1855 and appeared as Macbeth and Richard III at the Theatre Royal in the following year. Montgomery shot himself at *Shelly's Hotel* in London in September 1871 only a few days after his marriage. He was 44. His real name was Richard Tomlinson and for some reason his place of birth is wrongly given in the *Dictionary of National Biography* as Long Island, USA.[56]

There were other theatres in Norwich in the 19th century, specialising in all forms of variety and popular entertainment. Full-blooded dramas were staged at the Adelphi Theatre in the Ranelagh Gardens which in 1848 put on a local drama called 'The Spirit of the Loom' showing 'Norwich as it is' with 'Effects of Vice, Drink and Misery, Burning of the Cotton Mill and dreadful conflagration'. The Adephi closed when Victoria Station was built on the site in 1849. Another short-lived theatre was the Vaudeville in St Giles Street offering a roller-skating rink, cycling, performing dogs and music-hall. It closed in 1882 after six years. In March 1898 the freehold of the *Norfolk Hotel* was bought by a syndicate for £9,500 to build on the site 'The Norwich Opera House and Theatre of Vanities'. It later became the Hippodrome Theatre.

It was in this period that Norwich gained the reputation of having a church for every Sunday in the year and a pub for every day of the year. Like all towns, Norwich had far more public houses than it does now but most were very small, often hardly more than corner terrace houses. The pubs are named on the Ordnance Survey map of 1883. The so-called 'Drink Map' of 1878 by W. Ratcliff also shows them. It lists a total of 655 licensed houses (there are also later editions of this map with slightly different numbers of public houses).[57]

One form of civic pride was the putting up of statues. The Nelson statue by Thomas Milnes, made of granite, was erected in St Andrew's Hill. The Duke of Wellington statue, of bronze, by C.C. Adams was unveiled in the Market Place by Samuel Bignold in 1854 in front of a crowd of 20,000. Nelson was a local hero, of course. Wellington had no direct connection with the city but his son had an estate in Norfolk and had been MP for Norwich. Both statues have, at different times, been moved to the Close. At the top of Agricultural Hall Plain is my favourite statue in the city, the bronze angel on the Boer War memorial by George and Fairfax Wade, with delicate drapery across the legs and gorgeous outspread wings. Another beautiful memorial is the Mother and Child in the grounds of the Norfolk and Norwich Hospital. This is by Joseph Boehm and was put up in 1876 as a drinking fountain at the junction of the Ipswich and Newmarket Roads. It was paid for by Sir John Boileau in memory of his wife Catherine. Some people say that the lady of the statue is a portrait of Catherine.

Norwich was the home of many other Victorian institutions. The Norfolk and Norwich Museum was erected in St Andrew's in 1839 and the castle was converted

84   *Statue of Horatio Nelson in the cathedral close*

into a museum when the building ceased to be the county prison. Norwich was one of the first to levy a rate for the purchase of books under the Free Libraries and Museum Act. The Free Library opened in 1857 in St Andrew's at a cost to the Corporation of £10,000. In 1883 it had a lending library of 7,000 volumes, the City Library of 1,800 volumes and the reference library of 1,100 volumes. Funds must have been available to pay staff: the reference library was open until 9.30 p.m. six nights a week. In April 1880 the librarian used £10 received from fines for overdue books to buy some local reference books: this was the beginning of what eventually became the Local Studies Library.[58] The privately funded Subscription Library in Guildhall Hill was much larger with 50,000 books and a specialist law library of 4,000 books.

In June 1875 a group of Norwich residents met at the Literary Institute and resolved 'That the establishment of a public swimming bath in Norwich is most desirable'. The estimated capital needed was £1,500 and a site was chosen near the river at Heigham; such facilities were still seen as being provided by private enterprise rather than by the City Council.

Literary life in Norwich, although not at the peak of the Georgian era, could still furnish some famous names. George Borrow, born at Dereham in 1803, went to Norwich Grammar School and the family lived in Willow Lane until Borrow's marriage to May Clarke in 1839. He was a favourite of William Taylor, the author, and in 1833 became an agent and translator for the Bible Society in Spain and Russia. His account of his travels, *The Bible in Spain*, was one of the best selling books of its time. His two books of autobiography, *Lavengro* (1851) and *Romany Rye* (1857), were not successful at the time but are now valued for the picture they give of Norwich and Norfolk life.

One way in which the city does remember Borrow is in the words 'Norwich–A Fine City' on all the signs into the city which are taken from his book *Lavengro*, but leaving out the word 'old':

> A fine old city … view it from whatever side you will; but it shows best from the east, where the ground, bold and elevated, overlooking the fair and fertile valley in which it stands … Yes, there it spreads from the north to south, with its venerable houses, its numerous gardens, its three twelve churches, its mighty mound … there is an old grey castle on top of that mighty mound; and yonder, rising three hundred feet above the soil, from among those noble forest trees, behold that old Norman masterwork, that cloud-encircled cathedral spire around which a garrulous army of rooks and choughs continually wheel their flight. Now, who can wonder that the children of that fine old city are proud of her, and offer prayers for her prosperity?

Mary Wright was born at Sutton, Suffolk, and went to a dame school in Norwich; her drawing master may have been John Crome. Mary's father and brother were ruined when their steam packet blew up in 1817, as already described. Mary married Isaac Sewell, son of a prominent Yarmouth grocer: their first child Anna was born in Yarmouth in 1820. Mary became famous for writing children's books and books for the poor. Her *Mother's Last Words*, published in 1860, was a long ballad about two young brothers who preferred poverty to thieving. One died of cold and went to heaven, the other lived to be an honest man. It was published by Jarrold's and sold well over a million copies. From 1867 Mary lived at The White House,

Catton, now 125 Spixworth Road, and devoted herself to the care of her sick daughter Anna. Anna herself wrote *Black Beauty* in 1877, also published by Jarrold's. It was an immediate success and remains one of the most popular children's classics of all time. Anna did not live to see its full success; she died within a year of its publication and is buried, with Mary, at the Friends' Burial Ground at Lammas in Norfolk. They are commemorated–appropriately–by a horses' drinking trough at the bottom of Constitution Hill, not far from their Catton home. This was put up by Anna Sewell's niece.[59]

James 'Fred' Henderson of Norwich was a poet before he was a politician. The prime minister W.E. Gladstone wrote to him: 'I fell on the two sonnets for London and I greatly value them as poetry and as civic patriotism'. In 1892 he appears to have thought of appointing Henderson poet laureate but it would hardly have been Henderson's style. Leifchild Jones wrote to him, 'you are a republican and a democrat as I am: and you could never, poet as you are, write birthday odes for the Royal family'.[60] Henderson's political career is described in the next chapter.

6

Norwich in the 20th Century

The new century was observed in the city on 1 January 1900 with great celebration. The 20th century saw more changes in Norwich–and in life in England in general–than the previous 900 years. However, this is a book about Norwich and the changes are discussed here only as they directly involve the city.

The first change in the way the city was governed was in 1907. Under the terms of the Local Government Act of 1888 the city boundaries were extended to include parts of the parishes of Sprowston and Catton. In 1909 Edward VII visited the city and so became the first reigning monarch to come to Norwich since Charles II almost 250 years earlier. The mayor was Walter Rye and he met the king not in formal morning dress but in his usual bowler hat and tweeds–some people thought this cost Rye the knighthood he might otherwise have expected.[1] The following year the chief magistrate of the city became Lord Mayor rather than Mayor.

The early 20th century saw the beginning of the break up of the old two party system and the rise of Socialism. Norwich played its part in this. The 1895 Trades Union Congress was held in the city: it advocated the nationalisation of the means of production, distribution and exchange and also of land. The Norwich by-election of 1904 was one of the first where Labour broke its alliance with the Liberals and put forward their own rival candidate. George Roberts, a printer born in Chedgrave, stood for the Independent Labour Party. The election attracted national attention but in the event the Liberals won by 1,820 votes with Roberts a poor third. However Roberts' career had only just begun: two years later he won Norwich for the Independent Labour Party.

The first Socialist member of the City Council was James 'Fred' Henderson, elected in 1902. When his wife Lucy was also elected they became the first married couple to serve on a local authority. Henderson, who was born in Norwich in 1867, had spent four months in Norwich Castle gaol following food riots in the city in 1885. He was one of the last people in England to be forced to work the treadmill. His poetry was mentioned in the last chapter and his greatest importance was as a writer. His most influential book was *The Case For Socialism*, published in 1911. This was based on Sunday evening meetings he held in Norwich and was translated into many languages.

The city led the way in the election of women to local office. Some women had become poor law guardians after an Act of 1894 removed property qualifications and

Lines through Time 9: 1900 to 1950

	1900	Trams come to Norwich
Queen Victoria dies	1901	Census; population 111,733
	1906	Norwich Union building started
	1912	Norwich floods
First World War starts	1914	
First World War ends	1918	
	1919	Edith Cavell buried in Norwich
General strike	1925	
	1933	Norwich airport opened on Mousehold
	1938	City Hall built
Second World War starts	1939	
	1942	Baedeker raids on Norwich
Second World War ends	1945	City of Norwich plan
National Health Service set up	1948	
	1950	

among them was Annie Reeves of Norwich. She stood for the City Council in 1907 and 1908 for the Independent Labour Party but was defeated. In 1910 Ethel Colman made civic history in England when she became the first ever female Lord Mayor. Her sister Helen acted as Lady Mayoress. The first woman to be elected to the City Council was Mabel Clarkson in 1913. She was elected as a Liberal but moved to Labour after the war. In her 1912 election address she wrote:

> I know many, in fact most, of the Courts and Yards in our poorer districts, and I do not hesitate to say that some of the dwellings in which some families are living today are a disgrace to the city. Those of us who care for the purity of our homes, for the right of little children to opportunities of health and development, for the prevention of infantile mortality, and of all the unnecessary sickness and suffering caused by overcrowding and bad housing, are bound to make every effort to get rid of the slums.

Norwich had three female council members in 1920, eight in 1950 and 18 in 1986, over one third of the City Council. Norwich's first female MP was Dorothy Jewson, who held one of the Norwich seats briefly between December 1923 and October 1924.[2]

Norwich hit national headlines in 1912 when the city was devastated by flooding. On 26 and 27 August 1912 torrential rain fell continuously for 29 hours: 7.34 inches

85   *The Norwich flood of 1912: Midland Street*

of rain were recorded. The streets flooded as the drains became blocked with debris. This was cleared but by midday on 27 August the river began to overflow. Eventually 3,650 houses were affected by the floodwater, especially in the low lying areas north of the river and off the Dereham Road. Work went on through the night evacuating the houses in the devastated areas. Three people were killed in the night and 2,200 people were put up in schools and other shelters.

Food was supplied by boat to those still in their homes. Caley's provided milk and hot chocolate in soda water bottles with a loop at the neck passed to upper windows with boat-hooks. The water subsided on 30 August but many houses were damaged: 43 Closing Orders were issued on homes made unfit for human habitation and a further 102 Dangerous Building Notices were given out. The parish registers of some of the churches north of the river were damaged by the flood, which explains their poor condition today. One of the consequences of the flood was a widening of the river near Fishergate to make it less of a bottleneck. The flood also drew attention to the poor quality of some of the housing stock. The *Daily Citizen* commented: '[Norwich] has literally hundreds of little, narrow, sunless courts, resembling nothing more than a series of rabbit runs, and the dampness which the waters left as legacy has never disappeared'. It was estimated that one house in three was below the standard laid down by the Local Government Board and that one in five was positively unfit for human habitation.[3]

86 *The Norwich flood of 1912: Westwick Street*

The First World War broke out in 1914: the city was affected both in the loss of many of its young men and in the life of those who remained behind. The names of the Norwich men killed in the war are given in the *Norwich Roll of Honour* published by the City Council: the total is 3,544.[4] The Roll gives the name of the regiment in which men were serving: this is necessary to find further details of a man's military career as all army records are arranged by regiment. 'All three battalions of the Norfolk Regiment that went over the top at the Battle of the Somme on 1 July 1916 suffered so many casualties that they ceased to exist as effective formations.' People's reactions to the horrors of the Western Front varied, of course. One Norwich-born soldier, Sidney Day, received the Victoria Cross for his bravery at the front in 1917 while serving with the 11th Suffolks.[5] However for Private John Abigail from Thorpe Hamlet, the battle front at Ypres in 1917 was too much to face; he was one of the 307 British soldiers shot during the war for desertion. He was serving with the 8th Norfolk Battalion.

Norfolk men fought in the Middle East campaign as well. The 4th and 5th battalions of the Norfolk Regiment suffered great losses in the failed attempt to capture Gaza in April 1917: every officer of the 5th battalion was killed or wounded except one. There are three memorials in the Rosary cemetery to Norwich men killed at Gaza, including one to Major W.H. 'Harry' Jewson.[6]

Nearly 45,000 wounded troops were treated at the county asylum which was used as a war hospital: the Red Cross also ran five small convalescent hospitals in the city itself. The Norfolk and Norwich Hospital also played its part. Many expected that the war would begin with a massive battle in the North Sea between the British and German fleets. On 5 August 1914, the day after war was declared, the hospital sent a telegram to the Admiralty. It read, 'Can give you fifty beds in this Hospital today, and fifty more on Saturday, and can erect six marquees in Hospital Grounds to hold 150 more beds. If this meets with your approval can you or War Office assist in Equipment?' The tents were given by Mr. Horsfall, chairman of the House Committee. In the event the sea battle did not happen and on 3 September the Hospital sent another telegram offering the beds to the War Office. This was accepted and the first 97 men from the British Expeditionary Force arrived at Thorpe station on 17 October. Fortunately they were lightly wounded and could make their own way to the Hospital as there was only one city ambulance drawn by one horse! The *Eastern Daily Press* opened an appeal for a special ward at the Hospital for soldiers and this was opened in 1915 with 60 beds. The military beds were maintained by regular sponsorships from businesses and individuals–for example, Boulton and Paul sponsored 10 beds.[7]

Air raids were expected and blackout rules were introduced to the city in January 1915. Public houses were affected too; they were ordered to close at half past nine each evening. In the event there were no air raids on the city but the Hospital did receive four people badly hurt after an air raid on East Dereham on 8 September 1915. Food rationing was not introduced until early in 1918. The city was forced to sharpen its attitude to foreigners in the city and all aliens had to register with the police and stay within five miles of their homes. There were about 2,000 registered aliens in the city, mainly Italians. The war also encouraged volunteer activity among the citizens.

87   *Soldiers in Blackfriars' Hall in the early years of the First World War*

In December 1914 a Volunteer Corps was formed for men too old to join the army: the minimum age was 38. These men patrolled railway lines, guarded bridges, and helped build the airship base at Pulham Market. Another 700 men became special constables to replace those policemen who had joined up, and to enforce the black-out.[8]

There was a small anti-war movement in the city. The Independent Labour Party which was opposed to the war tried to hold a party conference in Norwich at Easter 1915. Almost everyone owning halls refused to let them use their property: they eventually met at Queen's Road Methodist church. The meeting was attended by Keir Hardie: it was the last public appearance of his hectic political career. The local I.L.P. leader was councillor Herbert Witard who was later criticised in the city for his refusal to help in any way with recruiting. Witard, who at 13 had run away to sea, was later leader of the Labour group on the City Council and the first Labour Lord Mayor, in 1927. George Roberts, however, was strongly pro-war and left the I.L.P. because of its anti-war stance. He was one of the founders of the Socialist National Defence Committee, which after 1916 became the British Workers' National League and advocated a punitive peace and economic reprisals on Germany after the war.

When Asquith formed a coalition government, Roberts was one of the ministers chosen from the Labour party and he joined Lloyd George's cabinet as Minister of Labour in 1917. When the Labour party withdrew from the coalition Roberts (and a few other Labour ministers) decided to stay in the government and they had to leave the Labour party. Roberts carried the people of Norwich with him in his decision. He stood not for Labour but as an Independent in the elections of 1918 and 1922 and was elected both times. In 1923 he completed his personal journey to the right by joining the Conservative party. He stood again for Norwich in the election of December 1923, this time as a Conservative, but he had gone a step too far for the electors and he was defeated. Roberts then retired from politics: he died in 1928.

As always, the war benefited some industries. Boulton and Paul made military aircraft on their Rose Lane site. They built a large number of Sopwith Camels and produced their own plane, the Bobolink, as a replacement, but it was not a success. They made a total of 2,530 military aeroplanes and over 5,000 miles of wire for the trenches. Mann Egerton began to supply seaplanes to the Admiralty in 1915. Howlett and White made Cossack boots for the Russian Army as well as R.A.F. boots.

The war also produced one of Norfolk's most famous heroines: Edith Cavell.[9] She was born at Swardeston in 1865, the daughter of Reverend Frederick Cavell. In 1890 she took a post in Brussels as a governess and she stayed for five years. In 1895 she began training as a hospital nurse in London. She went back to Brussels in 1907 and was soon in charge of a training school for nurses there. She was on a visit to her mother who then lived in College Road when she heard that Germany had invaded Belgium in August 1914. She returned at once to Brussels which was soon occupied by the German army. Edith Cavell looked after wounded soldiers of all nationalities–including Germans–under the Red Cross. She also helped over 100 British and allied soldiers to escape to neutral territory in Holland from where they were able to get back to this country and continue the war effort. She was arrested in August 1915 and kept in solitary confinement. At her trial she agreed that she had helped soldiers to leave Belgium and she was executed by firing squad on 12 October. Her last words, as she received the sacrament, were: 'Standing as I do, in view of God and eternity, I realise that patriotism is not enough: I must have no hatred or bitterness towards anyone'. Her body was buried on the rifle range where she fell but in 1919 she was reburied just outside Norwich Cathedral–her family preferring this to a burial in Westminster Abbey. At their request the grave was marked with the same form of simple cross that was used for the graves of soldiers killed in action.[10] A statue showing her in nurse's uniform and with a soldier hanging up a laurel wreath can be seen in Tombland: it is by J.G. Gordon Munn. Pevsner and Wilson see in it a resemblance to a man playing hoopla.[11]

The city war memorial was designed by Lutyens and was set up in front of the Guildhall in 1927. It was moved in 1938 to its present site opposite City Hall and expanded to form a small memorial garden. The war is commemorated in literary form in *The Spanish Farm Trilogy* by the Norwich author R.H. Mottram, which catches

88   *Queen Alexandra unveils the Edith Cavell memorial*

the flavour of life in the trenches. Mottram died in 1971 and the plaque on St James' lookout showing the buildings of Norwich was put up as a tribute to him. The chapel at the east end of the cathedral was built as a war memorial by public subscription but some people thought it did not harmonise well with the ancient building. The former mayor Ethel Colman wrote to the Dean that she would not have contributed if she had known how controversial the new building was going to be.[12]

The population of Norwich in 1931 was 126,236. The census of this year shows the large size of the institutional population in the city. There were 168 people in the Great Hospital, 380 in the Cavalry Barracks, 389 in Britannia Barracks, 128 in the Bethel Hospital, 537 in the Norfolk and Norwich Hospital, 875 in Norwich Institution (the old workhouse on Bowthorpe Road) and 117 in Norwich Prison.

In 1933 the City Council fell to Labour and they have remained in control ever since, apart from two years in opposition. However in the 1935 general election the Labour candidate Fenner Brockway lost his deposit.

Unlike the First World War which took most people by surprise, events in Europe in the 1930s meant that the next war was anticipated well in advance. One life-saver during the war was the blood transfusion service which was set up in Norwich in 1939. There were large numbers of volunteers giving blood throughout the war years and many lives were saved both in Norwich and abroad, much of the blood being sent to military hospitals overseas. In the 1930s many people expected that bombing of cities would have a devastating effect on life. The actual results were not nearly as bad as feared. Indeed the plans drawn up before World War Two anticipated such a disaster that they continued to be used as the basic plans of action to be carried out in the case of nuclear attack in the 1950s and later. Between 1940 and 1943 there were about 45 raids on the city, resulting in a total of less than 400 deaths but in damage to some 30,000 houses. Just over 1,000 people were injured but only 401 of these had to be taken to hospital. However the Hospital also had to cope with emergency illnesses and accidents among the many troops stationed in the area during the war.[13]

By the outbreak of war Norwich had built air-raid shelters to take 17,000 people but it was not until the start of 1942 that there were enough shelters for everyone in the city. The old chalk-working tunnels under Gas Hill and Earlham Road were pressed into service and fitted up with bunks which are still there, perhaps kept through the 1950s and 1960s in case of nuclear war. Anderson shelters were individual shelters made of two curved walls of corrugated, galvanised steel bolted together and covered with earth. They were put up in back gardens and a few still survive, used as garden sheds. Although they could not stand a direct hit, they undoubtedly saved many casualties. In bombing raids up to 75 per cent of wounds came from flying glass and the shelters provided protection against this danger.

The first air-raid siren in Norwich sounded on the night that war was declared, 3 September 1939 but the first raid was not until 9 July 1940: there was no alert. Two planes bombed the Barnards factory on Mousehold Heath and one of the planes backed away towards the centre of the city, dropping a bomb at the top of Carrow Hill. More bombs fell on Boulton and Paul's factory on Riverside and on the nearby locomotive sheds. In all 27 people were killed in this first day's raid.[14]

By far the most serious air raids on the city were the 'Baedeker' raids on the nights of 27/28 and 29/30 April 1942. These were in retaliation for R.A.F. raids on German civilian populations at Rostock and Lubeck. A German foreign office spokesman announced that the Luftwaffe would bomb every English building marked with three stars in the *Baedeker* guide book–the cities bombed were Bath, Exeter, Canterbury, Norwich and York. On the Monday night some 185 high-explosive bombs and a large number of incendiaries were dropped: 162 people killed and 600 wounded. After a respite on Tuesday night, the raids resumed on Wednesday night when 112 high-explosive bombs were dropped and even more incendiaries than on the Monday: 69 people killed and 89 admitted to hospital. About two thirds of those who died in air-raids in Norwich during the war were killed on these two nights, including 11 elderly people killed in a hit on Bowthorpe Lodge on 28 April. The hospital admitted 118 casualties from the two raids, dealt with 137 out-patients and also coped with damage sustained to its own buildings in both raids.[15]

89   *Caley's Factory burning after being bombed*

90   *St Bartholomew's church, Heigham*

Later raids were again on a relatively small scale. It was in the raid of 27 June 1942 that the cathedral was almost lost. Some 1,000 incendiaries fell in the Close on this one night. A very large number were in containers that failed to open but at least eight fires were started setting ablaze the roof beams of the north and south transepts of the cathedral. Fortunately these fires were dealt with but some houses in the Close were destroyed including two once part of the 12th-century Infirmary; a car park now occupies the site. It was on the same night that the family shop of R.H. Bond and Sons Ltd on All Saints' Green (which incorporated within it the Old Thatched Theatre) was reduced to a burnt-out shell. St Mark's Primary School in Lakenham was destroyed in this raid too. As the head teacher wrote in the school log book, 'I ran through the churchyard just before the "all-clear" to see whether the school was safe, and found it a blazing inferno, nothing to be done'. The school reopened two days later in the Church Hall.[16]

Other major buildings were destroyed in the raids. They included the churches of St Benedict, St Julian, St Michael at Thorn and St Paul in the city, St Bartholomew in Heigham, the synagogue off King Street and St Mary's Baptist chapel in Duke Street. The Hippodrome Theatre in St Giles was badly damaged and the manager and his wife were killed.

91 *Remembrance Parade, 1945*

The last conventional air raid was on 6 November 1943 when high explosive bombs fell on the municipal golf-course in Bluebell Road and incendiaries caused small fires in houses off the Unthank Road. No-one was hurt during this raid. On 26 June 1944 Hitler's secret weapon, the V-1 flying bomb, could be seen in the skies of Norwich but none fell in the city. On 3 October a V-2 bombardment rocket fell on Hellesdon golf-course. This was the only V-2 rocket that fell on Norwich. However, they caused a tremendous amount of damage in London which led to a second evacuation of women and children from there into Norwich. This evacuation only lasted a very short time, however, and the threat of the V-2 was soon ended as the allied armies advanced across Europe capturing the places from which they were fired. On 29 November 1944 an American B24 Liberator, returning to Horsham St Faith, struck the tower of St Philip's Church, Heigham. The pilot made every effort to avoid coming down in a built-up area and the plane crashed in the Corporation yard off Barker Street: all nine crew members on board were killed.[17]

The contributors to *Within Living Memory* have some telling details on life in Norwich in wartime. One recalls: 'When the blitz was on in Norwich in April 1942, I can remember seeing people walking with prams and barrows out of the city at night

Lines through Time 10: 1950 to 2000

	1950	
Festival of Britain	1951	
	1961	St Augustine's swimming pool built
	1963	University of East Anglia opened
England win the World Cup	1966	
	1969	New Norwich Airport opened
	1974	Norwich loses County Borough status
	1985	City win League Cup final
	1993	Norwich City win 3-2 at Bayern Munich
	1994	Norwich City library burnt down
	2000	

to sleep in the country'. Another contributor remembers: 'I was five years old when the war started. I went to Hillside Avenue School, Thorpe St Andrew. I remember being fitted for a gas mask which I had to take everywhere I went.'[18]

The bombing, added to the slum clearances of the 1930s, created an opportunity for a comprehensive new vision of how the city might be reconstructed after the war. Leonard Hannaford was the City Architect and his vision of Norwich in 1943 envisaged the demolition of all property between City Hall and Chapelfield Gardens and the creation of a new city centre. In 1945 *The Norwich Plan* was published: its introduction quotes Aristotle: 'Men come together in cities to live; they remain together in order to live the good life'.

Many of the council's grand plans came to nothing as the money ran out. Perhaps the greatest achievement was not in grand visions but in the huge quantity of new housing. Between 1945 and 1955 some 6,500 new council houses were built in Norwich. These include large new estates like West Earlham and Tuckswood and smaller developments such as Heigham Street, Guardian Road and Hellesdon Road. An *Eastern Evening News* report in 1948 praised the West Earlham estate: 'There is no group of more than 12 similar houses together … Different types of houses are blended, giving relief in roof heights and pitches and breaking the monotony of similarity.'

Reconstruction work took many years because of the shortage of labour, of materials and of cash. Steward and Patteson submitted plans to the city engineer to put up a temporary wooden building behind the shell of the bombed-out *Dolphin* inn in

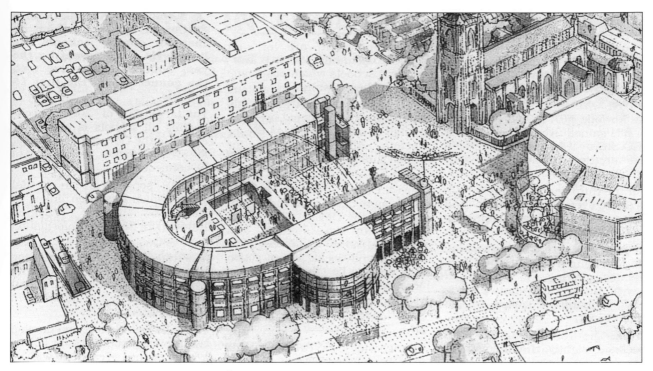

92 *The proposed Millennium Library in Bethel Street*

November 1943. Plans for the restoration of the *Dolphin* were not submitted until 1958: the work was completed in 1960.

Since the war the population of the Norwich area has spread well beyond the city limits and some boundary adjustments have been made. Under the 1950 Norwich Extension Act the city was extended to include a portion of Caistor St Edmund, the river Yare, and a portion of Thorpe St Andrew. In 1967, following a Boundary Commission report, the city boundary was extended to bring in most of the area of Norwich airport. To the west the area of Bowthorpe was taken in at the same time. This includes the Bronze-Age burial site described in the Introduction which is now the oldest site of known human occupation within the city boundary. The 600-acre site has been developed as a residential and industrial area. However, many suburbs remain outside the city boundary.

An important change to the running of the city was brought about by the Local Government Reform Act of 1972, carried out in 1974. Norwich lost its county borough status and some of its powers, such as control over education and libraries, passed to the County Council. The city tried to redress this 20 years later but after debate the status quo was confirmed.

The population of Norwich was 122,083 in the 1971 census, 122,300 in the 1981 census and 122,611 in the 1991 census (these figures seem to vary slightly in every publication on the subject perhaps depending on whether visitors are included in the totals as well as residents).

1993 and 1994 were dramatic sporting years for Norwich. In 1992-3, Norwich City achieved their highest position ever, finishing third in the new Premier League.

This qualified them for European competition and they became the talk of Europe when they beat the mighty Bayern Munich in Germany on 19 October 1993. Their run came to an end with two narrow defeats by Inter Milan in the following round.

On 1 August 1994, the Central Library was burnt down following an electrical fault. Many books were lost as were items held by the Local Studies Library including rare prints and photographs. The Norfolk Record Office shared the building and thus lost its home: fortunately no records were lost. In April 1995, the historic Assembly House was burnt out. The Assembly House has already been restored to its former glory but, at the time of writing, the Library and the Record Office are still in temporary buildings. However a major new library is to be put up for the new Millennium.

The Making of Livings

The first half of the century saw the rise of the shoe making and engineering trades in the city. These sectors declined during the post-war years and were replaced by an extremely wide range of manufacturing and service industries. Boot and shoe making had replaced weaving as the main industry in Norwich before 1900; in the 1901 census there were over 7,500 people employed in the boot and shoe trade and the number rose to 10,800 by 1931. Hawkins wrote in 1910,

> In light shoes and in women's and children's boots–men's are scarcely made at all–Norwich can now compete on equal terms with any other centre. The best ladies' evening shoes, which were till recently made in Paris and Vienna, are now, for example, being made in Norwich.[19]

In 1961, 10,000 people were employed in clothing in the city and 9,000 in shoe making. Norwich was making eight million pairs of shoes and ranked fourth as a footwear manufacturer. It specialised in ladies' fashion shoes and children's shoes. A 1961 report noted that teenagers were now buying five pairs of shoes a year:

> Fresh from the restrictions of school life, the teenager looks for style rather than durability. She has had enough of gym tunics and good strong sensible Oxfords. Now she looks for the prettiest shoes she can find, for the most delicate pastel colours, the highest heels, the most pointed toes. But though appearance is all to her at this stage, and though her desire for style must be fulfilled, she must not be disillusioned about quality. She may not look for durability but, if her pretty shoes fall apart at the first summer shower, she is not likely to spend her money on that particular make again.[21]

The trade has since declined and most of the factories are closed. In the 1984 Census of Employment, only 3,000 were employed in footwear and clothing in the city, about 3 per cent of the working population. There was only one textile firm in the city, Francis Hinde and Sons, employing about 275 people.

The manufacture of food and drink continued to grow in the 20th century. Colman's led the way again in care for its workers. In July 1905 they introduced a graduated pension scheme which reached a maximum of 8s. a week in the case of those who reached 65. In addition everyone contributed 2d. a week which produced an extra 2s. a week making a total pension of 10s. a week; or if the pensioner preferred he could take the extra as a lump sum. Foremen received extra money. The *Eastern Evening News* commented: 'The pension scheme has been often enough described, but as far as we are aware, it has never yet been paralleled. It has been again and again commended in disinterested quarters as the most liberal thing of its kind known to British industry.' In 1910 there were 97 elderly former workers of Colman's receiving pensions. Wages were generous too; Hawkins wrote,

> the best wages are earned at Carrow where the minimum for labourers is 21s. a week. On the mustard and starch floors the earnings are rather higher and not less than 22s. 6d. a week. There is only one other employer in Norwich where labourers are paid so much, namely the city itself. Street sweepers and other unskilled workers are given a minimum of one guinea a week.[21]

In 1961 Colman's employed 1,300 people and was still making good use of its riverside site: some 12 per cent of the inward traffic of grain was coming by river. In 1988, the firm employed 1,500 people. It has since become part of the international group Vandenberg Foods.

Caley's was another major employer in the food and drink business. One of their advertisements ran:

93   *Caley's advertising*

Believe It Or Not! In one year the manufacture of Caley Chocolate uses more than enough milk to float a 10,000 ton Ocean Liner. This amazing fact is particularly interesting to Norfolk people for a large proportion of this milk is produced on Norfolk farms.

Their factory near Chapelfield was destroyed in World War Two and later rebuilt on the same site. The firm was taken over by Mackintosh and in 1961 was employing 2,100 people. In 1987 they were trading as Rowntree Mackintosh and 2,000 people were employed on the Norwich site making Yorkies, Rolos and Munchies: the factory has since closed down.[22]

Another firm to close in the 1990s was the grain milling firm of R.J. Read in King Street. It was one of the last firms to make extensive use of Norwich as a port; foreign grain came up the river and was used for flour and for animal feed.

Brewing in Norwich was at its height in the late 18th and 19th centuries. There were four major breweries until 1957 when Bullard's bought up Youngs, Crawshay and Youngs in King Street, reducing the number to three. In 1961 the three breweries were employing 900 people. In that year two of the breweries combined against the third: Bullard's and Steward and Patteson together bought up Morgan's for the 400 public houses it owned and sold the brewery to Watney's. This was the beginning of the end. Watney's took over both Bullard's and Steward and Patteson in 1963. Brewing

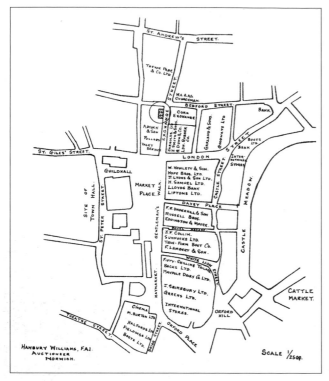

94 *Plan showing shops in the centre of the city in the 1930s*

stopped at the Anchor site in 1963 and eventually no beer was brewed in the city at all. In 1974 'real' or unpressurised beer could only be bought in two pubs in the city. However, the demand spread and some small breweries were eventually established again in the city, beginning with those at the *Reindeer* on Dereham Road and then the *Coach and Horses* on Thorpe Road.

Engineering also flourished in the city in the 20th century only to decline towards its end. As we have seen, Boulton and Paul prospered in the First World War and laid out an airfield on Mousehold Heath to test planes. In 1920 they moved to larger premises on Riverside: at the time they were employing nearly 3,000 people. Afterwards they made the framework for the airship R101 and when the great airship was completed it flew over the city watched by an enormous crowd that cheered as she passed overhead. Unfortunately she crashed at Beauvais in France while on her way to India in October 1930 but it was agreed that the Boulton and Paul frame was in no way to blame for the disaster. In 1961 manufacturing still employed 8,500 in the City, 3,500 at Laurence, Scott and Electromotors, making rotating electric engines, ships' winches and associated control gear. Boulton and Paul still gave work to 1,300 people and together with Barnard's they made about half of the total British production of chain link fencing and wire netting. Barnard's came to an end as an independent company in 1955 when they were taken over by the Sheffield company Tinsley Wire Industries Limited. They finally ceased to trade in 1991.

New engineering firms were established too. In 1920 Heatrae Ltd. began making electric heaters and in 1961 they employed 500 people. Factories set up after the Second World War included Autowrappers Ltd., Marston Caravans Ltd., Miller Organ Co., and Roneo Ltd.–the last three all on the new Salhouse Road industrial estate. In the 1980s new high quality engineering firms emerged like United Closures and Plastics bought by Metal Box from the Guinness group in 1987; Anglian Windows, a double glazing firm employing 1,000 people, and Diamond H. Controls employing about 800 people.

Banking and insurance has been a continually expanding field throughout the century. The Norwich Union Head Office was built in 1905 and modelled on the old Amicable House in Sergeants Inn, Fleet Street, London. The architect was George Skipper. Pevsner wrote of being 'knocked out by the smashing Norwich Union building

95 *Norwich Market Place: the stalls and the market church*

which, without any doubt, is one of the country's most convincing Edwardian buildings'. However the Norfolk antiquarian G. Colman Green was not convinced, writing: 'I still detest the huge building which is not in accorde [*sic*] with traditional architectur [*sic*] in the Ancient English Capital and retain a sense of shock to think that the Architect perpetuates Greek style into a city with its own characteristics'. The inside is as spectacular as the outside, making use of marble originally intended for Westminster (Roman Catholic) Cathedral.[23]

In 1925 the Life Society acquired the shares of the Fire Office from the Phoenix which had bought them in 1920. By 1961 the total assets of the Norwich Union Assurance group were over £250 million and in 1987 the company employed 4,500 in Norwich in several office blocks in the centre of the city. Gurney's Bank had amalgamated with Barclays' Bank in 1896 and their Norwich branch at Bank Plain became one of the largest in England, employing over 80 staff in 1961. Other large financial companies include the Sedgwick Group employing over 800 in 1987. The Norwich and Peterborough Building Society has helped spread the city name, especially during their sponsorship of Norwich City Football Club.

Printing and publishing have flourished too, with 1,000 people working for Jarrold's in 1961. In 1967 H.M.S.O. moved from London to Norwich and in 1986 provided employment for 1,100 people. Eastern Counties Newspapers were described by Townroe as 'a national leader in the difficult area of regional newspaper publishing ... the company has been a leader in newspaper production technology'. In 1987 the *Eastern Daily Press* was selling 92,000 copies a day.[24]

96   *Norwich Cattle Market in 1897*

97   *Fun at the fair in the 1930s*

In 1961 the construction industry was employing 7,000 people. By far the largest firm was that of R.G. Carter with over 900, men but most others employed less than 300 men. One of the older firms was J. Youngs and Co. which built the 300,000 gallon water tower on Thorpe Heights in 1932-3. They featured it in their advertisements as 'a Norwich landmark'. It is still a landmark and has a historical resonance too: it is close to the site of Kett's Oak of Reformation. The 1961 *Report* said: 'Norwich Corporation itself employs over 600 men in construction, for there are in the city nearly 16,000 council houses and flats, representing 40% of all dwellings'.[25]

The historic attractions of Norwich have made it an important holiday destination: in 1987 tourists were estimated to have spent £16 million a year in the city.

Norwich has declined as a port with the development of road transport, in spite of the poor quality of road links to the city. In 1998 there is still not a single mile of motorway in Norfolk. In 1961 there were 400 feet of public quay and several private wharves along the river below Foundry bridge. The main imports were coal, grain, meal, granite chippings, paper, steel and wood. The main export was scrap metal but the port was not making a profit; money from shipping tolls was all used up in dredging work to maintain the channel in the river.

Norwich continued to be the shopping centre for a large part of Norfolk. The two markets on either side of the castle were still the centre of the city. There were some changes in shopping trends. Before 1960 market stalls did not open on Mondays and Thursdays but after that they opened six days a week. Greengrocers and fruiterers sold an increasing proportion of foreign produce; in 1961 only 10 stall holders also grew their produce and only two sold just their own produce. There was a change in the character of Central Norwich when the Cattle Market was moved to Harford, on the edge of Norwich, in the early 1960s. It was replaced by a public car-park and then by the Castle Mall shopping centre which opened in 1993: most of it is hidden under the park, emerging only as a 100-yard-long glasshouse. The funfair, which had traditionally occupied part of the Cattle Market site at Easter and Christmas, has since been sited at Castle Meadow and at the Bethel Street car park but neither seems likely to provide a permanent home.

Housing

After the First World War the talk was of 'building homes for heroes' and Norwich led the way in the quality of its council housing in estates such as that at Mile Cross. In the 1920s and 1930s standards were reduced to save costs but the later estates still provide homes of impressive quality to former dwellers in slums and yards. The size of the gardens compared very favourably with any housing in the private sector.

There were continual disputes between local and national government about the costs of housing but by any standards the achievement was considerable. A Housing Committee report of July 1930 sums it up: since 1919 they had built 2,878 houses (332 under the 1919 (Assisted) Scheme; 48 under the 1923 Housing Act; 2,498 under the 1924 Housing Act). Counting the ones currently being built they will have erected 3,324 houses and used up all the land the Corporation has bought for housing except part of the Earlham estate. 896 houses have been built by private enterprise with

98 *Council houses in George Borrow Road built in the 1920s*

Government assistance—'these houses have in the main been built for sale and it seems unlikely that many will be built for letting in the near future for the working classes'. There was room for a further 355 houses at North Earlham when sewers were available. The committee proposed buying land for 40 houses at Elm Grove Lane, for 400 at Mile Cross Lane and Catton Grove Road and for 500 at the Mousehold House estate.[26]

According to the *Norwich Guide* of 1935 there were about 36,000 houses in the city. The council had built a total of 4,727 houses on six main estates with a few smaller sites on slum clearance areas closer to the city centre:

> There is every type of house from the small one bedroom flat let at an inclusive rent of 5s. 1d. to the 1919 non-parlour type at 16s. inclusive. Over 3,000 are of the three bedroom non-parlour type for which there is the greatest demand; these are let at a net rent of 5s., with 3s. 3d. rates, 7d. electricity assessment charge with, in some cases, additional charges of 6d. for hot water or 2s. 5d. for electric current.

While building council houses the City Council was also clearing slums. The 1935 *Norwich Guide* summed up progress:

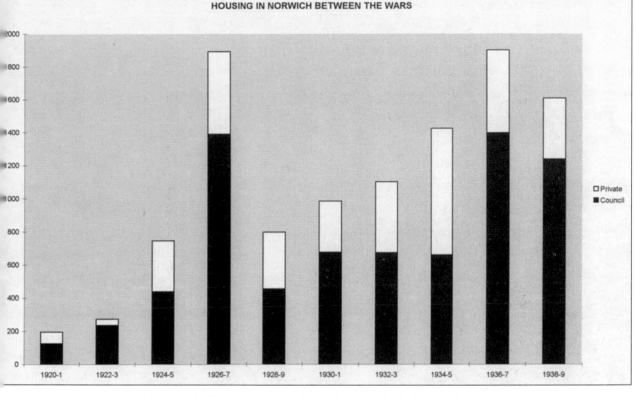

HOUSING IN NORWICH BETWEEN THE WARS

99   *Graph showing private and council housing built between the wars*

As to Slum Clearance in Norwich a good start has been made. Up to December 1933, several Clearance Areas had been declared, involved the building of over 300 houses and flats. A five-year programme to commence from 1 January 1934 was approved in September 1933 and this provided for the building of 1,400 flats and 645 houses, which it is estimated will re-house 8,099 persons ... Up to the present re-housing has mainly been carried out on the Catton Grove and Mill Hill estates, but it is intended to build on the site of the Clearance Areas and this has already been done in the case of a small area in Oak Street. In particular, three-storey flats are to be built in the Barrack Street and Cowgate Area as there is a great demand for accommodation in that neighbourhood.

These solid and substantial flats, so close to the city centre, are still very much in demand. The building of houses by the council was effectively ended by central government policies which encouraged the sale of council houses and the work of housing associations. Whereas in 1978-9 work had begun on 528 new council houses, in 1990-1 just one new house was being built–and over 5,000 council houses had been sold under the government's 'Right to Buy' scheme.[27]

The private sector was building some houses, of course, either as individual speculations or in larger groups. The houses along the Plumstead Road are characteristic of 1920s' ribbon development. Private development also occurred around council estates, like the houses adjoining the Mousehold estate at Wolfe Road and Montcalm Road.

As always, house prices depended on the location, size and condition of the property. An account book in the Norfolk Record Office describes a 'typical' private sector house. In 1929, a house in Upton Road was purchased for £400: the new owner then spent about £11 on small repairs and a further £2 to the Corporation to have electric light installed. The roads in this area had not been laid out and there was a charge to the owner of £109 7s. 10d. for the private street works five years later. The outgoings on the house in the 1930s were £7 13s. 0d. a year for rates, 6s. 8d. a quarter for water rates and 4s. 6d. a year to the Norwich Union for fire insurance.[28] Similar prices are given in the *Eastern Daily Press* in February 1937.

Electricity made a great difference. In *1920s Depression and Norfolk Memories* Fred Sampson remembered, 'Most of the houses had gas downstairs: one gas light in the front room, one in the living room and one in the kitchen'. A contributor to *Within Living Memory* recalled:

> Most people lived in terraced houses, streets of them, a great number of which were destroyed in the air raids in the war. The roads and streets were lit by gas lamps; these had two hanging chains 'on and off' which were operated by lamplighters on cycles at dusk and dawn each day. Houses mostly had gas for lighting and cooking but many people had oil lamps.[29]

The other great improvements were in the lavatory and bathroom facilities which transformed daily living for most people in the first half of the century. As Sampson recalls:

> The lavatory was at the bottom of the garden and was a crude brick-built structure, back to back with next doors. It had a corrugated iron roof and a full width box-like seat over the pan and we used newspaper. You had to take a candle to light the way and in winter the water pipe and tank would often freeze over.

As standards improved, expectations inevitably rose too. In 1970 it was said,

> Poverty is most apparent, most hurtful, where income is lower than that of friends and contemporaries–of a person's own 'community'. The deserted wife with small children is poor by comparison with her happily married sister; the young woman who has left home and is trying to support herself and perhaps a child as well on a wage which assumes that every woman is part of the household of a wage-earning man cannot keep up with a teenager living at home; a family man of below-average ability may well earn less money in a week than is deemed necessary for subsistence or Supplementary Benefit.

However there is still real poverty in the city. In 1991 there were 28,727 people in Norwich claiming Income Support, of whom 13,758 were pensioners.[30]

According to the 1981 census there were 47,791 houses in the city, including about 13,000 terrace houses. The size of the average household was down to 2.47. The number of households with exclusive use of a bath was 46,479: the rest were flats or bedsits where the bathroom was shared.

Norwich has been notably successful in rejuvenating the inner city by developing housing on the sites of closed factories. The large block of land between Coslany Street, Colegate and the river was the factory of Barnard, Bishop and Barnards from 1851. It was turned into houses and flats by the City Architect, David Percival, in the 1970s and 1980s. Further east, a large area of derelict warehouses was replaced by the Friars' Quay development erected by Feilden and Mawson in 1974: its most striking feature is the high pitch of the roofs.

100 *The Friars' Quay development in the heart of the city*

City Buildings

The 20th century saw a growing interest in preserving the city's building heritage. This took time; Norwich rumour says that at one time the Guildhall was only saved from destruction by one vote in a council debate. This seems to be an exaggeration. E.A. Kent in his book on the Guildhall says that in 1908 it was suggested that it would be cheaper to pull the building down than to restore it. Councillor Louis Tillett apparently said that the vibration of nearby trams was threatening the building and questioned whether it was preserving it for sentimental reasons. He criticised the view of Councillor Wild that the Guildhall should be preserved at any cost. However, I have searched the City Council minutes from 1904 to 1909 and found no record of any vote being taken on whether or not it should be pulled down.[31]

A case of a botched attempt at preservation is that of Whitefriars Bridge. The 16th-century bridge was taken down in 1924-5, each stone being numbered so that it could be re-erected elsewhere. Unfortunately all the stones then disappeared. They were probably used as rubble for the foundation of Aylsham Road. The iron structure of the early 19th-century Duke's Palace Bridge has been better handled and has survived to be re-used as the car park entrance to the Castle Mall complex.

Several old buildings in Norwich have been given to the city. Strangers' Hall and Folk Museum was given to the city by Leonard G. Bolingbroke in 1922. The Bridewell was given to the city by N.H. Holmes in 1925. Lord Mancroft gave George Borrow's house in Willow Lane to the city to be made into a Borrow museum. Unfortunately, due to the expense of maintaining these old buildings, several are now closed. Borrow House closed in 1948 and the City Council are even selling off Lord Mancroft's gift.

Other historic buildings, including the Assembly House, have been preserved by the goodwill of the citizens. The Assembly House had been used by the Norwich High School for Girls but they moved out to Newmarket Road in 1932 and the building became a warehouse. Alan Colman, Sir Ernest White and Harry Sexton bought it before the Second World War, intending to make it a headquarters for the Y.M.C.A. and Y.W.C.A. The war put paid to this scheme: later Harry Sexton spent £70,000 on restoring the building and on turning the annex (built in the 19th century as a ballroom) into a cinema. The architect was Rowland Pierce. The cinema closed in 1992 and the roof and interior of the building was badly damaged by fire in 1995: it has very quickly been restored to its former glory.

No survey of preservation work in Norwich is complete without a mention of Walter Rye. Born in London, he spent most of his holidays in Norfolk and retired to Norwich in 1900. He was responsible for the sensitive preservation of three buildings that would otherwise have been pulled down: the *Maid's Head Hotel*, Bacon House in Colegate and the Lazar House in Sprowston Road. He was also responsible for buying and preserving many manuscripts, pamphlets, books and prints about Norwich and Norfolk, including the city's *Book of Customs*. This was lost for many years and restored to the city archives by Rye in 1905. The manuscripts he collected are now in the Norfolk Record Office and his books and prints in the Norfolk Studies Library, although some of the latter were destroyed in the 1994 fire. Walter Rye died in 1929 and is buried in Lammas.

The number of medieval churches in the city centre meant that most were surplus to religious needs. Norwich led the way in finding other uses for them when St Peter Hungate was turned into an ecclesiastical museum.[32] A variety of uses has been found for the others and none has been lost apart from those bombed in the war.

Norwich is not noted for 20th-century architecture but it does have a few glorious buildings. The best ones from the early century are those by G.J. Skipper, especially the superb Norwich Union Building already mentioned. Other interesting buildings before World War Two reflect the importance of the city as a banking centre. They include the National Provincial Bank in London Street built in 1924 by F.C.R. Palmer and W.F.C. Holden (which looks like a Wren church), and Barclays Bank of 1929-1931, by local architect Boardman, with its huge and impressive banking hall.

The most impressive city building of the 1930s is the City Hall. The design for this was by competition and well over 100 designs were submitted which were reduced to a short list of four, photographs of which are preserved at the Norfolk Record Office. The winning design was by C.H. James and S.R. Pierce. It has attracted differing judgements. James Wentworth Day did not like it: 'A pity that [the market] is overshadowed by that modernistic monstrosity, the City Hall, which has the

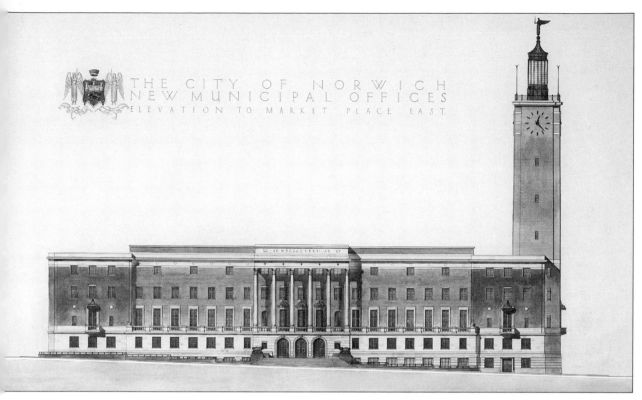

THE CITY OF NORWICH
NEW MUNICIPAL OFFICES
ELEVATION TO MARKET PLACE EAST.

101 *City Hall*

proportions of a brick and the complexion of brown Windsor soup' and 'It looks like
a precocious modern railway station, only the hoot of engines and the stink of diesel
are absent'. However George Nobbs disagreed: 'The dramatic flight of steps, the noble
civic lions, the imposing balcony, and the magnificent tower convey more, to me at
least, of the spirit of Norwich than any other building can ever do'.[33] The large bronze
doors are works of art in themselves, with portrayals of trades of the city past and
present. They are by James Woodford. The elongated lions, also in bronze, are by
Alfred Hardiman.

Post-Second World War buildings in the city included the Central Library by
David Percival in 1960-1962, which burnt down in 1994. Other major buildings include the University of East Anglia and the Sainsbury Centre, referred to later. Clearance of the old Boulton and Paul site, between the railway station and the football
ground, has created a huge opportunity for the city to invest in the finest architecture
of the new Millennium.

Health and Education

The great change in health was of course the introduction of the National Health
Service in 1948, offering free access to doctors and hospitals to everyone.

The first half of the century saw an extension of local authority and charity care
for the sick. At the turn of the century the City Council bought Greenborough farm

on the Salhouse Road to use as a hospital for smallpox patients. The hospital continued in use until 1939 when it was requisitioned by the Air Ministry. After the war it
was felt to be surplus to requirements and it was pulled down to make way for the
Heartsease housing estate, which was started in 1954.

The century saw an increasing concern with mental health. Eaton Grange was a
former private school for young ladies. In 1929 the Council bought it to house 'defectives'
and it opened the following year for 30 female adults and seven children. As the council
had not had anywhere locally to put these patients, they were in institutions as far away
as Chesterfield and Bristol and they were now brought back to the city. The report
quotes the case of a 34-year-old woman. She had lost her parents when young and had
been brought up in the Orphanage in Chapelfield Road. In 1912 she was sent to Stoke
Park Colony where she stayed for 19 years, largely forgotten one suspects. Certainly
when she was moved to Eaton Grange in 1931 her improvement was rapid: 'After only
a short stay at Eaton Grange she has now been able to go out to service for the first time
to a freedom which has hitherto been unknown to her'. In 1932, 16 of the patients were
well enough to be employed in service, earning between 5s. and 10s. a week.[34]

Fund raising for the Norfolk and Norwich Hospital was boosted in 1904 with the
start of the Hospital Cup—every year Norwich City played a top national team for this
trophy and the proceeds went to the hospital. In 1919 a tombola was organised which
raised £13,000, but the Bishop of Norwich and many others wrote strong letters to the
Eastern Daily Press disapproving of the gambling element in this fund-raising effort. 'Egg
Week' was started in 1923 and for one week every April people gave eggs for the
hospital patients.[35]

Private beds were first opened at the Norfolk and Norwich Hospital in 1928 to
raise money for the hospital. The private patients' ward was in the former Eye Hospital building at 80 St Stephen's Road and its 12 beds were immediately filled. Other
hospitals were already offering private beds but the Norfolk and Norwich was the first
to give each patient a single room. It also led the way in introducing an insurance
scheme by which people who were earning less than £350 a year if single or £450
a year if married could pay 30s. a year to cover future hospital expenses for themselves
and their families. In the first full year, 1929, 305 patients were admitted of whom 66
were members of the insurance scheme. In 1938, 361 insured patients were admitted
and only 169 uninsured patients.

In 1925 the Norfolk and Norwich Eye Infirmary amalgamated with the Norfolk
and Norwich and in 1930 a new building was opened for eye, ear, nose and throat
patients. After the war the hospital was united with the former isolation hospital and
workhouse in Bowthorpe Road, renamed the West Norwich Hospital. The hospital
was taken over by the state under the National Health Service Act of 1946. It was
administered by the Norwich, Lowestoft and Great Yarmouth Hospital Management
Committee until 1974 when the Norfolk Area Health Authority came into being. In
1990 land for a new hospital for Norwich was bought in Colney Lane.

The Bethel Hospital reached the end of its long and useful life. After the war it
became an annexe to Hellesdon Hospital and in 1974 an out-patient unit for disturbed
children and adolescents: this has since closed.

The city played a key role in the education of its children between 1902 and 1974. Under the 1902 Education Act both the Board Schools and the church schools came under the control of the City Council which became responsible for primary, secondary and technical education. Under an Act of 1918 all children were to stay at school until they were 14 years old. The city's education system is described in the 1935 *Official Guide*: 'Young children are admitted to Infants' schools at 4 or 5 years and for the first time in their lives become members of a community ... Formal instruction in reading and numbers is introduced by means of toys, apparatus and pictures'. At the age of seven children moved to Primary School: 'At first the methods employed are similar to those in the Infants' School and the child gradually enters upon a more varied curriculum, in which academic and cultural subjects are included ... the curriculum includes English, Arithmetic, History, Geography, Music, Art, Handiwork, Physical Training and Hygiene.' At the age of 11 children went on to one of the various types of Post Primary education.

The 1944 Education Act raised the leaving age to 15 and introduced three types of secondary school–grammar, technical and modern. The City Council can be proud of the speed with which it responded to the Act. In 1961 it was noted that 21 new schools had been built in Norwich since the War–9 infant, 7 junior and 5 secondary schools. In 1974 control of schools in the city passed to Norfolk County Council.

The University of East Anglia is one of a clutch of universities built in the early 1960s. After the war it was proposed to have the university in the centre of town on Ber Street and later the redundant Barracks on Mousehold was suggested as a possible site. The basic concept of the design and the early buildings were by Denys Lasdun and these include its best known features–the 'teaching wall', the 'ziggurats' or students' residences and the artificial broad. In 1973 Sir Robert and Lady Sainsbury gave their arts collection to the university and the Sainsbury Centre was built to house it: the architect was Norman Foster. In 1989-1990 he added the Crescent Wing. In 1987-8 the UEA had 4,866 undergraduates, 1,079 postgraduates, 423 teachers and provided employment for over a thousand other people.

In the same year City College had 2,700 full-time students, or 4,000 full-time equivalents when part-time students are taken into account. It had 300 full-time and nearly 400 part-time teaching staff. City College was started in 1937 but not completed until after the war. The Technical Institute has become the Norwich School of Art and Design and is expanding to take over the old Duke Street school. This, along with the Norman Centre and the Crome Centre, had been run by the City Council as a sports and leisure centre. Unfortunately, financial difficulties in the 1990s have forced the closure and sale of the Duke Street and Crome Centre sites.

Transport

The great increase in population in the suburbs of Norwich together with new engineering ideas changed the face of the city. The most obvious change was the introduction of the tram system. The first horse-drawn bus services had been started in 1879 by the Norwich Omnibus Company but this firm was wound up in 1899. Norwich Electric Tramways began laying rails and the first services opened on 30 April 1900 when services were run on Magdalen Road, Earlham Road, Dereham Road and Thorpe Road. On the first day 25,000 passengers were carried. When the trams first appeared, 'so great was the enthusiasm that men ran out of a barber's shop, their faces still covered with lather, to see this amazing spectacle'.[36]

At its peak the firm had over 40 trams and ran services along the Dereham, Earlham, Magdalen, Thorpe, Aylsham, Newmarket and Unthank Roads and to Trowse and to Mousehold. However, trams were destined to be a short-lived feature of city life. The first indication of decline came after 25 years when the Aylsham Road trams were replaced by buses and the number of bus services in the city steadily increased, some replacing trams and others acting as feeder services.

In 1932 the City Council decided to buy the Tramways Company. It held a referendum on 10 January 1933 but the people of Norwich voted against the purchase by 11,033 to 7,775 votes. In December of the same year the Eastern Omnibus Company

102   *Tramlines in St Giles Street, c.1930*

took a controlling interest in Norwich Electric Tramways and over the next two years all the trams were replaced with buses: the last service to run was from Newmarket Road to the Cavalry Barracks which closed in December 1935. According to the Bus Company this was a popular change:

> No longer were [people] compelled to ride on an exposed top deck in bad weather, nor were there any irritating delays through the limitations of a single track. Householders also expressed great appreciation from the point of view of their wireless sets, free at last from irritating interference caused by the overhead electric wires.

The Company promised 'a large and up-to-date bus station' and this was opened in Surrey Street on 24 March 1936. It was hit by a bomb on 30 July 1940 and 16 buses were damaged. The buses were nationalised in 1948. In 1950 fares were raised for the first time in 30 years, after which fare rises became an almost annual event.[37]

Other attempts at a public transport system came to nothing. In 1904/5 the Great Eastern Railway put an Act through Parliament to build a railway from Norwich to Loddon and Beccles, the idea being to use trams. At the same time the Midland and Great Northern drew up plans for a branch from City Station that would tunnel under the centre of Norwich and meet up with this line at Lakenham. Due to the high costs involved, neither line was ever built and a bus service to Loddon was introduced instead.

The first person to fly over Norwich in an aeroplane appears to be Bentfield Hucks on 10 August 1912. The First World War speeded up interest in air transport. The cavalry training field on Mousehold Heath was taken over by the Royal Flying Corps in October 1914. In 1915 the first aircraft built by Boulton and Paul made its maiden flight here. In 1933 the field was opened as Norwich Airport. Crilly Airways ran daily services to Leicester, Bristol, Liverpool, Nottingham and Northampton.[38]

During the Second World War the Mousehold airfield acted as a decoy site for the R.A.F. field at Horsham and dummy planes were placed on it to deceive the Luftwaffe. There were two fatal crashes on Mousehold Heath in 1942. In February the pilot of a bomber was killed when forced to make an emergency landing at Long Valley: the other four crew members survived. In July a plane from Lyneham in Wiltshire attempted a forced landing and the crew were all killed. In 1990 a plaque to the memory of those killed in both crashes was erected on the heath. The site of the airport was later used for the Heartsease housing estate and school, but some of the hangars can still be seen on the west side of Salhouse Road.

In 1969 the present Norwich Airport opened on the R.A.F. Horsham site.

Like most historic cities Norwich has had problems coping with the rise of the motor car. By the 1930s cars were becoming more affordable. In February 1937 second-hand cars were being advertised for as little as £50 for a five-year-old Morris Oxford saloon and £240 could buy you a one-year-old Triumph Gloria saloon. The *Norwich Plan* envisaged an inner ring road around the centre of the city with adjacent car parks. Part of the ring road was built, including the flyover across Magdalen Street, but the most expensive civil engineering project involved a huge viaduct across the river Wensum near Read's Mills. Funds never became available for this and the inner ring road remains incomplete.

103   *Emigrants for Canada leaving the city station in about 1910*

Norwich led the way in pedestrianisation when London Street was closed to traffic in 1967. This was the first time in England a shopping street had been closed to traffic. The ban on traffic has spread to Gentleman's Walk and to several narrow lanes in the Market Place area of the city. According to the 1981 census there were 47,791 households in the city and 22,042 were without a car.

The County Council Transport Strategy of 1997 said that the first two 'Park and Ride' schemes in the city–at Harford and the Airport–had been a great success. Its objective is to have seven such sites in a ring around the city and to restrict parking in city residential streets to the people who live in them. The plan also aims to create a network of safe cycling routes into the city centre for commuters.[39]

Leisure

The century saw a great increase in leisure time and in the city's leisure facilities. The Theatre Royal flourished until 1934 when it was burnt down. It was rebuilt the following year with a faience front. David Percival remodelled it in 1970 but the faience front is said to still exist behind his dull brick frontage. The Hippodrome was erected in 1902-3 and lasted until the Second World War when it was bombed.

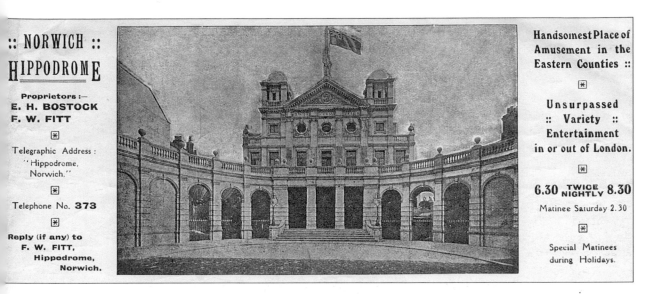

104   *Norwich Hippodrome*

Some of the greatest names in entertainment trod its boards between the wars including Charlie Chaplin, Marie Lloyd and Gracie Fields. It reopened after the war and featured famous acts including the Goons. After a brief spell as a repertory theatre it finally closed in 1966 and the building was demolished. Its site is now the St Giles' car park.

Nugent Monck began producing plays in Norwich in 1910, first in his house at 6 Ninham Court, then in the Music House where there was seating for just 99 people. In 1921 he paid £600 for the 18th-century Roman Catholic chapel and filled the auditorium with 200 Georgian chairs for which he paid 1s. 6d. each. The first play Monck put on at the Maddermarket Theatre was *As You Like It* in 1921 and this was also the last play he produced before his retirement in 1952. In between he had staged all Shakespeare's plays as Shakespeare himself had intended them to be performed, the first time this had been done since the 17th century. It was W.B. Yeats who convinced Monck he was a producer not an actor telling him, 'When I watch you produce I want you to play all the parts, but when I see you act I wonder how an intelligent man can be so bad'.[40]

In January 1897 George Gilbert introduced 'The Royal Cinematographe–

105   *The Maddermarket Theatre*

The Animated Photographs—presenting with marvellous accuracy scenes of everyday life' at the Agricultural Hall in Norwich. The scenes included a pleasure boat at Yarmouth, a boxing kangaroo, and the Prince of Wales at Marlborough House. Films were also being shown by travelling fairs when they visited Tombland. The first 'chain' cinema in Norwich was the Theatre de Luxe in St Andrew's Street, opened in 1910.[41]

The first purpose-built cinema in Norwich was the Cinema Palace in Magdalen Street which opened in 1912 with 850 seats. Norwich also boasted what must have been one of the very few thatched cinemas in England, the Thatched Theatre on All Saints' Green. This was originally a ballroom and became a cinema in 1915. It flourished in the age of silent movies but it was never fitted up for sound so its demise was inevitable. It closed in 1930 and became part of Bond's store: it was destroyed in World War Two.

The Odeon chain first opened in the city in 1938 and this was replaced by the present Odeon which in 1971 won the Quigley Award for Cinema Design. In 1923 the Regent opened in the Alexandra Mansions with 1,800 seats: the first film shown was *The Prisoner of Zenda*. This cinema is now the ABC, but its original name can still be seen at the back. In 1937 there were eight cinemas advertising in *the Eastern Daily Press* but numbers declined from the 1950s. As a 1961 Report said, 'The trend in local entertainment services is that which is common in other parts of the country, namely the decline of the cinema in the face of competition from television'.[42] With the close of the Noverre in 1992, there were only two mainstream cinemas left—the Odeon and the ABC. However both boasted

106 *Building works at Eaton Park*

several screens so the number of films on offer was almost as many as fifty years earlier. In addition, Cinema City, in Stuart and Suckling House, continues to show 'arthouse' and other films not shown in the main cinemas.

The rise in the number of television owners increased dramatically after Anglia Television opened on 27 October 1959. There were 13,295 TV and wireless licences issued in 1955 in Norwich: in 1959, 50,788 such licences were issued. Townroe writes: 'Being the home of Anglia Television Ltd. is a significant plus for Norwich. Not only is the company a major employer and significant income generator, but through its news and documentary programmes it also undertakes a considerable public relations function for the city and its surroundings.'[43] Norwich can also claim to be the first City in England to have postcodes: they were introduced here on a trial basis in 1959 and have been with us ever since.

The 1935 *Guide* listed 10 Gardens and Pleasure Grounds: Eaton Park, Earlham Hall, Chapelfield, Wensum Park, Heigham Park, Mile Cross Gardens, Woodrow Pilling Park, Mousehold Heath, Hellesdon Recreation Ground and Waterloo Park. The parks have had a varied history. Mousehold Heath of about 180 acres was a gift to the City by the cathedral chapter. As animals no longer graze on the Heath, trees have grown over much of it. Chapelfield was formally converted to a public park in 1880. According to the 1935 *Guide*, 'The Police and other bands perform here on various evenings during the season'. The Woodland pleasure ground, a gift of Mrs. Radford Pym, was opened in June 1904.

Waterloo Park opened in 1933. 'It covers 18 acres of land of which the rose gardens and herbaceous gardens, with a pavilion and bandstand, occupy 6 acres; there are lawn tennis courts, bowling greens and cricket and hockey grounds; in the children's' playground is a large paddling pool'. Waterloo and Eaton Parks were laid out by the City Council partly to provide work to the unemployed during the Depression.

The Woodrow Pilling Park, off Harvey Lane, opened in 1929: it was presented to the city by Mrs. Mary Pilling of Withington, Lancashire, in memory of her father Jeremiah Woodrow. She bought the site for £2,000 and gave it to the Corporation who were to maintain it for ever and to name it the Jeremiah Woodrow Recreation Ground: her father, who had left Norwich in 1829, had retained fond memories of the city. The council committee report says 'she preferred that the Gift should take the shape of a recreation and playing ground for young people of both sexes, without any limit as to age, and in particular mentioned that it should be for the benefit of young people having left school, and be available for tennis etc. The donor also hoped that it would be possible to set aside a small piece for young children and provide for sand hills for them to dig in.'[44]

The Council has slowly been developing a walk along the river through the city. The section from Bishop Bridge to Foundry Bridge was originally planned in the 1920s and finally opened in 1972: the willows planted in 1972 are now well-grown.

To conclude, Peter Townroe in 1987 listed seven major developments to revitalise the city over the following 12 years:

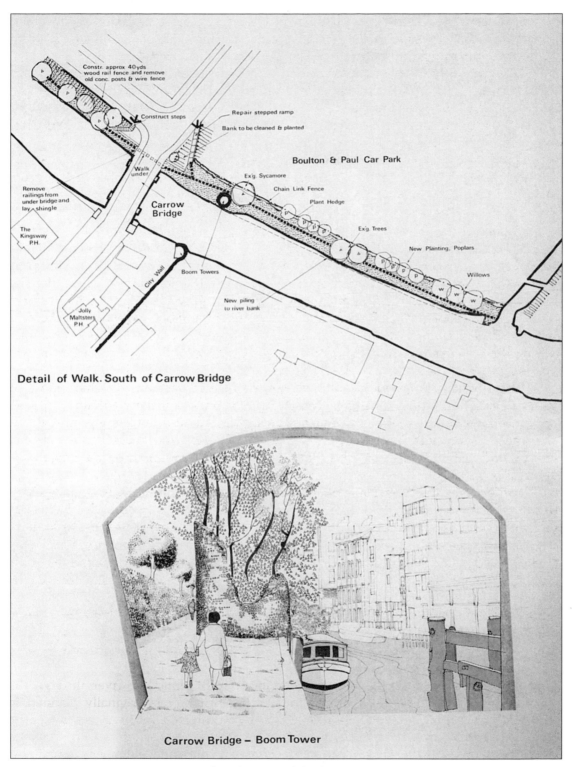

Constr. approx 40yds
wood rail fence and remove
old conc. posts & wire fence

Construct steps

Repair stepped ramp

Bank to be cleaned & planted

Boulton & Paul Car Park

Ex'g. Sycamore

Chain Link Fence

Plant Hedge

Ex'g. Trees

New Planting. Poplars

Willows

New piling
to river bank

Boom Towers

Carrow
Bridge

Walk
under

Remove
railings from
under bridge and
lay shingle

The
Kingsway
P.H.

City Wall

Jolly
Maltsters
P.H.

Detail of Walk. South of Carrow Bridge

Carrow Bridge – Boom Tower

107 *Planned river walk by the Boom Tower*

1. A47 Southern Bypass
2. District General Hospital
3. Castle Mall Shopping Development
4. Office construction for Norwich Union with redevelopment of the Bus Station
5. Development of Lotus Cars with an increase of 800 in the workforce
6. Development of Norwich Riverside for housing, offices, a tourist attraction, shopping and a swimming pool
7. (possibly) Completion of the Inner Ring Road across the river between Queen's Road and Riverside Road.[45]

The first and third of these have been achieved and the second and sixth are on stream. However, the people of Norwich will have to ask themselves if this is still the way ahead for the City or whether the new Millennium is a time for new dreams. As Edith Henderson concluded her *Child's History*: 'The past is not all, the story of the city still goes on ... Each new generation must carry on the story, making Norwich a still more noble city, the fairest in all England.'[46]

Notes

Chapter One

1. Ayers, B., *English Heritage Book of Norwich* (1994), p.16.
2. Green, B. and Young, R., *Norwich, The Growth of A City* (1981), p.7.
3. Poole, A.I., *Domesday Book to Magna Carta* (1951), p.80.
4. Wymer, J., *The Palaeolithic Sites of East Anglia* (1985), pp.60-1.
5. Castleden, R., *Neolithic Britain* (1992), p.141.
6. Castleden, *op. cit.*, p.142.
7. Ashbee, P., *The Ancient British* (1978), p.84.
8. Lawson, A.J., in Ayers, B., *Digging Under the Doorstep* (1983), p.7.
9. Salway, P., *Roman Britain* (1981), pp.113-22.
10. Ashbee, *op. cit.*, p.253.
11. Salway, *op. cit.*, p.656.
12. Toulson, S., *East Anglia: walking the ley lines and ancient tracks* (1979), pp.65-6.
13. Green and Young *op. cit.*, pp.8-9.
14. Ayers, *op. cit.*, p.19.
15. Atkin, M., *Norwich, History and Guide* (1993), p.7.
16. Ayers, *op. cit.*, p.21.
17. Myers, J.N.L., *The English Settlements* (1986), pp.96-101.
18. Carter, A., *The Anglo-Saxon origins of Norwich: the problems and approaches: Anglo Saxon England 7* (1998), pp.175-204.
19. Carter, A., *pers. comm.*
20. Green and Young, *op. cit.*, p.9.
21. Sandred, K.I., and Lindstrom, B., *The Place-Names of Norwich and Norfolk—Part 1: Norwich* (1989), p.140.
22. Ayers, *op. cit.*, p.24.
23. Atkin, *op. cit.*, p.12.
24. Stenton, Sir F.M., *Anglo-Saxon England* (1971 edition), p.248.
25. Ekwall, E., *Concise Dictionary of English Place-Names* (1959 edition).
26. Margeson, S., *The Vikings in Norfolk* (1997), p.27.
27. Green and Young, *op. cit.*, p.10.
28. Campbell, J., *Historic Towns—Norwich* (1975), p.2.

29.   Atkin, *op. cit.*, p.19.
30.   Blake, E.O. (Ed.), *Liber Elienses*, Camden Society 3rd Series, xcii, (1962), p.100.
31.   Whitelock, D. (Ed.), *The Anglo-Saxon Chronicle, a revised translation* (1961), p.87.
32.   Mottram, R.H., *Success to the Mayor* (1937), p.19.
33.   Henderson, E., *The Story of Norwich* (1918), p.69.
34.   Page, R.I., *Chronicle of the Vikings* (1995), p.159.
35.   Rumble, P., *The Reign of Cnut* (1994), p.222.
36.   Green and Young, *op. cit.*, p.11; Sandred and Lindstrom, *op. cit.*, p.148.
37.   Ayers, *op. cit.*, p.33.
38.   Ayers, B., *Digging Under the Doorstep* (1983), pp.11-19.
39.   Gilchrist, R., in Morris, R., *Churches in the Landscape* (1997 edition), pp.186-7.
40.   Campbell, J., *The East Anglian Sees Before The Conquest* in Atherton, I., Fernie, E., Harper-Bill, C., Smith, H. (Eds.), *Norwich Cathedral: Church, City and Diocese* (1996), pp.3-22.
41.   Duffy, E., *The Stripping of the Altars* (1992 edition), p.203.
42.   The two wills are transcribed in Whitelock, D. (Ed.), *Anglo-Saxon wills* (1930).
43.   Ayers, B., (1983), *op. cit.*, p.13.

Chapter Two

1.   Stenton, *op. cit.*, pp.611
 2.   Domesday Book: 33 Norfolk (1984 edition), Chapter 1; 61, 63, 66; Chapter 21; 37.
 3.   Hudson, W., and Tingey, J.C., *The Records of the City of Norwich* (1906, 1910), Vol. 1, pp.xv, xvi.
 4.   Blomefield, F., *The History of the City of Norwich* (1806 edition), Vol. 1, p.53.
 5.   Hudson and Tingey, *op. cit.*, Vol. 1, pp.xviii, xix.
 6.   Henderson, *op. cit.*, p.115.
 7.   Dodwell, B., *The Charters of Norwich Cathedral* (1974), p.xii.
 8.   Fernie, E., *An Architectural History of Norwich Cathedral* (1993), p.171.
 9.   Hudson and Tingey, *op. cit.*, Vol. 1, p.xlii.
10.   Hudson and Tingey, *op. cit.*, Vol. 1, pp.xxvi, xxvii.
11.   Froissart, quoted in Blomefield *op. cit.*, Vol. 1, p.101.
12.   Blomefield, Vol. 1, *op. cit.*, p.108.
13.   Mckisack, *The Fifteenth Century* (1959), p.418; John Capgrave, quoted in Jebb, M. (Ed.), *East Anglia, an Anthology* (1990).
14.   John, T., 'Sir Thomas Erpingham, East Anglian Society and the Dynastic Revolution of 1399', *Norfolk Archaeology* 35 (1970), pp.96-109.
15.   William of Malmesbury, *De Gestis Regum Anglorum*, Vol. 2, pp.386, 387.
16.   Goulburn E., and H. Symonds, *The Life and Letters of Bishop Herbert de Losinga* (1878), pp.131-135.
17.   Rose, M., and Hedgecoe, J., *Stories in Stone: the medieval roof carvings of Norwich Cathedral* (1997), *passim*.
18.   Fernie, *op. cit.*, p.179.

19. Rose and Hedgecoe, *op. cit.*, p.97.

20. NRO, RYE MSS 4, Vol. 1.

21. Hayes, R., 'The 'Private' Life of a Medieval Bishop' in *Harlaxton Medieval Studies*, Vol. 4 (1994), p.5.

22. Greatrex, J., *Biographical Register of the English Cathedral Priories of the Diocese of Canterbury* (1997), p.65.

23. Heslop, T.A., *Norwich Castle Keep* (1994), pp.1-13.

24. There are also drawings by Samuel Woodward in Woodward, S., *The History and Antiquities of Norwich Castle* (1847).

25. Appleby, J.T. (Ed.), *The Chronicle of Richard of Devizes* (1963), p.66.

26. NRO, NCC wills Joan Erpyngham 1404 (307-8 Harsyk).

27. Lipman, V.D., *The Jews of Medieval Norwich* (1967), *passim*.

28. NRO, DCN 40/7, transcribed in Dodwell *op. cit.*, p.241.

29. Lipman, *op. cit.*, p.117.

30. Foreman, J., *Haunted East Anglia* (1976 edition), pp.29-31.

31. Sutermeister, H., *The Norwich Blackfriars* (1977), p.2.

32. Kelly, S., Rutledge, E., Tillyard, M., *Men of Property, an analysis of the Norwich enrolled deeds 1285-1311* (1983), pp.5-13.

33. Barron, C., Rawcliffe, C., Rosental, J. (Eds.), *East Anglian Society and the Political Community of late Medieval England: selected papers of Roger Virgoe* (1997), p.89.

34. NRO, NCC WILLS Margaret Wetherby, 1458 (83-4 Brosyard).

35. Donald Logan, F., *Runaway Religious in Medieval England c.1240-1540* (1996), p.251.

36. Gilchrist, R., and Oliva, M., *Religious Women in Medieval East Anglia* (1993), p.57.

37. Hudson and Tingey, *op. cit.*, Vol. 1, pp.319, 320.

38. Sister Wendy *Julian of Norwich* (not dated), p.6.

39. Llewelyn, R., (Ed.), *Julian: Woman of Our Day* (1985), p.69.

40. Dunn, F.I., 'Hermits, Anchorites and Recluses' in *Julian and Her Norwich* (1973), *passim*.

41. Blomefield, *op. cit.*, Vol. 2, p.80.

42. NRO, NCR 4b, private deeds: St Peter Hungate. Transcribed in Hudson and Tingey *op. cit.*, Vol. 2, pp.358, 359.

43. NRO, NCC Wills William Blackdam 1479 (230-1 Gelour).

44. Tanner., N.P., *The Church in Late Medieval Norwich 1370-1532* (1984), pp.113-140; Atherton (Ed.), *op. cit.*, p.193.

45. NRO, NCC Wills Roger Aylmer 1497 (49-50 Multon); Katherine Kerre, 1498 (89-91 Multon).

46. Rutledge, P. (Ed.), *The Will of Oliver Wyth 1291,* Norfolk Record Society 56 (1971).

47. NRO, NCC Wills, John Cambridge 1442 (192-5 Doke); John Gilbert 1466 (47-9 Jekkys); John Daniel 1418 (32-3 Hyrning); Walter Daniel 1426 (4-6 Surfleete, 148-50 Hyrning).

48. Virgoe, R. (Ed.), *Illustrated Letters of the Paston Family* (1989), p.44.

49. Finucane, R., *Miracles and Pilgrims: Popular Beliefs in Medieval England* (1995 edition),

pp.161-2.
50. NRO, NCR, *The Old Free Book* fo. 162r.
51. Rose and Hedgecoe *op. cit.*, pp.123-39.
52. Anderson, M.D., *History and Imagery in British Churches* (1995 edition), pp.157, 161.
53. Davies, N. (Ed.), *Paston Letters* (1976), Vol. 2, letter 782.
54. NRO, MS 11606.
55. NRO, COL 5/19.
56. NRO, NCR, *Book of Customs,* transcribed in Hudson and Tingey *op. cit.*, Vol. 2, pp.209-11.
57. *Men of Property, op. cit.*, pp.13-31.
58. Jessopp, A., and James, M.R. (Eds.), *Life and Miracles of St William of Norwich* (1986) p.14; James Wentworth Day, *Norwich Through the Ages* (1976), p.36.
59. Blomefield, *op. cit.*, Vol. 1, p.59.
60. NRO, NCR *The Old Free Book, passim.*
61. Hudson and Tingey, *op. cit.*, Vol. 1, p.222.
62. NRO, NCR Assembly Book 1426.
63. Kerling, N.J.M., *Commercial Relations of Holland and Zeeland with England* (1984), *passim.*
64. Public Record Office, Court Rolls SC 2 (May 1275).
65. Anon: *Evidences Relating to the Town Close Estate* (1887), p.4. Hereafter cited as Evidences.
66. Rackham, O., *The History of the Countryside* (1986), pp.299-303.
67. Public Record Office, Assize Rolls, Norfolk 52 Henry III, pp.22-3.
68. NRO, NCR Assembly Book 1354.
69. NRO, DCN 45/33/62.
70. Evidences *op. cit.*, pp.32-3. Original document is Public Record Office, Inquis. p.m., 15 Richard II, p.2, no. 100.
71. NRO, NCR *Mayor's Court Book,* 15, 1615-24 fo. 117r.
72. Hudson, W., *Leet Jurisdiction in the City of Norwich,* Selden Society (1892), p.28.
73. Hudson and Tingey, Vol. 2, pp.xxv-xxvii.
74. NCC WILLS Moundeforde, Helen, 1458 (109 Brosyard); L'Estrange, J., *Calendar of the Freemen of Norwich,* 1317-1603 (1888), pp.9, 16, 148; Leyser, H., *Medieval Women* (1996 edition), pp.160, 1.
75. *Men of Property, op. cit.*, p.31.
76. East Anglian Archaeology 26 (1985), pp.83, 4.
77. Paston letters no. 149, quoted in Bennett, H.S., *The Pastons and Their England* (1990 edition), p.56; Campbell *op. cit.*, p.7.
78. Hudson and Tingey, *op. cit.*, Vol. 2, p.214.
79. Smith, R., and Carter, A., *Norwich Houses before 1700* (offprint from *Vernacular Architecture* Vol. 14, 1983), p.2, note 16.
80. Hudson and Tingey, *op. cit.*, Vol. 2, p.218.
81. NRO, NCR, Assembly Book 1420, cited in Evidences, *op. cit.*, p.46.
82. Dunn, I., and Sutermeister, H., *The Norwich Guildhall* (no date), p.4.

83. Transcribed in Hudson and Tingey, *op. cit.*, Vol. 2, pp.50-2.

84. Hudson and Tingey, *op. cit.*, Vol. 2, p.51 (the volume is NRO, NCR *Norwich Domesday Book*); NRO, NCR *Liber Albus* fo. 1.

85. Tillyard, M., in *East Anglian Archaeology Report* 37 (1987), pp.172-4.

86. Hudson, W. (1892), *op. cit.*, pp.6, 7; NRO, NCR 8a2.

87. NRO, NCR 8a2, transcribed in Hudson and Tingey, *op. cit.*, Vol. 1, p.204.

88. NRO, NCR 8a2, transcribed Hudson and Tingey, *op. cit.*, Vol. 2, p.206.

89. NRO, DCN 45/40/44, 53.

90. They are analysed by Rutledge, E., in *Men of Property, op. cit.*, pp.41-64.

91. Atkin, M., *Life on a Medieval Street* (1985), *passim.*

92. NRO, NCR, 24b. Transcribed in Hudson and Tingey, *op. cit.*, Vol. 2, pp.360-2.

93. B.L. Add. Roll 63207, quoted in Dyer, C., *Standards of Living in the late Middle Ages* (1989), p.63.

94. NRO, DCN 67/1A; Dyer, *op. cit.*, p.248.

95. Smith and Carter *op. cit.*, pp.2-6.

96. NRO, DCN 9/5.

97. Blomefield, *op. cit.*, Vol. 1, pp.333-4.

98. Ayers (1983), *op. cit.*, pp.27-8.

99. Kirkpatrick, J., *The Streets and Lanes of Norwich* (1889), p.20, note 5; p.28, note 9.

100. NRO, NCR Assembly Roll 1380, transcribed in Hudson and Tingey, *op. cit.*, Vol. 2, p.84.

101. NRO, NCR Assembly Book 1453, transcribed in Hudson and Tingey, *op. cit.*, Vol. 2, pp.90-1.

102. Margeson, S., *Norwich Households, The Medieval and Post-Medieval Finds from Norwich Survey Excavations 1971-8*, East Anglia Archaeology Report 58 (1993), pp.4-68.

103. Rawcliffe, C., *The Hospitals of Medieval Norwich* (1995), *passim.*

104. Batty Shaw, A., *Norfolk and Norwich Hospital, A Retrospect* (1992), p.10.

105. NCC WILLS, Wells, Henry, 1448 (9 Aleyn); Greatrex, *op. cit.*, p.246.

106. Blomefield, *op. cit.*, Vol. 1, pp.92-4.

107. NRO, NCR *Book of Pleas*, fo. 112.

108. Rutledge, E., *Immigration and population in early 14th century Norwich: evidence from the tithing roll*, in Urban History 15 (1988), 17-18.

109. DOM. Watkin, A., 'Inventory of Church Goods temp. Edward III', *Norfolk Record Society* Vol. 19, part 1 (1947), pp.26-7.

110. Virgoe, *op. cit.*, p.208.

111. Hudson, W., *The Wards of the City of Norwich* (1891), p.19.

112. Hudson, W., *Leet Jurisdiction in the City of Norwich*, Selden Society Vol. 5 (1892), *passim.*

113. P.R.O, Assize roll, transcribed in Evidences *op. cit.*, pp.10-12.

114. Hanawalt, B., *Crime in East Anglia in the 14th century*, Norfolk Record Society Vol. 44, pp.28-9.

115. Hanawalt, *op. cit.*, p.30.
116. NRO, NCR Assembly Book January 1492.
117. Cattermole, P., in *A History of Norwich School* (1991), pp.5-10.
118. Goulburn and Symonds, *op. cit.*, pp.19-37.
119. NRO, DCN 41/77.
120. Clanchy, M.T., *From Memory to Written Record* (1993), pp.237-40.
121. Duffy, *op cit.*, p.220.
122. Greenwood, J.R., 'The Will of Thomas Salter of London 1558', *Norfolk Archaeology* 38 (1983), pp.280-95.
123. Virgoe, *op. cit.*, is the most accessible and attractive edition.
124. Stoker, D., *Discovery and first publication of the Paston manuscripts* (no date), p.4.
125. Pollett, M., *John Skelton, poet of Tudor England* (1971 translation), pp.47-9.
126. Margeson (1993), *op. cit.*, pp.211-20.
127. Lasko, P., and Morgan, N.J. (eds), *Medieval Art in East Anglia 1300-1520* (1973), pp.18 ff.
128. NRO, DCN 2/3/36.

Chapter Three

1. Mackie, J.D., *The Early Tudors* (1952), p.73.
2. Blomefield, *op. cit.*, Vol. 1, pp.182-3.
3. NRO, DCN 1/6.
4. Derry, P. (Ed.), *Poets' England–16 Norfolk* (1994), p.41. Skelton's poem is in Latin–this translation is by Gray, I.E.
5. Evidences, *op. cit.*, pp.51-61.
6. Atherton, (Ed.), *op. cit.*, pp.507ff.
7. Taylor, R., *Index Monasticus* (1821), p.12.
8. Russell, F., *Kett's Rebellion in Norfolk* (1859). This transcribes many relevant records.
9. Blomefield, *op. cit.*, Vol. 1, p.236.
10. NRO, PD 12/1.
11. Blomefield, *op. cit.*, Vol. 1, p.244.
12. NRO, PD 12/1.
13. Hudson and Tingey, *op. cit.*, Vol. 1, p.45.
14. Mile Cross History Research Group: *Milestones to Mile Cross* (1995), p.5.
15. Hudson and Tingey *op. cit.*, Vol. 1, p.362.
16. Moens, W.J.C., *The Walloons and their church at Norwich* (1887-8). This is the basic 'source-book' for anyone with Walloon ancestry.
17. Forster, L., *Janus Gruter's English Years* (1967), p.27.
18. NRO, ANW WILLS, Peter Peterson (191 Wiggot).
19. Forster, *op. cit.*, p.32.
20. Charles, Amy, *The Shorter Poems of Ralph Knevet* (1966), pp.25-30.
21. Blomefield, *op. cit.*, Vol. 1, p.351.
22. Colthorpe, M., 'Queen Elizabeth and Norwich Cathedral', *Norfolk Archaeology*,

40 (1989), pp.318-23.

23. Blomefield, *op. cit.*, Vol. 1, p.364; Hudson and Tingey, *op. cit.*, Vol 2, p.cxxv.

24. Blomefield, *op. cit.*, Vol. 1, p.364; NRO, PD 106/4.

25. Evans, J.T., *Seventeenth Century Norwich* (1979), pp.67-9.

26. Quoted in Evans *op. cit.*, p.94; Laud, *Works* V, p.339.

27. Jewson, C.B., 'Transcript of Three Registers of Passengers from Great Yarmouth to Holland and New England 1637-9', *Norfolk Record Society*, 25, (1954).

28. Blomefield, *op. cit.*, Vol. 1, p.381.

29. Hall, Joseph, *Hard Measure* (1647).

30. NRO, PD 58/38; NCR, Mayor's court book 9 March 1643/4, fo. 415r.

31. Atherton, (Ed.), *op. cit.*, p.556.

32. NRO, NCR 12c1. Calendared in Bateman, F., and Rye, W., *The History of Bethel Hospital* (1906), pp.84-163.

33. NRO, PD 26/16, 71; PD 484/1.

34. NRO, NCR Quarter Session Book, December 1648; PD 58/1.

35. NRO, MC 500/26; NCR Mayor's court book 1655.

36. NRO, NCR Assembly book 1658.

37. Hill, R., 'Correspondence of Thomas Corie', *Norfolk Record Society*, 27 (1956), p.33.

38. For the 1702 election see Hayton, D., 'A note on the Norfolk Election of 1702', *Norfolk Archaeology*, 37, part 3 (1980), pp.320-4.

39. Baskerville is transcribed in Historical Manuscripts Commission, Portland MSS ii, 269; Morris, C. (Ed.), *Journeys of Celia Fiennes* (1949), p.148.

40. NRO, NCR Liber Albus fo.95; Hill, *op. cit.*, p.11.

41. Mackie, *op. cit.*, Vol. 1, p.463.

42. NRO, NCC WILLS 1626 p.220, Hayward, John; DN/INV 58B/33.

43. NRO, NCR Mayor's Court Book, 20 fo.422.

44. Baskerville, *op. cit.*,

45. NRO, ANW 23/5/113; Priestley, U., *Shops and Shopkeepers in Norwich 1660-1730* (1985), pp.19-20.

46. NRO, NCR Assembly Books, transcribed in Evidences *op. cit.*, *passim.*

47. NRO, NCR Assembly Book 1553, transcribed in Evidences, *op. cit.*, p.73.

48. Hudson and Tingey, *op. cit.*, Vol. 2 p.lviii.

49. Transcribed in Evidences, *op. cit.*, *passim.*

50. NRO, NCR 12a1. Transcribed in W. Rye, *Depositions Taken Before the Mayor and Aldermen of Norwich* (1905), p.87.

51. NRO, PD 461/57.

52. NRO, NCR Mayor's Court Book, 13, p.345. Quoted in Pelling, M., 'Healing the sick poor', *Medical History*, 29 (1985), p.131.

53. NRO, NCR Mayor's Court Book, 7 January 1559, 6 December 1561. Transcribed in Hudson and Tingey, *op. cit.*, Vol. 2, pp.177, 179.

54. Pound, J.F., 'The Norwich Census of the Poor', *Norfolk Record Society*, 40 (1971).

55. Hudson and Tingey, *op. cit.*, Vol. 2, p.389.

56. Harrington, Sir John, *Nugae Antiquae* (1804 edition).

57. NRO, NCR Mayor's Court Books 1622, 1633.

58. PRO, PCC Wills, Anguish, Thomas, 1622 (80 Savile), Tesmond, Thomas, 1626 (108 Hele).
59. NRO, NCR Mayor's Court Book 1675-6; Blomefield, op. cit., Vol. 2, p.60.
60. NRO, NCC WILLS Doughty, Thomas, 1688 (OW 74).
61. NRO, PD 461/57; MC 500/50.
62. NRO, NCR Assembly Book 1573.
63. Pelling, M., 'Illness among the poor in an early modern English town', *Continuity and Change*, 3(2) (1988), pp.282, 286.
64. Pelling (1985), *op. cit.*, p.131; Hudson and Tingey, *op. cit.*, Vol. 2, p. 190.
65. Batty Shaw, *op. cit*, pp.10, 11.
66. Pocket County Campanion: Norfolk (1896), p.109. Hereafter cited as Companion.
67. Hughey, Ruth, 'The Correspondence of Lady Katherine Paston', *Norfolk Record Society* 14 (1941), pp.81, 126.
68. Pelling (1985), *op. cit.*, pp.115-37.
69. Slack, P., *The Impact of Plague in Tudor and Stuart England* (1995), pp.128-33.
70. NRO, NCR 10f; *Norfolk and Norwich Remembrancer* (no date), p.32; NRO, NCR Mayor's Court Book, 1666; Hill *op. cit.*, p.20.
71. Hill, *op. cit.*, p.30.
72. Rye, W., *Extracts from the Court Books of the City of Norwich 1666-8* (1905), p.109.
73. Houlbrooke, R.A., 'Church Courts and People in the Diocese of Norwich' *Ph.D. Thesis Oxford* (1970), pp.354-5.
74. NRO, NCR Mayor's Court Book 1578; Blomefield, *op. cit.,* Vol. 2, pp.292, 3.
75. Atherton (Ed.), *op. cit.*, pp.560, 1.
76. There is a very detailed calendar of the records of the Society of Friends in the NRO.
77. Staffordshire RO, MS 33; xerox copy NRO, MS 21489.
78. NRO, NCR, Quarter Sessions Book, September 1657; Blomefield, *op. cit.*, Vol. 1, p.401.
79. NRO, NCC WILLS James Hopkins, 1634 (Fo.233).
80. NRO, C/S 3/41A.
81. NRO, NCR Assembly Book 18 May 1509. Transcribed in Hudson and Tingey *op. cit.*, Vol. 2, p.107.
82. NRO, NCR Assembly Book 14 April 1570. Transcribed in Hudson and Tingey, *op. cit.*, Vol. 2, pp.137-41.
83. Priestley, U., and Corfield, P., 'Rooms and room-use in Norwich housing 1580-1730', *Post-Medieval Archaeology* 16 (1982), pp93-123.
84. NRO, COL 1/114; PD 68/132; NCR 6a1/35.
85. NRO, NCR 10c.
86. Blomefield, *op. cit.*, Vol. 1, p.427.
87. Houlbrooke, R., 'A Mousehold Abduction 1548', *Counties And Communities: Essays on East Anglian History* (1996), pp.115-28.
88. Companion, *op. cit.*, p.105; Priestley, U., *The Great Market* (1987), p.16; NRO, MC 1026.
89. Young, J.R., *The Inns and Taverns of Old Norwich* (1975), p.56; NRO, PD 185/3.

90. NRO, BOL 4/156, 7.

91. NRO, NCR Mayor's Court Books, 1561, 1563.

92. Fuller, T., *The Worthies of England* (1662); De Beer (Ed.), *The Diary of John Evelyn* (1959).

93. Rye, W. (1905), *op. cit.*, pp.107, 8.

94. Prideaux's letters have been published by the Camden Society N.S. 15 (1875).

95. NRO, NCR Mayor's Court Book 25 February 1589. Transcribed in Hudson and Tingey, Vol. 2, p.195.

96. Greene, Robert, *A Groatsworth of Wit* (1592); *Dictionary of National Biography.*

97. *Cambridge Guide to Literature in English* (1993 edition), p.249; *Dictionary of National Biography.*

98. Stephenson, G., *Three Centuries of a Norfolk Library* (1917), *passim.*

99. Fuller, *op. cit.*, II, 154.

100. Hill, *op. cit.*, pp.36-7.

101. Seaman, P., 'Norfolk and Norwich Tax Assessment, Lady Day 1666', *Norfolk Genealogy*, 20 (no date), p.79; Baskerville, *op. cit.*

102. De Beer, *op. cit.*

103. Batty Shaw, *op. cit.*, p.117; Cleveland, A.J., *A History of the Norfolk and Norwich Hospital* (1948), pp.138-43.

Chapter Four

1.   NRO, MS 453; Monod, P.K., *Jacobitism and the English people 1688-1788* (1993 edition), pp.174, 177, 182.

2.   Blomefield, *op. cit.*, Vol. 1, p.437.

3.   *The First Report of the Municipal Corporations Commission* (1835).

4.   NRO, NCR 17b, quoted in Hamon, S., *Norwich* (1973), p.66.

5.   Gilmour, I., *Riots, Risings and Revolutions* (1992), p.227; Blomefield, *op. cit.*, Vol. 1, p.449.

6.   NRO, NCR 6h/1-10. All quotations in the next three paragraphs are from these documents, except that in note 7 below.

7.   Cozens-Hardy, B., and Kent, A.E., *The Mayors of Norwich* (1938), p.130.

8.   Jewson, C.B., *The Jacobin City* (1975), pp.12-20.

9.   Steven Watson, J., *The Reign of George III* (1960), p.358.

10. NRO, N/TC 71/2; NCR Chamberlains'accounts 1800-1.

11. Jewson, *op. cit.*, p.50.

12. *Dictionary of National Biography*: William Smith.

13. Mackie, C., *Norfolk Annals* (1901), Vol. 1, p.127. Hereafter cited as Annals.

14. Macauley, *History of England* (1913 edition), Vol. 1, p.324; Millican, P., 'The Freemen of Norwich 1714-52', *Norfolk Record Society* 23 (1952).

15. Defoe, D., *Tour Through the Eastern Counties* (1724).

16. Cornwall Record Office, HL(20) 593.

17. *Norwich Mercury* 7 April, 28 April and 19 May 1753.

18. Young, A., *A Farmer's Tour Through the East of England* (1771); Beatniffe, *The*

Norfolk Tour (1808).

19. J.L. and Barbara Hammond, *The Skilled Labourer* (1979 edition), p.116.
20. Clabburn, P., *The Norwich Shawl* (1995), pp.10-16.
21. NRO, MC 26/1.
22. Scarfe, *op. cit.*, pp.206-8.
23. Cozens-Hardy, B. (Ed.), *The Diary of Silas Neville* (1950), p.127; Simpson, *op. cit.*, p.52.
24. Blomefield, *op. cit.*, Vol. 1, p.449.
25. NRO, BOL 4/127.
26. Peck's *Directory* 1802.
27. Mantle, J., *Norwich Union, the first 200 years* (1997). As he does not mention the luggage quotation it may be apocryphal.
28. NRO, KIM 6/24.
29. NRO, BOL 2/142/2.
30. Cozens-Hardy, B., 'Mary Hardy's Diary', *Norfolk Record Society*, 37 (1968), p.21; Parson Woodforde's Diary 6 July 1778; Kennett, D.H., 'The pattern of coaching in early 19th century Norfolk', *Norfolk Archaeology* 36 (1977) pp.355-72.
31. Annals, *op. cit.*, Vol. 1, p.145, NRO, NCR 6a/23/9-17; MC 26/1.
32. Edwards, J.K., in Barringer, C. (Ed.), *Norwich in the Nineteenth Century* (1984), p.124.
33. NRO, NCC WILLS Samuel Chapman 1700 (Fo.33).
34. Bateman and Rye, *op. cit.*, pp.1-21; Winston, M., 'The Bethel Hospital', *Medical History* (1994), pp.27-51.
35. Cozens-Hardy, B., (1968) *op. cit.*, p.25.
36. Cleveland, A.J., 'The Norfolk and Norwich Hospital', *Medical Press and Circular*, 5 January 1944; Batty Shaw, *op. cit.*, pp.56-9; NRO, NNH 1, 64.
37. Batty Shaw, A., 'Benjamin Gooch, Eighteenth Century Norfolk Surgeon', *Medical History* (1972), 16 number 1, pp.50-60.
38. Stoker, D., 'The Correspondence of the Revd. Francis Blomefield', *Norfolk Record Society*, 55 (1992), pp.15-22.
39. White's *Directory*, 1854, p.123; Atherton (Ed.), *op. cit.*, p.651.
40. BL Add MSS 27966, xerox copy NRO, MS 534; NRO, NCR, 6a/8/141; NCR, 6a/11a/2, 25.
41. NRO, NCR, 22a/6; 16e/88, 91; 6a/17/3; 6a/19/41.
42. NRO, NCR, 6a/26/8, 9, 24.
43. NRO, NCR, 6a/12/1; NCR 6a/33/2.
44. NRO, NCR, 6a/13/31.
45. Scarfe, *op. cit.*, p.206; NRO, NCR 20e (minute books of the Guardians of the Poor).
46. The letters are transcribed in Crowley, J., and Reid, A., *The Poor Law in Norfolk 1700-1800* (1983), pp.56-7.
47. NRO, NCC WILLS John Norman 1724 (p.60). Printed copy NRO, MC 1213/2.
48. Corfield, P., in *The Early Modern Town* (1976), p.239; NRO, NCR 15c; N/S 15/1.
49. Essex Record Office, Braintree Vestry Minutes D/P264/8.

50. NRO, PD 499/7.
51. NRO, DCN 82/10.
52. NRO, PD 26/4.
53. Hudson, W., *History of the Parish of St Peter Parmountergate* (1889).
54. NRO, DCN 48/130.
55. NRO, NCR 6a/7/118.
56. NRO, NCR 6a/9/74-8; Remembrancer, *op. cit.*, p.13.
57. Remembrancer, *op. cit.*, p.9; *Dictionary of National Biography*: 'Peter'.
58. Scarfe, *op. cit.*, pp.204-5; Pevsner, N., and Wilson, R., *Buildings of England Norwich and North East Norfolk* (1997), p.316.
59. Pevsner and Wilson, *op. cit.*, p.269; *Notes and Queries*, September 1902.
60. Wearing, S.J., *Georgian Norwich: its builders* (1926), pp.34-5.
61. BL Add MSS 27966, xerox copy NRO, MS 554.
62. NRO, NCR 6a/6/95-7.
63. NRO, MS 579, pp.211ff.
64. David Smith, W., 'Politics, Religion and Education', in Barringer (Ed.), *op. cit.*, pp.199-214.
65. Cozens-Hardy (1950), *op. cit.*, p.17, 65; Wesley, *Journals*, Vol. 4, p.485.
66. Atherton (Ed.), *op. cit.*, p.557; Simpson, *op. cit.*, p.13.
67. NRO, BOL 4/157; Jolly, C., *The Spreading Flame* (no date), pp.3-30.
68. Wesley, *op. cit.*, Vol. 3, p.315.
69. Anon, *A Great Gothic Fane* (1913), p.75.
70. Annals, *op. cit.*, Vol. 1, p.58.
71. Annals, *op. cit.*, Vol. 1, pp.174, 305; NRO, PD 11/25.
72. NRO, MS 453; Annals, *op. cit.*, Vol. 1, p.190; Cozens-Hardy and Kent, *op. cit.*, pp.156, 7.
73. *Australian Dictionary of National Biography* (1967): Kable, Henry.
74. Annals, *op. cit.*, Vol. 1, pp.60 1.
75. Annals, *op. cit.*, Vol. 1, p.219.
76. NRO, NCR 6a/29/11; Annals, *op. cit.*, Vol. 1, p.219.
77. Rose, J., *Elizabeth Fry* (1980), *passim*.
78. *Dictionary of National Biography*: Elizabeth Fry.
79. There are 46 volumes, two at the NRO, the rest at the Library of the Society of Friends in London.
80. NRO, MC 1694; MS 21820 (press-cuttings and notes about the history of the Theatre Royal).
81. Young, J.R., *op. cit.*, p.74; *Woodforde's Diary*, 19 December 1785.
82. Remembrancer, *op. cit.*, p.23; Annals, *op. cit.*, Vol. 1, p.142; *Norfolk Chronicle* 18 and 25 January 1817.
83. Le Strange, H., *History of Freemasonry in Norfolk* (1896), pp.10ff.
84. NRO, MSS 579 p.218; BL Add MS 27966, xerox NRO, MS 554.
85. Fawcett, T., 'The Norwich Pleasure Gardens', *Norfolk Archaeology* 35 (1972), pp.382-99.
86. Elliott, C., *Aeronauts and Aviators* (1971), pp.15-18.

87. NRO, NCR 6a/8/36-9; 6a/9/42-5.
88. Annals *op. cit.*, pp.184, 214.
89. Millican, *op. cit.*, *passim.*
90. *Dictionary of National Biography*; Jewson, *op. cit.*, p.155.
91. NRO, BOL 4/166. The quotations in the next three paragraphs are taken from this source.
92. Jewson, *op. cit.*, p.155.
93. Rennert, J., *William Crotch–Composer, Artist, Teacher* (1975), *passim.*
94. Hamon, *op. cit.*, pp.165-6.
95. Moore, A., *The Norwich School of Artists* (1985), *passim.*
96. Nobbs, G., *Norwich, City of Centuries* (1978), p.28.

Chapter Five

1.   Annals, *op. cit.*, Vol. 1, pp.347, 359.
2.   *Champion* 10 November 1838, p.37.
3.   NRO, KIM 6/40.
4.   Nuthall, T., *Christ Church, New Catton; biography of a church* (1980), pp.4, 5.
5.   WARD, J.T., *Chartism* (1973) p.96; NRO N/S 2/3.
6.   Young, G.M., *Early Victorian England* (1934), Vol.1, p.210; *Barclay's Complete and Universal Dictionary* (1842).
7.   Quoted in *East Anglian Studies, the 19ᵗʰ Century* (1984), p.19.
8.   Gurney-Read, J., *Trades and Industries of Norwich* (1988), pp.71-6.
9.   Annals, *op. cit.*, Vol. 1, p.447.
10. The Market was regulated by the Market Committee (NRO, N/TC 8/1-18).
11. Annals, *op. cit.*, pp.214, 386.
12. *A Second Report of the Royal Commission for inquiring into the state of large Towns and Populous Districts 1845.* Appendix: Norwich.
13. NRO, NCR 6a/23/1.
14. 1851 Census: some Norwich parishes have been published in *Norfolk Genealogy.*
15. NRO, MC 389/23.
16. Nobbs, *op. cit.*, p.52.
17. Pevsner and Wilson, *op. cit.*, p.279.
18. Gibson, Brian, 'Water Water Everywhere', B.A. Thesis (1996): copy in the Norfolk Studies Library, Norwich.
19. Pound, J.F., *Poverty and Public Health 1800-1880* in Barringer (Ed.), *op. cit.*, p.61.
20. Lambert, R., *Sir John Simon* (1963), p.399.
21. *Norfolk Chronicle*, 2 July 1872.
22. NRO, N/TC 4/1-5; N/TC 57/9.
23. Bateman and Rye, *op. cit.*, *passim.*
24. Annals, *op. cit.*, Vol. 1, p.467.
25. NRO, BR 35/2/73a, 75; BR 35/1/181.
26. Batty Shaw (1992), *op. cit.*, pp.61-4; Annals, *op. cit.*, *passim.*
27. NRO, N/S 9/1.

28. Hodgkinson, R., *The Origins of the National Health Service* (1963), pp.121, 185-7.
29. Batty Shaw (1992), *op. cit.*, p.113.
30. Quoted in *East Anglian Studies: the nineteenth century* (1984), p.19.
31. *Annals*, *op. cit.*, Vol. 1, p.454.
32. *Annals*, *op. cit.*, Vol. 1, pp.6, 185.
33. *Annals*, *op. cit.*, Vol. 1, p.361.
34. *Annals*, *op. cit.*, Vol. 1, p.261.
35. NRO, N/S 2/1. The NRO has a typed list of people transported by the Norwich
     Quarter Sessions Court.
36. 'The 1851 Religious Census', *Norfolk Record Society*, Vol.62 (1998), pp.120ff.
37. Pevsner and Wilson, *op. cit.*, p.330.
38. NRO, BOL 4/157.
39. NRO, NCR 6a/18/26.
40. *Annals*, *op. cit.*, Vol. 1, p.139.
41. Gordon, D.I., *A Regional History of the Railways of Great Britain* (1977 edition),
     passim; Brooks, E.C., *Sir Samuel Morton Peto* (1996), pp.168, 310.
42. *Annals*, *op. cit.*, Vol. 1, p.437.
43. *Annals*, *op. cit.*, Vol. 1, p.451.
44. *Norfolk Chronicle*, 25 April 1845, 17 January 1846.
45. Wood, E., *Historical Britain* (1995), p.443; Gordon, *op. cit.*, pp.178-9.
46. Joby, R., in Longcroft and Joby (Eds.), East Anglian Studies: *Essays presented to
     Chris Barringer* (1995), p.120.
47. Ransome, A., *Coot Club* (1934), p.1.
48. Clayton, *op. cit.*, p.23.
49. Digby, A., *Pauper Palaces* (1978), p.128.
50. Wilson, D.M., *Awful Ends* (1992), p.87.
51. White's *Norfolk Directory* (1845), p.128.
52. NRO, DCN 120/2 for letters to Dean Pellew about Mousehold Heath.
53. Dugdale, T., *England and Wales delineated* (c.1845), Vol. 7, p.534.
54. Bayne, A.D., *A Comprehensive History of Norwich* (1869), p.107; DCN 120/2Q/1.
55. Bayne, *op. cit.*, p.61.
56. Bosworth, Harcourt, *The Chronicles of an Old Playhouse* (1903), p.67; *Dictionary of
     National Biography*.
57. The different editions are listed in Chubb, T., and Stephen, G.A., *Norfolk and
     Norwich maps* (1928), pp.233ff.
58. Hepworth. P., and Alexander, M., *City of Norwich Libraries—History and Treasures*
     (1957), p.14; Kelly's *Norfolk Directory* (1883), p.409.
59. Chitty, S., *The Woman who Wrote Black Beauty* (1971), *passim*.
60. NRO, MS 4265

Chapter Six

1. Palgrave-Moore, P., *The Mayors and Lord Mayors of Norwich 1836-1974*, p.43.
2. Hollis, P., *Ladies Elect* (1987), pp.445, 480.

3. NRO, NCR 4g10.
4. *The Norwich Roll of Honour of Citizens who fell in the Great War 1914-1919* (1924).
5. Gliddon, G., *Norfolk and Suffolk in the Great War* (1988), *passim.* The quotation is from the article by N. Mansfield p.27.
6. Hamlin, *op. cit., passim.*
7. Long, S., *Norfolk and Norwich Hospital, Twelve Months War Service,* offprint from *Eastern Daily Press* 3, 4 August 1915; Cleveland, *op. cit.,* p.131.
8. Kent, P., in Gliddon, *op. cit.,* pp.61-73.
9. Clark-Kennedy, A.E., *Edith Cavell: Pioneer and Patriot* (1965), *passim.*
10. NRO, DCN 24/12.
11. Pevsner and Wilson, *op. cit.,* p.293.
12. NRO, DCN 106/40.
13. Cleveland, *op. cit.,* p.154.
14. Banger, J., *Norwich at War* (1974), *passim.*
15. Cleveland, *op. cit.,* p.170.
16. NRO, N/ED 1/86.
17. NRO, MC 376/157.
18. Norfolk Federation of Women's Institutes (Ed.), *Norfolk Within Living Memory* (1995), pp.188, 215.
19. Hawkins, C.B., *Norwich, A Social Study* (1910), p.26.
20. British Association, *Norwich and Its Region* (1961), p.193. Hereafter cited as Region.
21. Hawkins, *op. cit.,* pp.45, 221.
22. NRO, Caley's business records, not yet catalogued.
23. Pevsner and Wilson, *op. cit.,* p.308; NRO, MC 322/5.
24. Townroe, P., *Norwich: the 1987 Norwich Area Economic Survey* (1987), p.46.
25. Region, *op. cit.,* p.195; Gurney-Read, *op. cit.,* p.11.
26. NRO, N/TC 29/6, 7.
27. Norwich City Council: *Poverty in Norwich* (1991).
28. NRO, MC 394/2.
29. Green, M., *1920s Depression and Norfolk Memories* (no date), pages not numbered; *Within Living Memory, op. cit.,* p.8.
30. Dickson, D.M., *Review of Local Charities* (1970), p.2; *Poverty in Norwich* (1991).
31. Kent, E.A., *Norwich Guildhall* (1928); NRO, N/TC 1/48-53.
32. Clifton-Taylor, A., *English Parish Churches as works of art* (1974), pp.17, 18.
33. Day, *op. cit.,* p.121; Nobbs, *op. cit.,* p.61.
34. NRO, N/TC 52/41; N/TC 18/2.
35. Cleveland, *op. cit.,* pp.28-42, 55-63.
36. Atkin (1993), *op. cit.,* p.97 adds that women appeared at their windows with their curlers still in their hair.
37. Doggett, M., *Eastern Counties, The First Fifty Years* (*c.*1981), pp.8-14.
38. Elliott, *op. cit.,* pp.146-53.
39. Norfolk County Council: *Norwich Area Transport Strategy Draft Plan* (1997).
40. NRO, SO 26.

41. Peart, S., *The Picture House in East Anglia* (1980), *passim*; Peart, S., *What Happened to the Cinema near you?* (1996), pp.58-94.
42. Region, *op. cit.*, p.222.
43. Townroe, *op. cit.*, pp.46-7.
44. NRO, N/TC 52/26.
45. Townroe, *op. cit.*, p.47.
46. Henderson, *op. cit.*, p.278-9.

Bibliography

Manuscript Sources

The Records of the City of Norwich are at the NRO. Those before 1834 were catalogued by W. Hudson and J. Tingey (1898). They have the prefix NCR. Records after 1834 have the prefix N/.

The NRO also holds *diocesan records* (including wills and probate inventories); *parish records* for the 35 Anglican churches in the city; records of many of the *free churches; business records*; records of *Norwich Cathedral*; and an enormous range of *private deposits* from residents of the city.

Printed Sources

There are full bibliographies in the two volumes of *A Bibliography of Norfolk History,* 1974 and 1991.

Some of the most important books are:

Atherton, I., Fernie, E., Harper-Bill, C., Smith, H. (eds.), *Norwich Cathedral: Church, City and Diocese*, 1996
Atkin, M., *Life on a Medieval Street*, 1985
Atkin, M., *Norwich, History and Guide*, 1993
Ayers, B., *Digging Under the Doorstep*, 1983
Ayers, B., *English Heritage Book of Norwich*, 1994
Banger, J., *Norwich At War*, 1974
Barringer, J.C. (Ed.), *Nineteenth Century Norwich*, 1984
Bateman, F., and Rye, W., *The History of the Bethel Hospital*, 1906
Batty Shaw, A., *Norfolk and Norwich Medicine, A Retrospect*, 1992
Bayne, A.D., *A Comprehensive History of Norwich*, 1869
Blomefield, Francis, *The History of the City of Norwich*, 1806 edition
British Association, *Norwich and its Region*, 1961
Campbell, J., *Historic Towns–Norwich*, 1975
Cleveland, A.J., *A History of the Norfolk and Norwich Hospital 1900-46*, 1948
Dunn, I. and Sutermeister, H., *The Norwich Guildhall*, n.d.
Fernie, E., *An Architectural History of Norwich Cathedral*, 1993

Gilchrist, R. and Oliva, M., *Religious Women in Medieval East Anglia*, 1993

Gliddon, G. (ed.), *Norfolk and Suffolk in the Great War*, 1988

Green, B. and Young, R., *Norwich, the Growth of a City*, 1981

Gurney-Read, J., *Trades and Industries of Norwich*, 1988

Hawkins, C.B., *Norwich, A Social Study*, 1910

Henderson, Edith, *The Story of Norwich*, ?1918

Hudson, W. and Tingey, J.C., *The Records of the City of Norwich*, 1906, 1910

Jewson, C.B., *The Jacobean City*, 1975

Kelly, S., Rutledge, E., Tillyard, M., *Men of Property, An Analysis of the Norwich enrolled deeds 1285-1311*, 1983

Kirkpatrick, J., *The Streets and Lanes of Norwich*, 1889

Lipman, V.D., *The Jews of Norwich*, 1967

Mackie, C.M., *Norfolk Annals*, 1901

Margeson, S., *The Vikings in Norfolk*, 1997

Moens, W.J.C., 'The Walloons and their Church at Norwich', *Huguenot Society*, Vol.1, 1887-8

Moore, A., *The Norwich School of Artists*, 1985

Nobbs, G., *Norwich, City of Centuries*, 1978

Pelling, M., *The Common Lot: Sickness, Medical Occupations and the Urban Poor in Early Modern England*, 1998

Pevsner, N. and Wilson, B., *The Buildings of England–Norwich and North East England*, 1997

Pound, J., *Tudor and Stuart Norwich*, 1988

Rawcliffe, C., *The Hospitals of Medieval Norwich*, 1995

Rose, M. and Hedgecoe, J., *Stories in Stone–the medieval roof carvings of Norwich Cathedral*, 1997

Sandred, K.I. and Lindstrom, B., *The Place-Names of Norwich and Norfolk–Part 1: Norwich*, 1989

Sutermeister, H., *The Norwich Blackfriars*, 1977

Tanner, N., *The Church in Late Medieval Norwich 1370-1552*, 1984

Townroe, P., *Norwich Area Economic Study*, 1987

Virgoe, R., *Illustrated letters of the Paston Family*, 1989

Index